D0490364

The
Longest
Tunnel

The Longest Tunnel

The True Story of World War II's
Great Escape

Alan Burgess

G.K.HALL&CO.
Boston, Massachusetts
1991

Published in Large Print by arrangement with
Grove Weidenfeld, a division of
Wheatland Corporation.

G. K. Hall Large Print Book Series.

Set in 16 pt. Plantin.

Library of Congress Cataloging in Publication Data

Burgess, Alan.
    The longest tunnel : the true story of World War II's great escape
/ Alan Burgess.
        p.   cm.—(G.K. Hall large print book series)
    Reprint. Originally published: New York : G. Weidenfeld, 1990.
    ISBN 0-8161-5103-2 (lg. print)
    1. Stalag Luft 3 (Zagań, Poland : Concentration camp) 2. World War,
    1939-1945—Prisoners and prisons, German.   3. Escapes—Poland—
    Zagań.   4. Large type books.   I. Title.
    [D805.P7B87   1991]
    940.54'7243094385—dc20   90-45904

Contents

Born of the sun they travelled a short while towards the sun,
And left the vivid air signed with their honour.
—STEPHEN SPENDER

Foreword

THEY WALKED ACROSS THE tarmac of a thousand airfields through the nights, pale dawns, twilights, and crimson sunsets: young men in flying suits, usually with a joke on their lips, sometimes a hangover in their heads, the beat of a tune and the kiss of a girl met the night before still in their memories. They were often apprehensive, tight-lipped at what lay ahead, but no different from the warriors of past ages—except that, this time, they flew like birds.

Nearly fifty thousand American and RAF aircrew were never seen again. They disappeared into the skies, as if they had never existed. In all, more than one hundred thousand Allied airmen were killed in World War II. Hundreds of thousands more were badly wounded. And almost the same number spent at least part of the war imprisioned in POW camps behind enemy lines.

This book concerns the prisoners of war in one camp, Sagan, Stalag Luft III, where, under a "moonless" sky in March 1944, seventy-six Allied airmen crawled out of a tunnel and escaped into the darkness.

Within days most of them were recaptured. On Hitler's express order, and against every tenet of the Geneva convention, fifty were executed—"shot while trying to escape." Of the remaining twenty-six, twenty-three were brutally reimprisoned, some after having spent several weeks on the run. Only three made it to safety.

This dramatic escape became the subject of Paul Brickhill's absorbing book *The Great Escape*, which was published shortly after the war, and, with a few fictitious additions, adapted as a movie some thirteen years later. However, there were many obstacles in the way of researching, collating, and assembling a full account of much of this truly amazing story: Europe was still shattered by the aftermath of war, while the thousands of POWs who had fought grim battles in fighter and bomber aircraft, and experienced camp life and a variety of escape attempts, were only then returning to their countries of origin.

It took years before the books and memoirs began to be published, and even longer for the classified documents from American, British, and German sources to be released, among them the official camp history of Sagan, Stalag Luft III; the History, with its invaluable stock of detailed information, has been an important source for this book. The personal stories of the aircrew themselves were always available for those who cared to listen to them. For a long time, it seems, no one did.

I began to listen after one of the Stalag Luft III reunions in 1986, my deep interest stemming, coincidentally, with the fact that as a BBC features producer from 1946 onwards I had dramatized and produced whole series of such epic war stories. And it seemed to me that no one had ever put this historic episode together in one continuous narrative, and in so doing isolated the stories of a handful of brave and determined men: how they arrived at Stalag Luft III; their experiences as POWs, and as escapers on the run; why so many of their comrades were killed; and the riveting story of how a small group of the RAF Special Investigation Branch returned to postwar Germany to bring the Gestapo murderers to justice.

I was priviledged to meet many of the surviving veterans who willingly contributed their recollections to this manuscript. It is to them, to their old comrades living or dead, and to the gallant fifty who died that *The Longest Tunnel* is dedicated.

Introduction

A Tunnel
Named
Harry

THAT MARCH OF 1944 the arctic wind drove across the flat Silesian plain, knife-edged and merciless, beading the barbed wire with ice, capping the watchtowers with a six-inch thatch of snow, and in Stalag Luft III, in the German town of Sagan,* the captured officers huddled around the stoves to warm their hands and buttocks.

In Hut 104 one warmed the bum with a certain reverence. Hut 104 contained a very special stove: special because it had survived dozens of German examinations and searches, and because concealed beneath it, thirty feet under the ice-hard earth, lay a tunnel paved with the dreams of two hundred escapers. A tunnel named Harry.

Because of Tunnel Harry, the faces of Wing Commander Harry "Wings" Day and Squadron Leader Roger Bushell were grim that morning. Collars turned up against the wind, feet crunching through the crisp snow, they trudged around the perimeter circuit—the exercise track that ran inside the barbed wire, around the circumference of the camp. Wings Day knew that if ever a man

* Located some 60 miles SSE of Frankfurt, Sagan is today the Polish town of Zagań.

needed reassurance, Roger Bushell needed it now. His was the final decision. To go or to cancel?

Wings Day was forty-six years old, tall, craggy-faced, with green eyes sunk under heavy brows. He had been behind the wire longer than anyone else. Shot down on a photoreconnaissance mission little more than a month after the outbreak of war, he had never fired a gun in combat. His contribution to the war effort as a trained and experienced commanding officer and pilot had been nil; his chances for promotion to the higher echelons of the RAF had vanished. And for the last five years Wings Day had felt very angry about his situation.

Roger Bushell, in his early thirties, known by all as "Big X," the organizing brain behind the entire escape plan, was also tall and stocky, but like all of them through those winters of short rations, lice, and bitter cold, he had thinned down; his shoulders had become a little huddled. Roger was a hard man: resolute, tough, coldly determined, driven relentlessly by his own emotional imperatives. His voice, as he spoke now, was deep and urgent.

"Wings, it's got to be 'Go!' It must be 'Go!'"

Wings Day said nothing. As acting senior British officer he shared responsibility, but Roger had to make up his own mind. After all, they'd churned it around for weeks as winter had turned to early spring. This was the crunch. They had to go by nightfall.

As if repetion might justify his decision, Roger went on: "We can't wait another month for the next moonless period. Four hundred sets of forged papers have to be stamped with today's date. . . ."

"Forgery gang ready and waiting to get started," said Wings, trying to sound encouraging, "Escape Committee called for eleven-thirty A.M. to hear what you decide. Can't postpone to tomorrow—no late trains run on Saturday."

This is crazy, thought Wings, and unlike Roger. He usually makes decisions like thunderclaps. But then, this was probably the most difficult decision he'd ever make in his life.

"The weather's going to be bloody awful, and will probably get worse," Roger continued. "Ninety percent of the hard-arsers will run into deep snow in the mountains."

"Doesn't matter. It would give the Nazis an almighty shock. Two hundred looney escape artists roaring around the countryside." Wings's face cracked into a smile. "It'll take all the police, Home Guards, Hitler Youth—thousands of troops to try and round us up."

They both knew what this would do to the morale of the camp. If "Go" was the directive, the faces of the two hundred chosen POWs would register a mixture of elation, relief, apprehension, and excitement. Out would come the escape clothes; the escape rations would be checked for the tenth time, the forged papers examined minutely. If the order was "Cancel," they would accept it, some with grumbles, others with patience. But many faces would drop, shoulders shrug dejectedly, and spirits diminish.

Six hundred officer aircrew shot down over Europe—American, British, Canadian, Australian, New Zealand, South African, Scandinavian, French, Polish, Czechoslovakian, and half a dozen other nationalities—were waiting for this signal. They had slaved for more than a year, digging three tunnels that were deeper and more complex than any in escape history. Harry was now ready and waiting.

They all understood the hazards: snow that in the mountains would be several feet deep, cold that entered a man's bones. The first forty, who would attempt to catch the early morning trains out of Germany, stood the best chance; they had earned that privilege by having the most experience in escapes, being the most fluent in languages, and being the hardest workers in the escape teams. The hard-arsers—the poor sods who were doing it the hard way, traveling on foot across country in heavy weather conditions, trying to jump freight trains, steal bicycles, boats, even airplanes—were most at risk. But they accepted those risks, often deliberately adopted them.

And Harry might not last another month. Even supported by hundreds of "liberated" bed boards, soft sand collapsed easily. German searches might strike it lucky. They had struck it lucky before this, and the guards knew that early spring heralded the escape season. Kommandant von Lindeiner's ground microphones, installed nine feet below ground at intervals of thirty meters around the perimeter fence, contained a highly sensitive swinging-pen mechanism that was set in motion by the slightest disturbance in the ground. The noise was transferred by cable to the control listening post in the Kommandantur, where a twenty-four-hour watch was maintained. The microphones had picked up plenty of vibrations. Thus, searches were constant, roll calls frequent, and head counts taken on the slightest suspicion. The "ferrets," specially trained guards with sharp eyes and longer, sharper probes, were on duty around the clock. Only George Harsh's security squad had so far kept them at bay.

George Harsh was the most unlikely member of a triumvirate whose activities were crucial to the success of the operation. He was Milwaukee-born, Atlanta-raised, and Georgia-chain-gang-educated—although no one but Wally Floody knew the details of that disastrous episode. Wally Floody, tunnel engineer in chief, insisted that George Harsh's soft Southern accent and his prematurely white hair and moustache made him seem like a favorite uncle, a sweet-natured, old-fashioned Kentucky colonel—a good camouflage for the tunnel security chief.

The "stooges"—lookouts—in George's wide network of spies would have endorsed that description. George's orders were always direct: "Not one whisper, one tendril of information, one ghost of a rumor, must reach the Germans about what we are planning. I want to know where every German is from the time he enters the compound until the moment he leaves. If he sneezes, farts, belches, looks happy, bored, or interested, I want to know why, when, and where."

George Harsh was in his thirties, Wally Floody ten years younger, but they formed a great friendship in the conspiratorial atmosphere of Sagan, Stalag Luft III. Wally was Canadian and had worked in the northern goldfields as a miner in prewar days; that gave him an edge over everybody else. The third member of the triumvirate could not have been more different. Royal Navy, Fleet Air Arm Lieutenant Commander Peter Fanshawe—nicknamed "Hornblower"—had an upper-crust accent and the background to go with it. "How," asked Wally Floody, "could we, two bog-rat North Americans, expect to associate with 'Hornblower' and work with him as a colleague?" But Hornblower had the right sort of brain, one that addressed a problem in neat, shipshape fashion. He knew that one had first to build the entrance to the tunnel through a trap that would be impossible to find. Then one had to dig a hole three or four hundred feet in length, so that it surfaced beyond the wire. And most important of all, one had to disperse and hide a few hundred tons of sand that, when freshly dug, was bright yellow in color and stank.

The Sagan escape attempt was an enormous community effort, in which literally hundreds of men were involved. On the other hand, no one disputed that Roger Bushell was the pivotal leader, the "Big X."

So it was out there on the snowy circuit that

Roger Bushell turned at last to Wings Day and grinned, no doubt for the first time in days. "Let's get inside and pass the word," he said. "It's 'Go!'"

On that night of March 24, North Compound of Sagan, Stalag Luft III, was alive with noiseless activity. From practically every hut, at regulated intervals, silent forms, evading the searchlights, slipped through the darkness to congregate in Hut 104. By around 8:00 P.M. two hundred airmen, dressed in a unique variety of escape disguises, were stacked like bees in rooms and corridors; the usual occupants had been dispersed to other huts much earlier.

Some of the escape outfits were utterly convincing: when a German sergeant marched down the corridor in full uniform, everyone nearly dropped dead from shock. It took a little time to reassure them that it was only the Polish Flying Officer Pawel Tobolski, who was making the break as companion to Wings Day.

Where had this assembly come from? How had they reached this place, whose name would soon become tragically significant in the history of prisoner-of-war camps? Their one point in common was that their arrival followed a dramatic exit from a blazing aircraft somewhere up in the skies, or an equally dramatic impact with earth or ocean in the same sort of flying machine. So thousands of airmen joined the company of "kriegies"—the POWs' shortening of the heavy German noun

Kriegsgefangen—to wait out the years of imprisonment . . . or escape.

The trap under the stove was open. Tunnel Harry, brightly lit from end to end (with energy illicitly drawn from German power supplies), lay waiting. Strips of blanket had been laid to muffle the sound of the wheels of the small trolleys that would carry the escapers over three hundred feet through the two-foot-square rabbit hole. One group was waiting at "Piccadilly Circus," the first changeover station; another small group was at the second station, "Leicester Square"; and at the exit trap itself, where the ladder pointed provocatively up to the top layer of earth and grass, Harry Marshall and Johnny Bull waited for their watches to tell them it was 9:00 P.M.—zero hour!

Roger Bushell and his escape partner, Frenchman Bernard Scheidhauer, had earned the right to be among the first through the exit trap. Roger wore a smart gray suit and a dark overcoat, with a trilby hat stuffed down the front; Scheidhauer had a similar sort of civilian outfit. They were the two most likely to succeed. Both were fluent in several languages; both were equipped with forged papers as perfect as human ingenuity could make them; both looked to perfection the role they were playing: that of middle-class Frenchmen traveling back through Germany to Paris.

Their first objective was to catch the night train to Breslau, then head to France via Dresden, Leipzig, and Frankfurt. In Paris, Scheidhauer had friends who would pass them through the underground Resistance.

Wally Floody, George Harsh, and Peter Fanshawe had been drawn into one another's company by the nature of their work. Others waiting in Hut 104 would be forced together by the exigencies and perils they would encounter on the run. Four of them in particular—Major Johnny Dodge, Flight Lieutenant Sydney Dowse, Flight Lieutenant Jimmy James, and Wing Commander Day—would face danger together.

Of the quartet, Johnny Dodge was the least typical. To start with, he was almost fifty years old. Next, Dodge was army, not aircrew. His sole connection with an airplane consisted of sitting, before the war, in a first-class seat on one of Imperial Airways' cross-channel flights to Paris, enjoying both the champagne and the view. Johnny was blue-blooded American, part of the wealthy East Coast Dodge family that had made its fortune in copper; he was also related to Winston Churchill's American ancestors, a fact that was to prove of significant value to him in the years to come.

At that moment, as he was sitting in Hut 104, waiting for his turn to nip down through the tunnel, Johnny's overcoat was packed so tightly with what he had decided were escape essentials—and he was a big man—that he looked more like the Michelin effigy than a normal human being. He did not utter a word of protest when some of the other men unpeeled about half of him at the tunnel entrance for fear he would block the hole completely.

Lying ahead of Johnny Dodge down in the tunnel was Flight Lieutenant Sydney Dowse, twenty-five years old. With his Polish partner, Stanislaw "Danny" Krol, he intended to head for the Polish border, where Danny was certain he would find friends.

Sydney's RAF flying duties in the first few months of the war had consisted of photoreconnaissance missions—swooping down over German submarine pens, battleships, railway yards, or ammunition factories. He would expend film instead of machine-gun bullets, and then, in his unarmored and stripped-down Spitfire, would waggle his tail fins contemptuously at pursuing Messerschmitts before landing back at base and handing over important evidence to Intelligence.

The Luftwaffe could be fooled—but not all the time. They laid traps for young men like Sydney. Against the sun, waiting at high altitude, they screamed down, employing maximum surprise and superior airspeed. They erased Sydney's plane with cannon fire, sending it plunging earthwards. Sydney parachuted out to become a POW at Stalag Luft III.

The third member of the quartet was Flight Lieutenant Jimmy James. He sat contentedly in Hut 104, knowing that after several years of exhibiting a great zeal for escape he had definitely earned his place as thirty-ninth man in line. No more than an hour earlier he had said goodbye to his roommates. They did not seem unduly sorry to see him depart—he had promised them the treasure trove of cigarettes under his bunk.

Number 22 on the list, Wings Day, did not hate the *idea* of escaping; he hated what had to be endured in order to escape. Surviving a series of tunnel crawls during his first years of captivity, he had discovered, first of all, that he suffered from excruciating claustrophobia. No one ever knew that, because Wings Day was immaculate in his execution of duty. But he suffered hell during those wriggles through coffin-dark holes, with, likely as not, the boots of the man in front kicking dirt back into his face and, likely as not, a burst of machine-gun fire to greet him when he emerged into fresh air.

And even apart from such hazards, Wings felt little elation. Being a hunted fugitive was not his style; nor did he think much of his costume and false identity: a double-breasted naval monkey jacket adapted to look civilian, its bright buttons concealed with cloth, and scruffed-up RAF trousers; and a cover story (with papers to match) of being a renegade Irish colonel—Browne by name —so indignant about the inhumanity of Allied terror-bombing that he was being given the opportunity of viewing it for himself—escorted, naturally, by a German guard.

Wings thought this was ridiculous. He would have preferred to escape as a Hungarian migrant worker. "But, Wings, you don't speak a word of Hungarian!" the Escape Committee objected. "That's the whole secret," he answered. "No one speaks Hungarian except the Hungarians, and their country's hundreds of miles away. With the right Hungarian papers, I could just jabber away like a lunatic, and any border guard would let me through just to get rid of me."

But the Escape Committee maintained its faith in the Irish colonel role. Besides, with his escape partner, Polish officer Pawel Tobolski, decked out as a German Feldwebel, they couldn't miss. They'd reach Berlin with ease.

That night the cast of two hundred, in their divergent costumes, assembled in the wings—the ramshackle rooms and corridor of Hut 104. That night they would break out through Harry, reach the pine trees, the snow, the star-filled sky, and smell the clean air of freedom. And to climb out of a hole in the earth, to know that they were beyond the wire, that they were free, if only for a few hours, a few minutes, was to experience a profoundly intense personal victory.

Part One

Captors
and
Captives

Chapter One

North Compound, Sagan, Stalag Luft III . . . April 1943

ROGER BUSHELL LOOKED DOWN at the group of airmen crowded into the small barracks room. As a former barrister for the prosecution, he was reminded of the prewar criminal courts, where one's opening address was crucial to the eventual verdict. It was a moment when the fresh and interested jury could be swayed. A persuasive, dramatic opening gambit might motivate opinions that—even after all the evidence was heard—the jurors would retain when the judge dismissed them to the jury room.

Roger had a similar task now. These men must believe in this escape as strongly as he did. He had to fire them with his own passionate conviction.

"Everyone here in this room is living on borrowed time," he began. "By rights we should all be dead! The only reason that God allowed us this extra ration of life is so we can make life hell for the Hun."

There were grins, some laughter, and a little applause.

Years before, a skiing accident had left Roger

Bushell with a facial scar and a slight droop in one eyelid. They gave his face a certain diabolical aspect that, when brought to bear, could be both accusatory and intimidating. Generally a friendly charisma was part of his personality, of his aura as a leader. But now, with an intention to shock, his voice was harsh.

"By rights our names should already be inscribed on the honor rolls in the parish churches." He stared around the room in silence before assaulting them with his warning. "And maybe, in the future, the names of some of us sitting here will still be found in those lists."

This time there was no murmur of approval. Roger expected none. The men in rows in front of him wore old, stained uniforms, sweaters, open-necked shirts. They were young and cheerful, but there were shadows behind many eyes, put there by the rigors of air combat and survival. Roger had their full attention. "Realistically, how many men do we think are going to make it back to England, the U.S.A., the Antipodes, and all the other places? Very few. But we're going to give the Germans as big a shock in their Wagnerian war score as they've ever had. Not a bang on a big bass drum but an explosion of howitzer proportions!"

More murmurs of approval.

"Not a breakout by ten, twenty, fifty men. Our intention is two hundred under the wire in one spectacular night of escape!"

Now the gasp was loud and mutual, a mixture of admiration and apprehension.

"I've called this general assembly of the Escape Committee to explain how we are going to achieve that ambition. We are now settled into this brand-new part of Sagan, Stalag Luft Three—North Compound. And from our recently vacated happy home in East Compound we have brought all our escape know-how. We've all dug tunnels in POW camps scattered all over Germany. In East Compound we dug, lost, or abandoned at least fifty tunnels. In North Compound we are concentrating our efforts on completing and escaping through *one* master tunnel. No private-enterprise tunnels allowed. Three bloody deep, bloody long tunnels will be dug—Tom, Dick, and Harry. One will succeed!"

Roger Bushell held up both hands to quiet the buzz of conversation.

"Practically everyone here has made an escape attempt—some have made several—during his time as a kriegie imprisoned in various stalags. As Escape Committee representatives in your separate barrack blocks, you have authority over your own setup of lookouts, stooges, penguins, contacts, and what-have-you. After this meeting it's your job to spread the word amongst them about what we are going to do"—again Roger emphasized his point with raised hands—"remembering all the time that security—total security—is vital."

Sitting among that audience, Wally Floody,

George Harsh, and Peter Fanshawe knew pretty well what Roger was going to say. And so they should have, for as part of the inner group of the Escape Committee they had discussed and helped to work out these plans.

Wally Floody and George Harsh's friendship dated from the time many months before when George, having been shot down in a bombing raid on Cologne and experiencing his first hour in Sagan, had lain on his bunk and hoped to Christ food and drink might materialize from somewhere. Instead, Wally Floody had appeared. He had stared at George with all the affability of a drill sergeant regarding a recruit with two left feet. "You're American?" he said.

George nodded. He felt that his nationality should give no cause for complaint, considering that he'd been occupying an air-gunner slot long before most of his compatriots even knew there was a war on. He also caught Wally's North American accent.

"You're Canadian," he retorted.

"Sure. And I'm just sending off a letter to my wife in Toronto. That letter will get to her about six months before the Air Ministry gets round to informing your next of kin that you are not a corpse, but safe and well. If anyone is worrying, my wife might ring them up and give them the news. Anybody in mind?"

George pulled himself up on one elbow. He understood this was a very warm gesture towards a very new boy.

"Thanks," he answered. "I sure do."

It was the beginning of a deep friendship between the two men.

"At this moment," Wally argued on one of their numerous walks around the perimeter track, "there are about eight hundred and fifty officer POWs in this camp. Half the buggers intend to lie on their backs, dreaming of the past, improving their education, and writing nice little letters home to Mom, or their girlfriend, and waiting until the war ends."

"Include me in that group," said George. "And what's bugging you about it?"

"The war might last for five or ten or twenty years," said Wally emphatically. "I do not intend to spend the rest of my life doing that and existing on one ersatz German beer a year. I'm getting out."

"Wally," answered George soothingly, "you know the figures as well as I do. Fifty percent of the camp don't want to escape. Forty-five percent would love to escape given the opportunity. Five percent are the demented escape lunatics like you. But ninety-nine percent are prepared, often anxious, to help any escape attempt in any way they can: the noise groups, the interference groups, the staged-fight groups, the music groups, the lookouts, the stooges, the sand carriers, the contact men. We're all prepared to do that."

"Good," said Wally, "you're getting a promotion."

George Harsh's face cracked into an enormous

smile. "You mean to the Escape Committee? An offer? Wally, they're all officers and gentlemen, and there are hundreds of them around here. Why me?"

"For security reasons."

The smile left George's face. "Wally, you haven't been talking—"

"Don't be a bloody fool," Wally snapped. "That's *your* business. But there are big plans taking place around here."

"I know," said George, "down in some two-foot-square rathole digging at the face, which is about a hundred yards from the only vertical escape shaft. Out of your mind."

"The Germans," said Wally, "have a nasty habit of driving heavy trucks around over ground which they think is being tunneled. Being buried in a collapsed tunnel is no fun. I want security people on top who can guard my ass. People I can trust."

"Floody," said George Harsh, "you really are a crafty bastard. What's your next move?"

"After roll call tomorrow morning, you are meeting three of the big chiefs of the Escape Committee: Wings Day, Roger Bushell, and Group Captain H. M. Massey," said Wally.

They had met in Wings Day's room. The furniture was sparse: a bare wooden table, and chairs for Wings in the middle, Roger Bushell on his left, Group Captain Massey on the right. Massey had flown with the Royal Flying Corps in the First

8

World War, and had reached his senior rank, promoted to station commander, during the Second. A desk job. But like dozens of old warriors before him, he had decided he must take one more farewell trip before he got rooted behind that desk. A big mistake: his plane was shot down over the target, and Massey, his foot severely injured by flak splinters, parachuted to captivity. Now he hobbled around with a stick, often in great pain.

It was Wings Day, more than any other single officer among RAF POWs, who had formulated the idea of the Escape Committee. Before Christmas 1939 he had arrived at Dulag Luft, the transit camp near Frankfurt am Main, through which would pass thousands of downed RAF and USAAF aircrew. Here they would be held for varying lengths of time, interrogated, and passed on to other stalags.

After one ingenious but unsuccessful escape attempt from Dulag Luft, Wings Day was dispatched to another camp at Barth near the Baltic Sea. And here, as at Dulag Luft, escape attempts were free-for-alls. Singly or in groups, POWs tried routes through the gates, under and over the wire, and through ingeniously complex tunnels. The results were chaotic. Tunnels ran into other tunnels. Diversionary activities—fights, brawls, massed bands, choral groups—found themselves competing with each other. Except that POWs were highly secretive and would tell no one of their master plan, security procedures did not exist. Clues to the existence of tunnels were easy to find, but the German guards were neither perceptive nor vigilant, and inventing escape plans was easily the POWs' most popular pastime.

Wings Day, as senior British officer, had decided that this was absurd. No one could dream up and implement an escape plan without the authority of a properly organized escape committee. And indeed, POWs soon exhibited their true commitment and, abandoning exercise and educational facilities, dedicated all their waking hours to a concerted effort to win freedom.

George Harsh, sitting opposite the Escape Committee on that first day, had begun to have reservations. His traumatic experiences had taught him that you found freedom inside yourself, not by crawling through holes in the earth. And after all, this setup was a trifle theatrical, wasn't it?

But then George had considered another point. This *was* a theatrical scene: a POW camp in the heart of an arrogant, aggressive, war-torn Germany, complete with high barbed-wire fences, searchlights, watchtowers, machine guns, guards trained to fire at the slightest provocation, vicious guard dogs. . . . Yes, it was theatrical—lethally theatrical.

And now here he was, over a year later: tunnel chief of security, listening to Roger Bushell's impassioned advocacy.

"The Germans might—no, rephrase that— probably *will* discover Tom, Dick, or Harry, because over the past few years they've become as clever at finding tunnels as we have at building them. But *three* deep and technologically expert tunnels should give us an edge. Which brings us to the next important point. From now on every one of us here has got to think *not* what the Germans think, but to get one step ahead of that thinking. When, and if, they find one of our tunnels, being German, and methodical and thorough, they'll realize exactly how much thought, labor, and skill have gone into making it. They'll think we've put everything we have into that one project. That's exactly what we *want* them to think. And if they find *two*, we hope they reach the conclusion that we've exhausted *all* our efforts. . . ."

Roger paused so that his next point would sink home.

"Everything hinges upon security. Our security measures must be faultless. From now on I never want to hear the word 'tunnel' mentioned in this camp, and I'll trust you to pass that directive on to every kriegie in every barrack block. I don't care if the person is dead certain that no ferret can hear him. The word is expunged from our vocabulary. Three new words have entered it—Tom, Dick, and Harry.

"Tom goes out of Hut One-twenty-three under the west wire," Roger continued. "Dick goes out of Hut One-twenty-two, also under the west wire." Roger paused to give them his imitation of a grin. "Harry—and I have a feeling that Harry might be our boy—goes out from Hut One-oh-four, under the compound, under the cooler, under the perimeter road, under the guard tower, and emerges in the woods . . . a total distance of around three hundred and fifty, maybe four hundred feet."

Four hundred feet! They had been close to that in East Compound, but at what cost! There was a groan from the audience hearing this fact for the first time, and Wally Floody, a prime architect of the scheme, smiled, pursed his lips, and made a whistling noise to join in the general consternation. What else had the buggers to do except learn to dig?

"Groan, gentlemen, groan," Roger went on, his smile real now. "But remember the Escape Committee are trying to outthink Germans, and Hut One-oh-four is the very last place the Germans would expect a tunnel to originate."

He glanced down at Squadron Leader John "Willy" Williams, a redoubtable Australian Spitfire pilot, who had raised a languid arm. "You got a question, Willy?"

"*Tunnel*, my friend. You just said a dirty word!"

The audience roared. Roger grimaced. "Dead right. And you can all see how easy it is to slip up. Let that be the last time we ever hear that word. After all, we learnt a lot from East Compound. You might even say we were born there."

Certainly Flight Lieutenant Ian M. Muir had played a major part in that birth when, one morning in East Compound, he came up with a new tunnel idea so simple and yet so revolutionary that it startled the Escape Committee out of its eternal skepticism.

The Germans had designated Stalag Luft III as an officer air-crew POW camp in April 1942, their intention being to build a major camp of five compounds: East, Center, North, South, and Belaria. East was the first completed, and officer aircrew from the USAAF, the RAF, and other European air forces were transferred there from camps all over Germany and Poland. Many were inveterate escapers who had broken out many times and been recaptured, for the melancholy truth attached to all escape attempts was that very few achieved a "home run."

But the blending of so many escape addicts from so many nations meant that escape activity was given a new resolution: the Escape Committee, which had flourished in many of the first camps —the brainchild of Wings Day—was now an accepted part of POW existence. A roster of expert veterans were always available to scrutinize escape proposals. Wings Day, Wally Floody, Squadron Leader Tom Ker-Ramsay, Lieutenant Commander Peter Fanshawe, and Harry Marshall had been on duty that morning. Flight Lieutenant Muir was not intimidated. "Practically all the tunnels that have been started so far—and there have been a hell of a lot of them—have been discovered because they were too shallow . . . never more than four feet below the surface. A heavy lorry can cave them in, and the sand dispersers have been too careless."

The Escape Committee stifled a mutual yawn. So what was new? If the committee okayed a project the applicant was free to choose his own team, his own sand dispersers, and left to go ahead in his own way. That was a democratic way to approach such attempts, wasn't it? And so if they messed up the whole project—which they usually did—it was their own concern.

Muir continued: "So we construct a shallow tunnel four feet deep, twenty to fifty feet long, and then abandon it. If the Germans find it, it's just an abandoned tunnel."

The Escape Committee were now dozing off; Wally Floody expected to hear snores at any moment.

"But after that fifty feet we install a disguised trap and sink another shaft—at least twenty feet deep—beneath it. So now we've got two tunnels, one at four feet and one at twenty-five, the *real* tunnel heading for the wire!"

In a single movement the Escape Committee sat up. James Watt had discovered the secret of the steam engine by watching a kettle boil; Archimedes, specific gravity by plopping into his bath and watching the water overflow . . . maybe Muir's idea wasn't quite as good as these, but damn close to it.

"If the Germans discover the shallow tunnel, which is likely—we might even drop a few clues as to its whereabouts—they are bound to believe that we will not try again from that particular hut or in that particular tunnel. But we shall not have

14

stopped work on our deep tunnel; we'll simply join up to it from other deeper shafts and linking tunnels."

There was a babble of enthusiasm. Wings Day quieted it with a quick summing-up. "It's a great idea, and I think we should give it top priority."

Other committee members voiced approving sentiments.

"What about stopping all other tunnel attempts while we push ahead with this one?"

"*One* man in charge of sand disposal—Peter Fanshawe—so the other careless buggers can't leave sand castles all over the place."

"Three teams of tunnelers working around the clock, in three shifts: Wally Floody to manage overall, Ker-Ramsay and Harry Marshall to take a team each. The tunnel to run from Hut Sixty-six."

"How many diggers do you want for each team, Wally?"

Wally did a quick mental calculation. "Seventeen to each shift."

"Right," said Wings Day. "It was Muir's idea, so he's deputized as overall leader. Let's get organized."

Flight Lieutenant Muir's suggestion had provided a blueprint for the three master tunnels of the future in North Compound. Deep tunnels were the answer, even though they confronted everyone with special problems. Air was the first one. If the roof fell in at four feet you had a chance of burrowing upwards and popping your head

15

through the surface; at thirty feet you were entombed.

Another problem was light to work with at that depth. Fat-lamps were the usual light-providers throughout the compound at night. A fat-lamp was a round cigarette tin filled with boiled margarine, strained and cooled, with a thread from a pajama cord embedded within it to act as a wick.

David "Tokyo" Jones, one of the first Americans to arrive in Sagan, remembers them well—just as he will always remember his first experience of descending a tunnel shaft. "We were down at twenty-five feet and there was just room for two of you at the bottom. And the damn fat-lamp kept going out. I'd send it up, and down it would come with the wick flickering, and within seconds it had gone out again. Then you'd realize that there wasn't enough oxygen down there to keep a fat-lamp alive, let alone a human being. I also began to understand the dangers and difficulties of digging a two-foot-square tunnel. You had to wear those awful long johns to prevent getting elbow and arm sores as you wriggled your way along a tunnel—they would give you away at once as a tunnel digger if the Germans happened to spot them in the showers. Those long johns were obscene: dirty, wet, stinking. You left them down in the shaft and had to put them on when you restarted. At the end of a shift, you might be a hundred feet away at the face; you'd have to back out, your feet or shoulders might precipitate a sand fall, and you'd feel your partner tugging away at your feet, and you'd be there with your head under the sand in darkness, and you'd say to yourself, 'What the hell am I doing here?'"

The air problem was eventually solved by a simple milk can. There were thousands of them in the compound. One simply cut out the bottom, and the top section—where the lid had been—was fitted snugly into the next can. The join was bound with tarred paper, and one had produced a perfect air conduit that could be buried in the sandy floor as the tunnel progressed.

Homemade bellows in a special chamber at the foot of the entrance shaft, operated by a kriegie with strong arms, drew air from a carefully concealed outside air brick and ventilated the entire tunnel at regular points. The air kept both fat-lamps and tunnel-digging kriegies alive.

Then they hit a snag.

They had intended to run the tunnel under the concrete foundations of the kitchen. They had taken close to three months to reach this obstruction, but now, even though all other tunnels were held in temporary abeyance, the amount of sand excavated from the exceptionally deep tunnel was creating severe problems.

The Escape Committee held daily conferences. Hornblower outlined the difficulties: "Roof spaces above huts are sagging with the weight of sand. Garden plots are being saturated. Glemnitz or Peschel—" he was speaking of Oberfeldwebel Glemnitz and senior Abwehr officer Major

Peschel—"is bound to pick up a clue sooner or later."

Ker-Ramsay came in with a suggestion. "There's a big empty space under Hut Sixty-eight, and its walls come straight down to earth level. We could stick it under there."

Hornblower raised his eyes to heaven. Dispersing sand in predictable areas immeasurably increased the risk of discovery.

Roger glanced across at Hornblower and shrugged his shoulders. "Got to put it somewhere, Peter. I think we've got to take a chance and give it a go. Trouble is, how do we get into and under Hut Sixty-eight without our sand dispersers being spotted? There's one hell of a lot of sand that still needs to be dug out."

"A tunnel might be the answer," suggested Wally. "We build a tunnel back from our entrance shaft in Hut Sixty-six towards Sixty-eight. The tunnelers and the sand dispersers never need show their heads above ground."

"Good idea," agreed Roger. "Let's get on with it."

George Harsh was quick to observe that the Germans were examining the terrain around Hut 68 with a certain amount of suspicion. Ferrets were probing the ground with more than their usual enthusiasm. Platoons of Wehrmacht hopefully dug several shafts.

Roger said, "Let's limit working hours to night-time only. That will lessen the risk."

"Seems to me," said George, "that Major

Peschel might be up all night hoping to make himself famous. Let's hope he gets carried away and does something stupid."

Two days later, Wally said happily, "I think he's taken your advice."

George went outside to see for himself. Under the hot summer sun, teams of sweating Wehrmacht infantry were digging a ditch eight feet deep and three feet across.

"Where the hell's that going?" asked George in amazement.

"Around the entire camp, according to our spies," grinned Wally. "Their theory is that if you ring the entire camp with a tunnel you must stumble across any other tunnel heading out."

"Bad thinking," said George. "Slip across and tell them they've got to increase their depth to thirty feet to strike gold."

Roger was elated. "Perhaps we can capitalize on this," he said. "Anybody got any ideas?"

Ker-Ramsay offered his: "Three of our blokes have worked it out and found a place in the ditch where they can't be seen from the guard towers. They want to hide in the ditch after roll call and try and rabbit-hole themselves under the wire during the night."

"Give them the go-ahead," said Roger. "Any diversion helps to give us more time. Tell them to be careful not to get themselves shot if they're caught."

It didn't work. The three hopeful officers managed to hide in the ditch, but the guards with their dogs discovered them. They were marched off to do their stint in the cooler.

The Germans completed their circular moat. They discovered nothing except that the POWs might use it as a starting point for other escapes. Major Peschel ordered the ditch to be filled in. From the noises emerging from the sweating, blaspheming infantrymen, it appeared that Peschel was not the most popular officer in the Wehrmacht.

But Peschel had the last word. A week later Ker-Ramsay made a hurried entrance into Bushell's room, shouting, "Come and look at this! Quickly!"

Together they watched the ferrets pouring into Hut 68 to flush out its occupants, while a jubilant Peschel watched a few boards being pulled out of the hut's sides to reveal the golden sand.

Chapter Two

MAJOR PESCHEL WAS DELIGHTED with his discovery, for it opened German eyes to the new efficiency of kriegie tunnel construction. It was not hard for the ferrets to find their way back through the sand channels to Hut 66 and there discover the deep tunnel. That made them really blink, for by this time it was close to four hundred feet in length. It was photographed for the camp museum, then flooded with water from fire hoses, collapsing it completely.

Although this turn of events was a setback, everyone sensed that a new chapter of deep tunnel building was about to start. A taut and determined Roger Bushell was holding meetings every day. Wally Floody fell asleep dreaming of deep tunnels. They'd licked the air problem with the milk cans; they had a way to go before solving the lighting problem; they'd invented trolleys to pull sand from the tunnel face, and soon would come up with the idea of mounting those trolleys on rails.

And there was one other aspect to be considered: East Compound was now beginning to fill with a great number of American aircrew, and was becoming wildly overcrowded. Rooms intended to hold six men were now filled with double that number. The Germans let it be known that a second, larger North Compound was about to be constructed and would be ready for occupancy in March 1943. Volunteers from the kriegie population were asked if they were prepared to form working parties: it was, after all, their camp that was being built, and they could, on parole, help in its construction. The Escape Committee decided that this was an opportunity too good to be missed. Wally Floody, George Harsh, and Peter Fanshawe were among the working parties who paced out the terrain, examined the drainage and sewage systems as potential escape avenues, made mental notes of distances from wire to woods, inspected foundations of future barrack blocks, and eyed building materials that could be "liberated." They just could not wait to move to the new North Compound.

The commandant of Sagan, von Lindeiner, thoroughly approved of what he thought was the commendable cooperation of his POWs. Kommandant von Lindeiner was a Prussian officer of the old school—honorable, severe, correct—who had served his country gallantly in the First World War. Accepting that it was his duty to keep his charges safely penned behind barbed wire, he looked upon them with a certain indulgence, observing quite proudly, "A budding diplomat could have received an excellent schooling here, studying the mentality of almost all the peoples of the globe."

Like most Germans, von Lindeiner was fond

of classifications. He listed most of the prisoners' professions: "Millionaires' sons, tram conductors, football players, racehorse trainers, professional hockey players, actors, photographers, racing-car drivers, professional dancers, schoolteachers, traveling salesmen, pianists, chefs, bandleaders, porters, plantation owners, hotel managers, jockeys, bacteriologists, scientists, organists, diamond miners, lawyers, coal miners, missionaries, private detectives, singers, artists, politicians, veterinary surgeons, doctors, reporters, stockbrokers, Indian princes. . . . no end to their diversity of employment."

But what von Lindeiner did not really appreciate was that the kriegies intended to use every skill they possessed to escape, and it is doubtful if he ever quite understood the intensity of that feeling. In the first two years of the war the Germans were quite unprepared for the gigantic influx of aircrew prisoners of war. The result: POWs who were hungry to the point of near-starvation, cold, and embittered by the conditions under which they had to live. By 1943, however, with mail and Red Cross parcels arriving regularly to supplement the meager German rations, and the Germans now building more camps, conditions were much improved. Sagan, Stalag Luft III, began to realize its full potential, especially in North Compound, where in April 1943 around 850 heavily laden kriegies were herded across from East Compound to North by guards armed with automatic rifles.

Although Sagan had been chosen by Reichsmarschall Hermann Goering himself as the site of a huge POW camp, Kommandant von Lindeiner disapproved. He felt that if the POWs themselves had been given the chance to choose their own site, they couldn't have done much better than Sagan. To start with, von Lindeiner didn't like Sagan's geographical location: 105 miles southeast of Berlin, 80 miles from Dresden, 125 east of Leipzig; main rail lines and spur lines running in all directions to help a POW make a quick getaway, should he manage to cover the few hundred yards between camp and station. And to help the escaper even further, thick, wooded areas spread in all directions. Von Lindeiner also viewed with disfavor the fact that the water level lay about 350 feet underground, so that the tunneling addict would never be bothered by underground flooding.

He would admit, however, that the sandy subsoil was an element in his favor. Even though there were clay strata about eight inches in depth every fourteen feet or so, the bright yellow sand possessed a quicksilver quality and was not conducive to the building of tunnels. When dug out it had a distinctive and easily discernible odor; it collapsed very easily with only a slight "crack" of warning, and was lethal in its weight and suffocating capacity. Wally Floody could have written a treatise on that—he had been buried beneath the sand enough times.

In the main, Kommandant von Lindeiner's philosophy was simple and humanitarian: Here we have hundreds of young men cooped up as prisoners of war. They are brave and patriotic and they have committed no crime. The misfortunes of war have placed them in German hands, as it has placed many German soldiers in Allied hands. Therefore it is our duty—a duty entrusted to us under the Geneva convention (and Germany was the first nation, in 1929, to sign that convention)—to provide for their welfare.

It was ironic, therefore, that this strange amalgam of young officer aircrew—eventually thousands of them—began to scheme and plan to make Kommandant von Lindeiner's life as complicated and turbulent as possible.

There were, in fact, occasions when Kommandant von Lindeiner and his staff thought they could not believe their own eyes, or the reports of their subordinates. For example, there was the day when Offizier Karl Pilz—known to the kriegies as "Charlie"—while walking through the compound, saw *himself* coming towards him. Charlie's character wavered between humanitarian kindness and outraged Nazi fury. He was a master at discovering tunnels, and amateurish efforts aroused only his contempt. Good tunnels were admired and photographed, and the photos were passed along to the Escape Museum, which was a permanent feature of every self-respecting stalag: a tribute to both observant ferret detection and brilliant kriegie invention.

Charlie was tall, with a long, sallow face and a

dour expression. The other Charlie approaching him was a mirror image. Charlie's mouth stayed open. Would this doppelgänger spring upon him? Only the voice saying in a clear English accent, "Well, what d'you know! What bad luck meeting the original version!" restored Offizier Pilz to his senses.

Charlie's face, hair, bearing, and walk had been studied carefully by the hopeful escaper during weeks of observation. A little chalk and makeup added to the deception. The RAF uniform had been darkened with the addition of soot and graphite, the badge carefully contrived from odd bits of material. The RAF POW received ten days in the cooler; Charlie eventually got over the shock.

The strange case of Offizier Hohendole was somewhat similar. He passed through the two gates of East Compound, showing his pass, and arrived at the Main Gate. The guard carefully examined his credentials and let him through. Ten minutes later a second Offizier Hohendole arrived at the Main Gate. The guard blanched. "But, Offizier Hohendole, you have already left the compound!"

Offizier Hohendole blinked, then exploded into infuriated German: "What are you gabbling about —fool! I am standing here in front of you. Touch me—I am human. That is my identity pass you are holding in your hand, complete with my photograph!"

The guard was now babbling, "But, sir, you

are now wearing light-colored trousers—last time you were wearing dark trousers—"

"I am the only Offizier Hohendole, idiot. You have let an impostor escape!"

The fake Offizier Hohendole was captured soon afterwards. He was not displeased; he had won quite a lot of large bets in cigarettes. Like the kriegie who had masqueraded as Charlie, there was also a distinct facial resemblance; the only striking difference between imitator and original was the color of the hair: Offizier Hohendole was fair-haired. The potential escaper had spent weeks carefully applying dabs of hydrogen peroxide to his own hair until he was an almost perfect match.

There was between prisoners and guards a certain reluctant admiration. None, for example, could dislike Oberfeldwebel Glemnitz, even though his job was precisely to prevent escapes. As Lieutenant Colonel Bub Clark, USAAF, said about him: "We respected him and he respected us. He was shrewd, highly intelligent, a good leader. He had under him a group of highly skilled young Luftwaffe personnel—the 'ferrets'—who wore dark-blue overalls, Luftwaffe Field Service caps, and leather duty belts. They were unarmed, but carried long, thin steel probing rods. They crawled under huts looking for tunnels; they drove their probes into the earth searching for tunnels; they drove heavy trucks around near the huts and other areas seeking to cave in tunnels. You could find them around any corner, behind any door, under the floorboards, or in the attic—eavesdropping—and one of the requirements of their job was the ability to speak excellent English. They could enter any room without knocking; in fact, they were free to wander where they liked, looking with eager eyes for any trace of escape equipment, maps, radios, clothing, papers, compasses. I was part of our security system for quite a few months, and it was a constant secret battle between us."

Roger Bushell's rallying shout about Tom, Dick, and Harry had already started to produce results. The entrance traps in Huts 122, 123, and 104, opening into vertical shafts dropping towards as yet undug tunnels, were marvels of kriegie ingenuity. The architects were three Polish officers: Gotowski, Minskewitz, and Kolanowski. Wally Floody—as tunnel engineer in chief—chose Harry as his own particular baby, delegating Tom to Harry Marshall and Dick to Ker-Ramsay.

Davie Jones felt honored when Wally suggested they do a little reconnaissance work on Tom's shaft. Wally showed him along the narrow corridor next to the kitchen. There was not much light. Wally said, "Even the guys who built this trap have a hard time finding it, second time around."

Fishing in his pocket, Wally produced a thin-bladed knife and began picking cautiously at the floor. With a "Hmm!" of appreciation, he felt it slide through the paper-thin crack brushed over with a mixture of damp cement and floor dust, and worked his way around a square of concrete

28

just wide enough to admit a man's shoulders. Gently he levered out the wires tucked down in the cracks on all four sides, which formed handles. With Davie helping, he lifted the concrete slab out onto the floor.

The need to drive holes through concrete foundations of huts and washrooms to start tunnels presented severe problems—the main one being noise. Somehow the crashing and banging had to be covered. Major Johnny Dodge had come up with one brilliant suggestion. At nearly fifty, the Dodger was cosseted as a sweet geriatric by his younger associates, who were fascinated by his ability to entrap them in his debates and discussions on every political, theological, or philosophical event since the world began. And they certainly enjoyed his massed choir practice. No auditions were needed. A steam-whistle tenor or a tractor-engine bass was welcome. At given signals in the vicinity of Huts 122, 123, and 104, Choirmaster Dodge climbed on his soapbox, raised his baton, and surprised every German guard staring down from a watchtower with the thunderous power of his choir's Christmas carols. The fact that it was early May did not seem to bother anyone.

At other critical hammering periods, Johnny Travis's pot- and pan-making teams would decide to work outside, and fill the vicinity with their factory noises. And if the worst became imminent, Jerry Sage's "hooligans" were always on standby to create a diversion of spectacular proportions, thereby preventing ferrets or suspicious guards from closing in on an objective. Jerry's boys could start a march, a brawl, an unarmed-combat session, or a football game of inexplicable ferocity. All the traps had been completed successfully.

In Hut 123 Wally Floody carefully removed the square wooden grille that lay beneath the concrete slab. It was packed with folded blankets. "Muffles all echoes or hollow sounds if you stamp around on top," he explained.

Davie Jones looked down into the vertical shaft. Wally continued his exposition. "A framework of four bunk-post uprights, locked into place as we go deeper with other bunk posts, the whole thing strengthened by bunk boards to form a solid vertical entrance." He indicated the ladder leading downwards. "So far there's just enough room for two to stand at the bottom. We've got to do a great deal more digging there. A working chamber to hold the tools and sledges. A chamber for the bellows operators."

Davie knew that Wally Floody had been half buried alive in stalag tunnels all over Germany, often hauled out with only seconds to spare. Nevertheless there seemed no stopping Wally's enthusiasm for a molelike existence.

They had reached the bottom of the shaft and Wally was standing with his head up, sniffing the air like a hound dog. He said, "Davie, I have a feeling that we'd better do our work down here pretty quickly and then get the hell out."

30

Davie Jones could sense no danger. "You think so? Why?"

"I've been doing this sort of thing for so long, you get a sort of feeling about it. This goddam place is gonna fall in on us if we're not careful."

Wally described the incident later: "Davie said, 'I can't see a problem.' And at that moment there was the usual 'crack' and the whole damned shaft caved in on us. We went up that ladder like scalded squirrels, but I can tell you Davie had no chance to beat me up. When I got to the top he was buried up to his armpits and the sand was filling in almost like water. I reached down and hauled him out, and we watched the shaft fill up almost to the rim."

All through that year when six hundred kriegies labored in their separate tasks to protect and build Tom, Dick, and Harry, collapsing sand was a constant hazard. So many tunnel diggers were buried, only to be saved by the frantic muscular efforts of their coworkers, that such activity had become almost a commonplace.

On the surface, problems were equally harassing.

Bub Clark was made chief security officer almost as soon as he arrived in East Compound. Bub had divided East Compound—as he did when they were all moved to North—into two zones: "D" for danger, and "S" for safety. "S" usually turned out to be "almost safe" because "duty pilots"—watching the entrance gate and logging in and out all German personnel—and "stooges"

31

(lookouts) had to be constantly on the alert, ready to anticipate the wily moves the intelligent, English-speaking young ferrets would make. It was the stooges' job to stay on the trail of every ferret or German official during every minute of his stay in North Compound.

Should a ferret enter D zone, the defensive network slipped into gear. It might mean a leisurely stretching of one's arms, a yawn, a scratching of the head, the closing of a book, an adjustment to a window shutter, the closing of a door—the signals were endless—but the next stooge operating fifty to a hundred yards away, or sometimes as close as ten, would be instantly alerted to pass the danger signal to the next in line, and the word was snapped to the forgers, mapmakers, and compass makers to close up shop.

There were many narrow squeaks. Wally remembers the time when George Harsh stumbled into his room, hand outstretched, moaning, "A large Scotch—a large Scotch!"

"In ten years' time," said Wally soothingly. "What's up?"

"That damned Charlie Pilz. Clever little bastard. Of course we've got him marked. A stooge in front, another on his tail, and me in my little room in Hut One-twenty-three where I sit like a spider, who has now been alerted to the fact that Charlie is behaving very strangely. Walking around between the huts, slowly then fast. Into Hut One-twenty-two, then out again. And somehow I have a gut feeling that it's Hut One-twenty-three he's after, so I rise to take the necessary evasive action because I know the trap in the corridor of One-twenty-three is open and the guys are working down below. Charlie's heading straight for the door which leads to it. There's another stooge in his way, naturally, and another stooge in my way, naturally. They both know the drill. We have a fiendish shouting match. 'What are you doing hanging around here, you stupid clod!' That sort of thing, knowing that if they're not going crazy to get that trap closed, Tom goes up in smoke. Charlie's at the door. Everybody's at the door. Charlie's turning the handle. I launch myself at him like a fifteen-inch shell! All of us crash through the door. Charlie's flat on his face with me on top of him and the stooge on top of me, and I'm howling blue murder about the goddam stooge tripping me up when I'm roaring to the john with a bad case of the green-apple two-step. Stooge dusts Charlie off. You know . . . usual British bull . . . 'Terribly sorry, old chap. These Yanks are just bulls in a china shop. Can't even go to the lavatory without making a scene. But of course he didn't expect to find a noncommissioned German officer taking a stroll along this corridor.'"

"The trap," said Wally, "the trap!"

George gave one of his dreamy Deep South smiles. "Trap? What trap? Oh, that trap. No trap there. The corridor was empty. A few guys working in the kitchen." George then added, "Do you realize, Flight Lieutenant, that there's more larceny, forgery, intimidation, and deception going on in North Compound every *day* then there would be in a small town this size in ten *years?*"

"I believe you," answered Wally. "Isn't it great?"

Chapter Three

CAPTAIN JOHN BENNETT OF the USAAF never forgot his arrival at Stalag Luft III. Within hours he was being interrogated by an RAF wing commander and Lieutenant Colonel Bub Clark.

"Captain Bennett," said Bub Clark sternly, "the Germans are always trying to plant informers and spies among us. Therefore we have to examine your credentials, find out that you are exactly what you say you are—the pilot of a B-17 shot down on a bombing raid on the submarine pens at Brest."

John Bennett, sure of his ground, said cheerfully, "Well, sir, I can tell you the names of my crew, the commanding officer of my squadron . . . and as a matter of fact, I know you, Colonel Clark."

Bub Clark's eyebrows shot up. "Oh?"

"Pendleton Field, Oregon, January 1942. I was a second pilot attached to Davie Jones's group. You were there, too."

A few more questions and Captain John Bennett was cleared for duties in Sagan, Stalag Luft III. "No time to waste here," said Bub Clark. "We can use your help. At the moment there's a vacancy for a sanitary officer. You're it."

"But I don't know anything about sanitation, sir," said Captain Bennett politely.

"You'll learn," answered Clark.

Lieutenant Colonel Bub Clark, twenty-eight years old, had arrived in the summer of 1942 to find Stalag Luft III in something of a turmoil—there was a crisis of sewage and garbage. A group of RAF kriegies had decided to sabotage the German war effort by eliminating the pig population of Stalag Luft III. Their contentions were logical: pigs produced pork, bacon, and sausages, welcome additions to the Reich's food supply. The pigs were fed mainly on camp garbage. Throw all used razor blades into that garbage and the pigs would perish. Good in theory. Harmless in reality. The pigs went on chewing garbage and razor blades with the same relish as always.

However, German orderlies noticed the razor blades, and several of them were cut while handling the garbage. They were angry and retaliated. Garbage was no longer collected; it was left to rot and stink in the hot summer sun. Sewage, treated in the same category as garbage, was also left unattended and uncollected. Sagan stank to high heaven and spawned untold millions of buzzing flies. Outbreaks of dysentery became commonplace.

After a month of fly pestilence, both Germans and Britons realized that some compromise must be reached. Wings Day gave strict orders that razor blades were to be banned from garbage. The Germans agreed to collect it again. But the flies had now proliferated to such an extent that there seemed to be no way of eradicating them.

Wings Day then heard about a bright young American lieutenant colonel who had been among the first half dozen men to arrive in Sagan. Wings Day believed in the theory that the Americans were the most hygiene-conscious people on earth. Maybe Lieutenant Colonel Clark could assist in this matter? By lucky chance Bub's father had once been in charge of camp construction sites in the wooded areas of Colorado. He had faced the same problems that now confronted Stalag Luft III. And as a teenager, Bub Clark had often worked with him. To clear flies one dug drainage ditches, covered all garbage dumps and sewage pits, used insecticide, and ventilated in all the proper places. Bub Clark won the Battle of the Flies, and was held in high esteem by both the British and the Germans. And by the time John Bennett arrived in Sagan, a completely new use had been found for old razor blades.

"Bub Clark," said John, "went around to all the new American arrivals—and they were coming in at a fairly steady rate by now—asking, 'What can you do? Any good at radio, draftsmanship, tailoring, carpentry, forgery?'"

And Davie Jones recounted: "The very first job I got, before I took up the more hazardous task of deep tunneling, was to move a wall—a wooden interior wall—to make a space where our escape gear could be hidden. Each room in a barrack hut was about fifteen feet square. If you moved a wall

37

about nine inches inwards, nobody noticed the decrease in space except the inhabitants, and they always thought the room was too small anyway, so what the hell. It wasn't all that hard to do. You'd pry out the nails, move the spacers, set them up in a different place, put the walls back on, and there you were . . . a nice big cubbyhole with secret traps in it through which all the goodies could be popped within seconds."

"When Bub Clark approached me," said John Bennett, "after I'd completed my spell as sanitary officer, I said I liked working with my hands.

" 'Good,' said Clark. 'Got just the job for you. Follow me!'

"That's how I entered the world of Al Hake and his compass-making factory. Al Hake was a great big dark, hairy Australian, and I've never met a nicer guy in my whole life. We shook hands, and Al introduced me to his friend who also worked in the factory—only one room really— with Al's guitar laying waiting on the bed, so if the ferrets made a quick search, all our stuff was behind the wall, and Al was strumming the guitar while we made an awful howl harmonizing 'Waltzing Matilda.' "

Al asked John, "I suppose you had one of those RAF button compasses with you when you were shot down?"

John answered, "Yes, darn useful too. When I hit the deck it gave me a clue as to how to head south towards Spain. Only trouble was I landed in northern France, and Spain was seven hundred miles away across the Pyrenees."

Al grinned. "Well, you know that without a compass the escaper is lost. We've got to make hundreds of them for the mass escape. As an apprentice your first job is to make the magnetic pointer, the sweeper hand which turns towards magnetic north. Here's your raw material." He handed John a used, double-edged razor blade.

John looked mystified. "What do I do with this?"

"You magnetize it," said Al. "Slow process but vital." Al had "liberated" a large magnet from some guard. He showed John Bennett the art of magnetizing an old razor blade: one stroked the razor blade, always in the same direction, for hours at a time.

"No one could call it an intellectual pursuit," said John, "but at the end of that first afternoon, triumphantly, I had produced one fully magnetized razor blade. Now, plainly you could not use one whole razor blade. The next trick was to split it into thin needles. Again Al Hake showed me the procedure. He had a vise—well, something as good as a vise: a hinge from one of the heavy shutters which barred every window of every hut every night. You stuck the razor blade between the two sections of the hinge, with a tiny strip showing . . . a sharp, expert tap . . . and voilà— one magnetized compass needle.

"Of course, being American, I was soon into the mass-production, Ford-assembly-line philos-

39

ophy. Why not magnetize twenty razor blades at the same time? I took a flat bed board, used powdered skim milk to make a glue, and secured all the blades. I used the same stroking technique and increased production overnight.

"That was only a part of the job. Next was the compass case. For that, as basic material we used phonograph records; the YMCA used to send us piles of these Bakelite discs, and naturally a lot got smashed in everyday usage. The plastic would melt under quite a gentle heat, and was easily molded, then would reset as hard as a nutshell.

"For the compass card Al used a small disc of thin cardboard—the Germans allowed us to buy this with 'lager-geld,' or prison money. Using a tiny brush made from his own hair, and white paint, Al would indicate the compass points on the card. When Jerry Sage—he was the wildest American boy in the whole stockade: he'd been in the OSS, he'd been a paratrooper, he'd been behind the lines in the desert—when Jerry calmly 'liberated' the Kommandant's alarm clock from his office (nobody ever wanted to know the details of that exploit), we chipped tiny slivers of luminous paint off the hands, stuck them to the tips of the razor blades, and lo! . . . night-visible compasses.

"Al had also managed to buy from a German guard a fine pair of German surgical scissors, and underwater they would cut out circles of glass we obtained from broken barrack room windows. Al himself finally put together every compass. First he balanced the strip of razor blade on the point of a phonograph needle securely welded into the base of the Bakelite case. Then he added the glass cover and sealed that in with a tiny drop of solder—we got those drops from the seals of every can of bully beef—and Al completed his master-pieces by stamping every one of them with the inscription 'Made in Stalag Luft III. Patent Pending.'"

After the war the *Official History of Sagan, Stalag Luft III*, included this tribute: "The compass makers were so skilful at their work that the few real compasses brought in by newly shot-down aircrew, and the small number smuggled in through secret channels, were quite superfluous. Five hundred were produced ready for the mass-escape in March 1944."

When the move from East Compound to North Compound was made in April 1943, John Bennett's task was to get the entire stock of Al Hake's compass factory moved with them. That required some careful planning.

"In those days the British used to receive their cigarette allowance in these beautiful round aluminum tins which held fifty cigarettes in a vertical position. They were common currency in the compound; there were thousands of them in circulation," said John.

"The tins were sealed, but stand them on a hot stove for a second, and you could flip off the lids with a penknife. I'd take out the cigarettes and stack the tins three-quarters full of compasses, then fill the remaining space with neatly clipped nubs about an inch long, and reseal the tins. The Germans hardly bothered to look."

In Germany during those war years no one could move or operate without papers. No escaper could hope to travel across country through towns and villages without documents detailing who he was, where he was coming from, where he was going, and what he was doing. Gilbert "Tim" Walenn's forgery department functioned to supply those papers, and was probably the most original such group in the history of escapes. First came the raw materials: pens, inks, papers, brushes, tracing cloth, and linen. Some were filtered in by M19 in private parcels to prisoners; others were supplied by contacts inside the camp, or were "liberated." And every sort of material was utilized: toilet tissue could be used as tracing paper, flyleaves of Bibles and textbooks for the same purpose; rubber from boot soles could be carved into official-looking stamps; and "contacts"—usually guards with friendly or greedy intentions—were indoctrinated into service by judicious bribery. Kriegies were better off than most of the guards: kriegies received chocolate, cigarettes, coffee, tea, and canned goods in their Red Cross parcels. A contact would be invited to sit in a warm room and chat over a cup of coffee while his POW "friend" made innocent conversation about the possibility that— who knows?—their roles might be reversed in the future. It was a quiet and insidious form of blackmail and it worked. Guards lent passes and documents for copying—and these were fantastically numerous. To name but a few: there were the *Dienstausweise*, a brown card printed on buckram entitling the holder to be on Wehrmacht property; the *Urlaubscheine*, a yellow form used as a leave-chit for foreign workers; the *Rückkehrscheine*, a pink form for foreign workers sent back to their own country; the *Kennkarte*, a light gray card printed on buckram used as an identity card; the *carte d'identité*, an identity card issued in France and bearing a 50-centime stamp; the *Sichtvermark*, a passport visa; *Ausweise* and *Vorläufiger Ausweise*, passes and temporary passes; the *Polizeitische Beschenigung*, a police permit authorizing the presence of a foreign worker in given areas; papers bearing letterheads belonging to important manufacturers such as Siemens and Focke-Wulf Flugzeugbau. Many of these documents were printed on a background similar to that of a bank note, with fine whorled lines and tiny print. One of these took a month to produce, a worker putting five hours a day into his forgery.

Attached to this beehive of forgery was a department of intelligence and language, which advised on every detail and was run by a gutsy Lithuanian member of the RAF, Flight Lieutenant Romas Marcinkus. Marcinkus also, through artful bribery, gained information about German railroad schedules and copied such little items as a police chief's signature from an area a hundred miles away.

As the war "got hotter" (to use Hermann Goering's phrase), and the tide of German success began to roll back towards a distant horizon, helpers became more accessible. Inside North Compound, when Gefreite Fischer—a secret anti-Nazi—went home on leave, he took stenciling and typing home from the various escape units for his wife to do. Hauptmann Peiber, also pro-Allies, a rather worried but decent Austrian on Kommandant von Lindeiner's staff, gave a helping hand, ostensibly to cheer up homesick prisoners who needed to send a snapshot home. He lent his Leica camera, and then developed and printed the photos the kriegies had taken. How could Hauptmann Peiber know they were being used for fake passports?

Probably the most outrageous and impudent use of a contact was that of a German who went on leave to Paris, with all his expenses paid by the Escape Committee, and returned with important documents giving details of the French underground and how a potential escaper might seek help from it.

That hot summer of 1943 saw a constant battle between the tunnelers and Oberfeldwebel Glemnitz and his crew of trained ferrets. The attitude of the kriegies was determined but cheerful. The Wehrmacht guards and the stalag officials had too much to lose to adopt that attitude. It was common knowledge that malignant power rested with the Gestapo and no one wished to tangle with them or oppose them. The Gestapo were doing their best to master POW affairs. If prisoners of war escaped, it was necessary to set in motion a whole chain of costly and time-wasting activities that Nazi Germany could ill afford. Cables had to be dispatched; telephone calls made; frontier guards, Home Guards, Hitler Youth organizations, foresters, and railway and shipping authorities alerted. For such incompetence, the Kommandant and senior officials were fired, transferred, or imprisoned; lower ranks could expect the most feared punishment of all—a transfer to the eastern front and the chance of a very quick death.

The kriegies held certain advantages: their system of duty pilots clocking every German in and out of the camp, and knowing exactly where each one was during that time through watchers, trackers, and stooges, preserved practically all their secrets. Physically, however, the Germans, with watchtowers, heavily armed guards, dog handlers, and constant patrols, were always in command.

The Germans knew that tunnels were being constructed, but they did not know where. So searches were carried out regularly, ruthlessly, and systematically. Huts were suddenly broken into and their contents scattered. To a certain extent this was countered through judicious bribery among contacts who would warn kriegies which hut or huts were to be searched. But as the weeks passed, the guards became edgier, and anger was roused more easily. There were snap roll calls. Without warning the Main Gate would open and a large detachment of Wehrmacht armed with au-

45

tomatic weapons would race in and surround a barrack hut they suspected. The racket of their bawled commands, *"Raus! Raus! Schnell! Schnell!"* was never amusing. It did not spread fear through the barrack blocks, but it often caused consternation, and highlighted the fact that security was priority number one.

Often George Harsh found that he had to spell out the facts of kriegie life to many of the newcomers. And they were arriving regularly.

One of the constant complaints was voiced by a young Canadian pilot: "George, don't you think this boot-faced interrogation of a poor guy who's just been shot out of the sky is a bit of a bore?"

"No," said George.

"I suppose the idea is to stop them from planting a spy or an informer."

"Yes," said George.

"But he'd be found out by the kriegies within days."

"Within *days*," said George, "that's a long time."

"Yeah—but all this stuff about does your mother come from Toronto or Alaska, and tell me the name of the Brooklyn Dodgers' pitcher in 1932 . . ."

George interrupted. "The Germans know they've got a buzzing nest of escapers. Just one informer planted here and we're dead. That's why the ferrets speak excellent English and hide everywhere—to listen."

"But to *plant* an informer. They'd never try that."

"They already have. Not so long ago. Here in North Compound. Nice guy. Perfect English. A pilot in the Egyptian air force. Nothing wrong with that. The British are fighting in the Western Sahara; the RAF has trained pilots from all over the world. So that part of the story held up. Shot down in the desert by the Luftwaffe. That held up too. Lots of Americans were shot down in North Africa by the Luftwaffe. This guy knew all the right names, all the best brothels in Cairo and Alexandria. But a lot of British aircrew, now residents of Stalag Luft Three, had been in Egypt during that period, and nobody had met this character. Peculiar. They put him under close arrest —immediately. Within a few hours he had confessed he was an agent. They handed him back to the Germans with a courtesy note saying that the next one they planted would end up in a barrel."

With the entrance traps completed, Roger Bushell gave Group Captain Massey a guided tour, spelling out, as they went along, the difficulties that had had to be overcome.

"The point being, sir, that we had to discover locations where in the natural course of things a trap could not possibly exist, and certainly in places where if a ferret crawled underneath a hut he would not for a second imagine one could exist."

"Which meant?"

"Cutting through concrete floors in huts, choosing places like washrooms and stove foundations which stood on concrete bases but were also supported underneath by brick foundations that went deep into the earth. And each trap, as I shall show you, sir, had to be a completely different setup. Now you've seen the entrance to Tom in Hut One-twenty-three, hidden in a narrow corridor."

Roger led the way to the washroom in Hut 122. To the German eye there was nothing strange about the senior British officer and a squadron leader making a tour of inspection.

"No hope of ever putting a trap in here, sir, is there?"

Group Captain Massey smiled. "Roger, I've met our little Polish officer Minskewitz. When he tugs on that little gray goatee of his and looks puzzled, I know he's probably planning a trap under my bed."

"All three Polish officers who planned them were expert engineers, sir. All that stuff about weights, stresses, and cantilever principles—second nature to them."

The washroom sloped gently to the center of the room where a square drainage sump covered with a grating had been sunk. It was half full of water.

"Trap lies under there, sir," said Roger.

"It's half full of water. How can it?"

"The sump hole is three feet deep," explained Roger, "but the actual drainage pipe takes the water away about halfway down, and there's always a sediment of sand and water in the bottom half. Bail that out and mop it out and you've got a dry hole. Minskewitz took out one side of the sump and replaced it with a concrete slab which fits tightly and can be pulled upwards. So, remove the grating, remove water, pull up concrete slab, dig out soil and sand, and start a downward shaft. Great thing about Dick, sir, is that there're always kriegies in the washroom and we can plant stooges there. The Germans can never jump us, and we can seal in a shift of underground workers and they can work day or night undetected."

Group Captain Massey frowned. "I don't see how this tunnel can ever be found."*

Harry, in Hut 104, was entirely different in conception. Harry's stove stood on a heavy concrete base inlaid with colored tiles. A stovepipe led up through the roof. Harry's stove never went out. An extension stovepipe that would bend when Harry was moved was necessary. Then a completely new concrete base was manufactured within a timber frame, and the old tiles removed, scraped, and cemented down in the concrete. Their absence was masked by sand and dirt. It took the replacement block four days to dry. Several of the colored tiles cracked, a giveaway that might invite disaster. Then someone remembered that a stove resting on a similar base of tiles existed in East Compound. A German guard was bribed to

*It never was. It is still there, maybe completely sand-filled by now, waiting for an archaeologist to discover it.

49

lift a few and bring them across to North. They matched and the cracked tiles were replaced.

Smashing through Harry's concrete base and removing the rubble was a noisy business. The Dodger's choir sang themselves hoarse. The new base, hinged on the back so that it could be tilted open, was slid into place. It fit perfectly. The stove could be removed by wooden handles and go on burning. Beneath its base Harry's shaft penetrated thirty feet through the sand.

Dispersing that sand undetected would prove to be a major problem. But for the moment, only one fact mattered: escape operations were firmly under way.

Chapter Four

THAT SUMMER, THE SIGHT of Russian prisoners cutting down swaths of pine trees beyond the wire and guard towers created some interest—and then quickly became a subject of increasing consternation.

The new South Compound was being built. It was intended to hold all the American POWs now mixed with the RAF in North Compound, as well as the increasing number of newly shot down U.S. aircrew. There were many groans. The mixed bunch in North Compound had learned to live together and like each other. Besides that there was the matter of Tom, Dick, and Harry.

The top echelon of the Escape Committee went into immediate session.

Roger Bushell said vehemently, "It's bloody unfair that all the Yanks who've worked just as hard as the rest, and taken the same risks, should be cheated out of a chance to break out."

"I agree," said Wings. "But what can we do? We've made approaches to Kommandant Lindeiner, but he won't or can't do anything about it. It's a direct order from High Command, and you can bet the Gestapo boot is behind it. We've already got the warning from them about escaping POWs being recaptured wearing civilian clothing—that they run the risk of being accused of espionage, sabotage, or just plain banditry. Penalty: a firing squad."

"There is one thing we can do," said Roger, his mind already made up. "We close up Dick and Harry, now!"

There was a slight murmur of disagreement. What good would that do?

"We go full out on Tom. Tom's at least sixty feet out towards the wire. I know Dick and Harry are not far short of that, but if we put all our eggs into one basket—all three shifts of diggers—we might make it before the autumn and before South Compound is ready."

There was a mutter of approval at that.

Roger went on: "Wally, how many feet do you think we make daily now from each tunnel?"

"Five to ten. But even with three shifts, with changeovers we couldn't guarantee to take Tom up to thirty feet a day. Then Hornblower here's got to distribute the sand. I know he's got a lot of penguins—guys scattering sand everywhere—but—?"

All eyes turned to Lieutenant Commander Peter Fanshawe.

"The system's working very well at present," he said. "The big metal water jugs used for hauling it up the shaft and spilling it into a blanket are giving us no trouble. We've got improved methods of putting bags of sand round the penguin's neck under battle-dress blouses when the weather's cold, and sacks inside the trousers when it gets hot . . . and so far, what with all the building that's still taking place and the drainage ditches still being dug, and all the new gardens being dug by the vegetable lovers, we're doing pretty well. I'd say we could cope."

Bub Clark spoke up. "This is a very generous gesture of yours, gentlemen, which we appreciate. But it might raise the risk factor to an unacceptable degree. If we hurry we might lose Tom, and then they might latch onto Dick and Harry."

Roger grinned. "It's a high-risk business, Bub. You and George Harsh have really got to get your security smarts together when the steam starts to rise from Tom."

The vote was unanimous.

Bub Clark repeated his feelings that the tunnel should not be jeopardized by rushing the job, but the Escape Committee were adamant. Tom had to get there somehow or other. More than that, the concept of one tunnel being pressed forward against a definite deadline gave the work an excitement and a purpose.

Tom went out another fifty feet.

There were alarms and perils. Wally was constantly getting buried. There were arguments about angles and inclines, but nothing stopped Tom's progress.

The discovery of sand by the Germans was always the great danger, and if any trace of it was ever found, Oberfeldwebel Glemnitz, the most able and knowledgeable escape-preventer, kept it to himself, watching and waiting to see if the little yellow trails might lead him to the jackpot.

Tom moved fifty more feet. They were close to the wire, then under the wire! Tension mounted. Would this tunnel be the answer? They went over their calculations. They must be closing on the trees by now, the perimeter lights dwindling into shadow. Could they risk a break if the situation got desperate?

There was a lot of argument about the shaft up to the surface. Should it go straight up, or slope up on an incline? But this was not as worrying as one other problem. One morning they looked through the wire and saw that the Germans were busy cutting down trees at the very spot where Tom was due to surface.

"For Christ's sake, why there?" fumed Roger Bushell. "Even if it's sand that's given us away, it could not lead to that particular area, it's all dispersed *here.*"

What the Escape Committee did not know, and what was revealed only at the court-martial of Kommandant von Lindeiner, was the "swinging pen" microphones buried in the ground around the perimeter barbed wire had revealed far more activity than usual. Von Lindeiner had never viewed the microphones very favorably. There had in the past been a lot of mining work in the neighborhood, and some was still going on. The mikes picked up all sorts of subterranean sounds; one could not spend all one's time and labor digging holes in the ground and finding nothing. This time, however, the constant intensity of the sound made it clear that a tunnel was being dug practically under the mike. That gave them a directional clue, but they still had no idea from which hut the tunnel was being built.

"The Germans are certainly up to something," said George Harsh. "Do they think we can't see them building their little 'hunting blinds' of brushwood and branches outside the wire and peering in with binoculars? They'll learn nothing from that. There is no unusual activity from or to any particular hut."

"But they're damned interested in One-twenty-three," said Roger. "Could it be sand? Hornblower, have you got any ideas where we might stow it in case it is?"

"Certainly," said Hornblower, his thin face and aquiline features betraying not a trace of emotion. "Dick's closed down and empty. For the time being, why don't we use Dick as a dump? It's the nearest and safest dispersal site."

Everyone blinked. It was an option of such obvious opportunity that they couldn't believe they hadn't thought of it before.

"Great," said Roger. "Do it at once. Wally, how many extra yards do we have to tack on to Tom before we get to the new line of trees?"

"We were within two days," said Wally. "Now we might make it in ten."

"Still within our time allowance. I think we might seal up all three traps solidly for a couple of days and see what the Germans are up to."

It was timely advice. The Germans suddenly increased roll calls and hut searches; ferrets became more active with their probes; those who had been quite forthcoming with their information suddenly clammed up. One morning after roll call a large body of Wehrmacht troops burst through the gates and raced into position, encircling Hut 123. Kriegies who were ordered out stood at a distance, watching events. Noises of smashing and banging were heard. The members of the Escape Committee at various vantage points had their fingers crossed.

The Germans found nothing.

They began to dig a trench between Hut 123 and the perimeter fence. Wally Floody eyed it with professional distaste. They had to dig a trench thirty feet deep. They gave up at five feet.

Cautiously, Tom was reopened. It reached a length of 285 feet. They were inside the tree line. The old argument about how to end the shaft started again. Wally was for the vertical shaft; they had already come up to approximately 19 feet from the surface. An incline meant that trolleys would pick up too much speed; the ropes were fallible enough as it was. If one broke, a tunnel collapse was inevitable. Roger Bushell ended the argument. Wally was right.

And then, out of the blue—disaster. A moment of sheer bad luck.

No one ever knew exactly what took place. Ferrets roamed everywhere. They were always a bit cautious about going alone into a room full of boisterous kriegies, but on this occasion there were few kriegies in Hut 123, and the ferret was alone. It is likely he was seeking a quiet corner for a cigarette, because Hut 123 had survived every search the ingenuity of German security forces could invent. As he went in he noticed that drainage pipes were being laid and that a careless workman had left a pickax in a trench. Knowing that, with their sharp eyes and magpie habits, the kriegies would spirit it away at the first opportunity, he picked it up and carried it with him. Whether by accident or design, he dropped it at the vital spot in the narrow corridor that housed Tom's trap. A chip of concrete flew up. That was odd. Old concrete does not chip that easily. The ferret peered closer, got down on his knees, let out a howl of glee, and rushed for Oberfeldwebel Glemnitz.

For the Germans there was joy and acclamation. Charlie could scarcely snap enough pictures for the museum. This was a tunnel of true magnificence. Visitors arrived to inspect it and to marvel at the POWs' labors.

There was gloom among the Escape Committee, and among the kriegies generally. There was also much concern on the part of Kommandant von Lindeiner. Among the visitors were high-ranking Gestapo officers who were now tightening their grip on every facet of German security. The POWs had been within a hairsbreadth of breaking out through that tunnel. Security measures in Stalag Luft III were plainly unprofessional. This was a very serious matter. Worse, a new Gestapo decree had been promulgated—the *Stufe Romisch III:* in the future all escaping officers would not be returned to their POW camps, but would be handed over to the Gestapo for special treatment. Kommandant von Lindeiner knew that would mean concentration camps—where life was often no more than an orderly wait for extermination or was immediately extinguished by a bullet in the back of the neck. It might also mean that Kommandant von Lindeiner would receive orders to liquidate *all* his prisoners as a retaliatory measure. When faced with this threat, Kommandant von Lindeiner made it clear to his officers, he would certainly shoot himself rather than carry out such an order.

His second dilemma was how much he should reveal to the senior British and American officers. He could not betray his own country's secrets; at the same time he needed to prevent further escape attempts. In confidence he talked to Group Captain Massey, urging him to take action. In turn Massey summoned Roger Bushell.

"The Luftwaffe," said Massey, "are meticulous in abiding by the rules of the Geneva convention. The Gestapo are not and their power is growing every day. They know that when the war ends they will have committed enough bloody crimes to put them away for years to come. So one more murder or execution will make no difference." He lifted his head and stared directly at his subordinate officer. "Yours, for example, Roger."

Roger had already made two escape attempts, the second earning him a ringside seat at the massacres in Prague the previous year and some first-hand experience with the Gestapo. The Gestapo had warned that his next encounter with them would be his last. Roger had arrived back in Sagan a changed and embittered man.

Now he looked at Massey and said quietly, "I appreciate what you are saying, sir. But I've learnt a lot over the past few years and I've thought a great deal about it. They won't catch me on this third attempt."

Losing Tom had been a major setback. Keeping Dick and Harry was all-important, and Harry was the more important of the two. Above all, German suspicions that there might be other tunnels must be allayed.

Witnessing the formal destruction of Tom was like attending the public execution of a friend. The German sapper summoned for the occasion indeed looked like an executioner plainly determined to do his job. He stuck his charge somewhere down the hole, added a hundred pounds of dynamite, pressed the plunger, and everything went sky-high.

There was one cheerful moment, however, when it was seen that the charge had passed through the whole length of the tunnel and shattered a drain that served not only North Compound but the German living quarters as well. Moreover, the drain's repair caused one watchtower to tilt slowly sideways until it was uninhabitable. At the very least, Tom had done a small but excellent job of undermining German morale.

Part Two

The Price
of
Admission

Chapter Five

Wing Commander Harry Day strode across towards his Blenheim bomber where his two young aircrew stood waiting. It was October 1939.

Wings Day was not overly superstitious, but after fifteen years of peacetime service he had had to recognize that this was his first real operational mission, and that all those barnstorming and aerobatic shows were not going to help very much. And he could not brush out of his mind that the date was Friday the 13th.

The two young airmen came smartly to attention and saluted. Wings touched his flying helmet with one finger, thinking, "Christ! They both look about nineteen!"

Navigator Hillier was just out of training school. Leading Aircraftsman Moller had not even been given time to complete his gunnery course. "There is a war on, you know. Just pick it up as you go along."

Wings Day had not slept well the previous night. His bedroll, stretched out on the floor of the crew room, was hard and uncomfortable, and the twenty-four-hour canteen service for French ground crews next door had not helped matters. So he had lain awake and contemplated his future.

It did not seem bright. He decided he did not wish to become a hero, particularly a dead hero. His group captain, a veteran of the Great War, had even offered a way out: "Wing Commander, I'm not stopping you from flying this first photographic reconnaissance, but I do not approve of it. You are far more useful organizing the squadron than dying for it. I appreciate your desire to set an example to your men, but really we have no time for romantic trivialities. I hope you will bear that in mind."

With hindsight, Wings now realized this was the moment to step back, throw up a smart salute and reply, "Well, sir, if that's the way you feel about it, I shall reconsider squadron flight plans and make other arrangements."

But he hadn't said that. He had already committed himself to the flight, and the whole squadron knew it, and he wasn't backing out now.

Intelligence had been quite understanding about the dangers. "Just get a few quick shots of the Hannover-Hamm railway lines running into the Ruhr. See if they're congested. Then get the hell out. The place is bound to be infested with Messerschmitt 109's, and you are no match for them."

Wings knew as well as Intelligence the difference between a Blenheim and a Messerschmitt 109. Sure, the Blenheim was a neat little plane. Twin engines, three-man crew. Its armament, however, was insignificant: one Bren gun fixed in the wing firing forward, one amidships—in aerial combat a little better than two peashooters. And if the pilot gave it full boost it might start nudging 250 m.p.h., while the ME-109 pilot was screaming past at nearly 400.

As they nosed along the runway and climbed into the sky, Wings had a good view of his squadron site adjacent to the airfield: two flights of nine aircraft each among France's pleasant Moselle countryside, situated hard against the German border. It had seen lots of action in the 1914–18 war: farmer's ploughs were still turning up old bones, bayonets, helmets, and bullets, rusty relics of that bitter attrition of trench fighting.

As they droned northwards towards the Rhineland, Wings was reassured that, for once, the French meteorological reports—usually as unreliable as the English—seemed to coincide with the real weather. Visibility, thank God, was no more than a mile: cloud cover started at two thousand feet, and allegedly would stay thick to twenty thousand.

It took only a few minutes to cross the German border. Fifty more miles and the cotton wool still enveloped them, streaming reassuringly past their wingtips.

Then, suddenly, the cloud cover was sliced across. It was as if they had flown through a stage curtain into a vast fishbowl of sunlight and airy space. At any other moment one would have caught one's breath at its beauty. Now, Wings felt apprehension race through his veins. They were poised between a distant earth quilted in autumnal

65

shades and an upward-stretching, endless, tranquil sky—with no place to hide.

Wings swung his head around in a 180-degree sweep. The clear space looked as if it stretched for hundreds of miles. He had to get back to cloud cover, check their position, see if he could wriggle through clouds to their target. Remaining exposed out here was tantamount to suicide.

Moller's voice from his midship turret buzzed through on the intercom. "Flak, skipper. Starboard side." Wings peered through his Perspex window. The puffy brown balls seemed miles away. No trouble there. He acknowledged Moller's sighting, knowing he had to make a final decision within seconds. Then Moller's voice again: "Flak getting closer, skipper." And at once Wings knew he had probably been caught in a trap as old as aerial combat. The flak wasn't *aimed* at him . . . it was signaling his position to marauding fighters somewhere out there in the sun. And by God, there they were! Three ME-109's hurtling towards them like evil insects—flyheads separated by two matchstick wings.

Wings stood the Blenheim on its port wing trying to steer clear of them. No hope. Cannon shells rocked the aircraft with thunderous resonance. Over the intercom he heard Moller's scream. Thick smoke, choking and oily, filled the cockpit. The instrument panel was blacked out. He couldn't breathe. He thrust open the escape hatch, forcing the helmet intercom hard against his face to try to snatch a mouthful of air, then thrust out a probing arm to find out if Hillier had already gone. He had. Then through a leaping gush of smoke and flame he forced himself upwards, sheer mindless terror propelling his action, the sudden thought entering his mind in a microsecond of panic: Miss the tail fin!

Then he was falling, arms and legs sprawling, somersaulting, with a quick glimpse of the Blenheim streaming flame. If Hillier was out, Moller must have got out, too. Where was the goddam rip cord? He couldn't find the handle through his heavy gauntlets. He tore them off, catching another glimpse of aircraft—this time a Messerschmitt wheeling triumphantly against the blue sky. Now he'd gripped the parachute release handle, but that quick glimpse of the ME-109 chilled him. No one had tested chivalry in the air yet—better free-fall as long as he dare. Far below he spotted a layer of diaphanous cloud. He was falling towards it. If he could make that without being sprayed by bullets he should be all right. It seemed only a second before he felt its cold clamminess on his cheeks. He tugged on the parachute handle, and was jolted by the fierce impact of air rushing into silk. Life returned to a slightly stunned normality. Suspended above a beautiful countryside, he drifted down towards woods, open fields, and a small collection of picturesque cottages. His face and forehead burned and throbbed: those bloody flames must have nipped him. That thought brought him back to Hillier and Moller. He hoped to God they had made it safely.

He squinted downwards, trying to gauge the direction of his drift: it seemed to Wings that he might well land astride the shoulders of the brawny farmer who was busy ploughing his field into furrows of bright burnt umber and, because of the racket of his engine, had no idea that an enemy pilot was descending onto his fields. Or he might miss him altogether and land in the shelter of a small copse of trees. If he did, and could get rid of his parachute quickly enough, he might be able to hide until nightfall and then make a break for it, heading west.

That hope disappeared as the noise reached up to him: men, women, children, dogs, chickens were streaming out of the cottages, no doubt alerted by the thump of pieces of Blenheim hitting the ground. They were pointing up at him, waving up at him, shouting up at him, and all running towards the approximate point where Wings anticipated starting his tour of the Reich.

The trees of the small copse rushed up faster than he thought possible. He hit the ground hard, rolled, and entangled himself in shroud lines and billowing silk. He couldn't move. He was dazed, powerless. Then the wide country face of the tractor driver loomed over him, his mouth stretched in a wide grin. He reached down and grasped Wings by the hand, working it up and down as if it were the village pump. He was plainly delighted by this unexpected visitor.

"Engländer! Engländer!" he exclaimed, as if he were greeting an old and treasured friend.

Wings was bewildered. Only one thought was clear to him: "God, here I go again. A mere two days before the end of the last war I found myself on the deck of a torpedoed battleship narrowly escaping being singed to death. And here I am only a handful of days into the next war, singed again, and this time captured. There must be something drastically wrong with my timing!"

Chapter Six

THE TWO SPITFIRE FIGHTER pilots, Squadron Leader Roger Bushell and Flying Officer Robert Stanford Tuck, first met in the mess of the old civilian airfield Croydon, some twenty miles south of London. It was May 1, 1940, a momentous month in one of the most critical years Britain has ever faced. The Battle of Britain had begun. These two were among the pilots who would carry the burden of her defense.

They eyed each other warily: Bushell, the senior in rank and age (by six years), five-feet-ten in height, broad-shouldered, burly. Tuck, in his mid-twenties, tall, slender, dark, a narrow Ronald Colman moustache, a scar down one cheek resulting from a near-calamitous midair collision, his RAF uniform cut in Savile Row: the prototype of the debonair, dashing fighter pilot.

Bob Tuck's eyes were probably more wary than Roger Bushell's, for Roger was by far the more worldly of the two. His parents were wealthy, his education typically English upper-echelon: Wellington public school; Oxford University. A fine athlete, a rugby blue, a brilliant criminal barrister, with a deep voice that commanded attention in court or on the theatrical stage, Roger was made for success.

Roger grabbed Tuck's hand. "Good to meet you, Tuck. Heard a lot about you. All of it good. As of now, you're promoted to flight lieutenant —you command your own flight. We've got one hell of a job to kick this squadron into shape. We're starting *now*! I'll meet you at dispersal point in half an hour."

Robert Tuck's admiration, devotion, and loyalty to Roger Bushell started at that moment, and never wavered for the rest of his life. He had found his hero. And that, considering Bob Tuck's sometimes arrogant and challenging nature, was an astonishing occurrence.

Roger Bushell had come in through the RAF Auxiliary and Reserve Volunteers, and joined the "Millionaires' squadron": young men who paid their own expenses and who were trained and learned to fly on weekends and on holidays. Bob Tuck came from a middle-class family and education, served three years in the Merchant Navy as an apprentice, and then abandoned his intended profession in the mid-thirties, when newspaper ads all over Britain invited young men to apply for commissions in the RAF.

By the time he met Roger Bushell, Bob Tuck was already known as "a born fighter pilot." The qualities that earned him this reputation were an instinctive, almost innate ability to fly fighter aircraft and a phenomenal sense of marksmanship. It also entailed a steely ruthlessness.

Precisely twenty-two days after that first meeting, on the morning of May 23, 1940, there was a certain tenseness in the mess as breakfast was served. Ninety-two Squadron had moved the few miles south from Croydon to Hornchurch, soon to become one of the most famous fighter bases in the Battle of Britain. Twelve Spitfires waited outside on the tarmac. Twelve pilots were available. None had ever flown a combat mission before. The situation in the skies over France was critical; the war being waged in the fields below and moving towards the beaches seemed already lost.

"Okay, chaps," said Roger cheerfully, "we've all heard the bad news over the BBC, so we know things are a bit tough. Our orders are to fly across to Boulogne, make a sweep left along the coast over Calais and Dunkirk, and then return by the same route. Intelligence believes we shall encounter large formations of ME-109's, and if we run into any of those dive-bombing Stukas which seem to be giving the army and the poor civilians bloody hell, so much the better. Okay, let's scramble!"

At ten thousand feet over the rolling green countryside of Picardy, where roses that bloomed in the First World War had matched the color of the blood flowing so freely in the trenches, they could see the fretted shoreline of France against a serene blue sea. It was a day for buckets and spades and sand castles on the beach, and Dad snoring under his open newspaper. Instead the beaches were being put to different purposes, and many dads were lying dead under spread capes, as bullets from low-flying Messerschmitts raked the sand.

They flew in tight V formation, straining to catch the merest metallic reflection from a marauding bandit high up against the sun, the slightest trace of a vapor trail—and all of a sudden here they were, knifing in from behind Roger's left shoulder, and a voice was yelling, "Bandits, bandits! Ten o'clock, ten o'clock!"

Roger Bushell heard the warning, and at precisely the same second Pat Learmond's Spitfire evaporated in an explosion of sound and flame, the ball of fire that he had become racing level with them for a few split seconds and then falling away beneath them. But there was no time for thought or grief, only instinctive, instantaneous reaction. The ME-109's, which had attacked them from a higher altitude, sliced downwards and through and over their wavering formation. Discipline had gone. Despite all the warnings of those careful briefing sessions, Bushell's headphones were full of shouts and screams of advice, orders, tactics, encouragement. "Shut up!" he yelled. "Shut up!"

He might just as well have shouted "Piss off!" to the swarming Messerschmitts. Every man was suddenly alone. He saw Tuck streaking skywards after a German aircraft that had ended its dive and spiraled upwards to start again. He swung his Spitfire around, turning as tight as a quarter horse around a barrel, and there in his sights, maybe a thousand feet ahead, was a Messerschmitt going like a bat out of hell but in level flight. And Roger was slightly higher, and going just as fast. Now, if he really squeezed the throttles. . . . He sped up, cut the distance to under a thousand yards. His finger was poised above the firing button, when a pail of whitewash was thrown across his windshield. Sight had gone, any sense of altitude or flight control had gone; he could be upside down for all he knew—he had run into thick cloud. He yanked back and sped upwards, breaking out of cloud cover into a clear blue sky. And all was silent, peaceful, lonely. The dogfight was over. Ammunition exhausted, fuel indicators flickering towards empty, the Germans sped back to bases in conquered France, and Roger Bushell towards Hornchurch.

Eleven Spitfires had returned. Only poor Pat Learmond was missing. Roger already knew that grief was not stylish; you had to invent a language of euphemisms: dead comrades had "gone missing," "gone for a burton," "caught a packet."

Bob Tuck had scored his first victory; so had three others in the squadron. All planes had been refueled; a replacement pilot had taken Pat Learmond's place. And a large van had arrived on the airfield with the new bulletproof windshields— technicians were already at work fitting them to the Spitfires. When the order came to rescramble, only three had been fitted—one to Bob Tuck's aircraft, a safeguard that was to save his life within a few hours.

Just before two o'clock they rose again into the golden sky, and, seen from above, each camouflaged Spitfire was a beautiful flying machine. A slender nose cone leading back to the curved wings, the wasp waist, the butterfly-shaped tail fins: a beauty that disguised the awesome capacity of the thundering, 1175-horsepower Rolls-Royce Merlin engine, and the eight lethal .303 machine guns nesting in the wings.

They made their first "tourist run" from Boulogne to Dunkirk, and had they swung back in a wider circle they might have seen down below, half hidden by the trees, the small gray-stone château of Premesques, where a singular part of history was being made. Had they dropped from eight thousand feet to window height, they might have glimpsed, sitting at his desk, a solitary figure wearing the red tabs of a British general. But they would never have guessed that General Viscount Gort, commander in chief of the British Expeditionary Force, was making the most crucial decision of his career. He was about to disobey orders.

His government and its military advisers were aware that he had been driven back by the devastating blitzkrieg of the German panzer divisions; that his forces were hemmed in on three sides; that French resistance had already crumbled and would crumble even further. Now he reiterated that General Maxime Weygand's order to turn south against the German panzers was neither practical nor realistic. He advised an eastward fighting retreat towards the port of Dunkirk and that an evacuation fleet be assembled to take them back to England.

Neville Chamberlain's government back in London, buoyed by disbelief and vain optimism, did not agree. General Weygand's order must be obeyed.

General Gort knew that he must act. That evening he gave the order for the British Army to fall back towards Dunkirk, and so Dunkirk became the British sticking point. Now it was do or die. No more fudging. No more appeasement. The battle was on. And Winston Churchill gave voice to their determination.

As Bushell's squadron wheeled back towards Boulogne, they were aerial spectators of the dramatic panorama below them, but they knew nothing of its implications; all they could see was the oily black smoke eddying up from the wrecked oil tanks in Dunkirk harbor, and the occasional yellow flash of a shell burst. And then they were too occupied to think of anything besides survival. From out of the sky came the enemy. Fifty, sixty, God knows how many Messerschmitt 110's, recognizable at once by their twin engines. The German pilot, using his nose cone as a sort of rifle barrel, spouted cannon-shell and machine-gun fire. Back-to-back with him sat a tail gunner swiveling a heavy-caliber machine gun. Down they hurtled, but this time not catching the Spitfires in their V formation. Bushell had grilled them on this between scrambles: "Keep off the bloody in-

tercom until you've got your orders from me."
And now here they were. "We're turning left—
turning left . . . a wide circle, a wide circle . . .
give yourself room . . . hang onto each other's tails
till we break."

It worked. The bulk of the Messerschmitts
poured through their circle. Then came the order
from Bushell. "Right, break—break—get after
them!"

The dogfight was on. As the 110's passed, the
tail gunner's tracer bullets arched red arabesques
through the clear sky. Into Bob Tuck's sights
came the rear end of a 110, its tail gunner squirting
bullets as if out of a hose pipe. He heard them
ricochet off his Perspex windshield, but was too
busy lining up his own guns to identify the opaque
splotches that, but for the newly installed windshield, would have blown his head off. He slewed
the Spit to follow the turning 110 and pressed his
firing button. The plane and its tail gunner took
a continued burst of machine-gun fire. Bits of
fuselage blew away as if wrenched by a sudden
typhoon; smoke poured from the port engine,
turned to flame, and in a split second enveloped
the entire plane. It fell earthwards.

Now once more, despite Bushell's warning, his
earphones were assaulted by noisy voices. There
was no way of stopping them. Then Tuck saw
another 110 approaching him head-on, with
flashes indicating shell fire emerging from its nose.
There was no time for any sort of logical thought:
they were approaching each other head-on at a

closing speed of around seven hundred miles an hour. Tuck knew that to pull up or tip down was equally fatal: an exposed belly or an exposed cockpit. But that was almost an afterthought as they crisscrossed in midair. Bob Tuck never knew if the 110 had gone under or over him, only that he was still alive, and the sky ahead was clear of planes. He looked around for Roger Bushell. Where the hell had he got to?

Roger was busy with the same sort of desperate scenario. As soon as they broke he found five 110's after him. He turned inside them, he slipped and dived and climbed to dodge them, knowing that his aircraft was at least as good as, if not better than, the 110's in this cataclysmic melee. He came up under one and got in a full deflection shot that sent the enemy plane into a long curving dive, one engine pouring smoke. He turned the Spitfire on one wing as he realized he had more 110's on his tail, and then, as he went into a dive, he saw another 110 coming up like a rising trout, red flashes spraying from its eyes. As with Bob Tuck, there was no time for conscious decision, only a determination to hold his line of dive and fire back. He was certain he killed the pilot as the plane screeched above him and he hurtled past, inches or feet away. He came around again in a tight turn and found he was sliding earthwards and trailing a long black train of smoke.

His engine was spewing glycol, and seemed to be on fire. His controls were loose and muzzy; he was losing altitude. He must have been down to around five thousand feet when the controls responded again. His fall seemed to have killed the flames, but the engine had conked out. Just to make sure, he switched it off. He went into a steep glide at just above stalling speed. There were fields below. A few hundred feet above them, the engine caught fire again. He hit the grass hard, taxied to a stop, slid back the canopy, and clambered out. There were a lot of holes in the fuselage. The engine was burning furiously. He sat on a grassy bank. After the cacophony and aerobatics of the last few minutes he felt disoriented and exhausted. He knew he must have been forced down somewhere to the west of Boulogne, certainly in territory still held by French or British forces. No doubt British soldiers from one of their anti-aircraft batteries would pick him up within the next few minutes. Then he heard the motorbike engine. Thank God! He stood up trying to wipe the blood from his eyes and nose, holding up his hand as a signal of recognition. Yes, here they came now. Then he realized that the uniform was not khaki, but field-gray. And the helmet was that German bucket shape. And the machine pistol that the soldier held was pointing at him.

The outstanding difference between Roger Bushell and Bob Tuck was not that, while Roger Bushell was never awarded a single medal, Bob Tuck became one of the most famous and highly decorated pilots in the RAF. Nor that some eighteen months later, when Bob Tuck was shot down over

Boulogne, he not only managed to land miraculously, but also aroused the admiration of the German anti-aircraft gunners because a cannon shell from his return of fire went straight down the barrel of one of their guns and splayed it open like a banana peel. No, the outstanding difference between the two pilots had simply to do with Lady Luck. In those tumultuous war years, Lady Luck never smiled upon Roger Bushell, but positively beamed upon Bob Tuck.

She was smiling when Bob Tuck came home from that mission which left Roger Bushell a prisoner. She was smiling when, halfway across the English Channel, Bob Tuck heard worrying noises from his engine and realized that the Spitfire was riddled with bullet holes but managed nevertheless to keep it airborne until he landed, skidding to a standstill near the control tower.

An hour or so later they added up the score: five out of the twelve in their squadron dead, wounded, or missing on their first day of battle. That evening the station commander approached Bob Tuck and said quietly, "How do you feel about taking over the squadron, Tucky?"

Bob Tuck nodded. He felt no elation. His chief concern was the fate of Roger Bushell. Bob Tuck prayed he had made a safe crash landing, but he also knew that very few people knew what was happening over there in France.

By an odd coincidence Roger Bushell, Bob Tuck, and Major Johnny Dodge would all meet in Sagan,

Stalag Luft III. But at that moment, only Johnny Dodge knew what was happening down on the battlefield—knew that the battle was already lost.

He had made one last attempt to swim from a lonely beach and intercept a passing ship, and had been forced to swim back. Now there seemed very little else to do except rejoin his comrades of the Fifty-first Highland Division and march off into captivity, consoling himself with the belief that such a march would surely give him other chances of making a run for it. He stared across the sea towards the harbor entrance of St.-Valéry-en-Caux.

Any old soldier—and at a few days short of his forty-sixth birthday, Johnny certainly considered himself that—could see that Hitler's panzer divisions had effectively defeated this section of France. Never before had he seen such carnage on the roads. Stukas screaming down like banshees out of hell to drop bombs on any target they could find, the easiest targets being the crowded roads full of fugitive men, women, and children, with their horses, dogs, carts, and trucks, mixed up with troops endeavoring to retreat—a kaleidoscopic, frantic mass of humanity. And fighter planes mercilessly strafing the same roads to spread chaos and panic.

As segments of the Fifty-first Highland Division were forced back towards the port, a Dunkirk-style evacuation was planned. But this time, because German batteries now held the hills around St. Valéry, and their planes had mastery of the skies, it had to be an evacuation under cover of darkness. Small ships and destroyers slipped in to take off as many soldiers as possible. But the plan failed. On the night of the attempt, fog rolled in, making nautical navigation impossible. By the time it lifted, the panzer divisions were already probing through the outskirts.

The town was packed with civilian refugees. A last-ditch, fight-to-the-death stand to defend a nonstrategic position and cause a massacre of French civilians was judged useless by the British High Command. The trapped regiments of the Fifty-first—six thousand men—were ordered to lay down their arms and surrender.

Johnny Dodge could not bear the thought. An army might surrender as a whole, but as an individual he felt he could take a chance on his own. A few beaches were still unconquered. It was unlikely he would even have made the twenty-one miles from Calais to Dover; the sixty miles or so from St. Valéry to the coast of England were beyond him.

John Bigelow Dodge was a rare American. In August 1914, bright-eyed Johnny Dodge, three months past his twentieth birthday, decided that with Britain and France at war the defense of liberty in Europe against what the newspapers called the "rapacious German hordes" was more important than sitting in an office and perusing *The Wall Street Journal*. He caught the next boat to England. There, with a little help from his kinsman Winston Churchill, he joined the newly formed Royal Naval Division, romantically identified as a "flying column of Royal Marines." It attracted artists, writers, and poets—among them the poet Rupert Brooke. Nineteen-fifteen found Johnny Dodge and company assaulting the shores of Turkey at the entrance of one of the world's most important waterways, the Dardanelles at Gallipoli. Waist-deep in bloodstained water, Johnny found himself helping to drag a shallow-bottomed barge full of troops, many of them wounded or dead, to the beach. Johnny Dodge was badly wounded in that first assault, and found himself in a hospital in Egypt, decorated with the Military Cross and promoted to the rank of major.

He was back in action at the closing Battle of the Somme in time to rejoin what was called "the remnants" of the Royal Naval Division, now reorganized into the 188th and 189th brigades. This campaign of the Somme had started in July and lasted until November, with the Battle of Ancre. The four-month battle for a few square miles of the pleasant chalk hills along the Somme River churned its terrain into a muddy wilderness unfit for human existence.

Johnny Dodge's commanding officer had been killed. The remaining men were isolated by Germans firing along the trenches from a redoubt that had already decimated an entire battalion. Then suddenly, clanking up out of the dawn, Caterpillar tracks squelching through the mud, came six ungodly machines! They were tanks, the first the British Army had ever used in battle. And their effect on the shocked Germans was almost un-believable. The redoubt was overrun in a matter of minutes, yielding up 600 prisoners, who were quickly joined by 180 more from the surrounding trenches.

Lieutenant Colonel John Bigelow Dodge emerged from the trenches, a bloom on his twenty-four-year-old cheeks, ready to put the "war to end wars" behind him and concentrate on the future of mankind. He heard the Russians were making great strides towards that future with their new revolution. He went over to see for himself, but his optimism was drained out of him within a few weeks. The final blow came when the secret police arrested him as a spy and clapped him into prison for several weeks. Indeed, he was lucky to avoid execution. Johnny Dodge returned, his enthusi-asm for the rights of man undiminished, but cer-tain that they would be better served elsewhere.

In pursuit of these ambitions, Dodge divided his time between the United States and Britain, stockbroking in the two countries. When war broke out in 1939, he returned to his old com-rades, who were now amalgamated into the Fifty-first Highland Division.

They had been marched up past Calais and Dun-kirk, along roads littered with the debris of the German victory: carcasses of animals, battered trucks, field guns, and tanks, the dead still un-buried, the living exhausted and hungry. Crossing the river Schelde, their captors had noticed the string of empty barges moored along the banks, and decided they would make excellent temporary accommodations for their prisoners while they decided what to do with them. The sentries they posted were inattentive and bored; they would much sooner be enjoying the victory beers in the local estaminets. After all, the war was over, wasn't it? What was the point of escaping? It wouldn't be long before all the prisoners were repatriated anyway, so why risk a bullet? The Dodger did not agree with that.

The evening was beautiful. When darkness fell it was a simple matter for Johnny to slide over the side of the barge onto the towpath, to walk through the darkness in the general direction of Holland, hoping to meet some kindly Belgian or Dutchman who might offer him shelter. As dawn began to break, he came upon a cheerful middle-aged man who spoke a few words of English and who appeared to understand Johnny's problem. He was going in the same direction. He seemed to be Dutch. He led Johnny straight into the arms of a Luftwaffe sentry guarding a small airfield. Johnny Dodge always liked to believe that the man thought he was doing him a favor and showing him where to give himself up!

The Luftwaffe officers were delighted. They had the same cheerful attitude of the sentries guarding the barges. The war was over. They'd achieved the most momentous victory in German history. "Do have a glass of this excellent Scotch whisky which the British kindly left behind in their mess, Major, and let us celebrate the end of hostilities. . . . A little more whisky, Major? You are lucky too. As we have captured you, we can now hand you over to our Luftwaffe prisoner-of-war authorities. They will treat you in a much more civilized fashion than the Wehrmacht."

Major Johnny Dodge decided that might not be a bad idea. After all, a period as an honorary member of the RAF would make a nice change.

Chapter Seven

EACH NIGHT IN YOUR barrack block you lay in your bunk, listening to the heavy breathing, the snores, the turns and movements of your roommates. And if you were George Harsh, you thought how lucky you were to be in Sagan at all.

Long ago George Harsh had discovered that to degrade and humiliate someone, manacles make a good start. Watch the fatalistic eyes of a black convict—a lifer in for murder—as he hammers someone's steel anklets into place, locking them together with the "stride" chain that forever regulates you to a peculiar hobbling gait. Then see him fix the vertical chain that comes up from between your ankles so that when you walk you have to hold it up, ready, if necessary, to be tethered like an animal to fellow members of the chain gang.

Smell the stench of the night bucket in the steel lattice cages where the convicts lie every night. Know the nausea of being hustled out at dawn every morning to the beating clang of a bell to begin the backbreaking fourteen-or fifteen-hour day, one gang loosening the rock and shale, the second shoveling it into mule-drawn wagons.

The food was revolting: corn pone, sowbelly,

cattle-feed beans; it never varied. In winter a man was ankle-deep in mud; in summer he breathed through a fog of red dust, and his sweat made little stripes down through it. At night the men were herded back to their cages, which were surrounded by high barbed-wire fences; guards with dogs patrolled.

Few attempted to escape. Fewer succeeded. Punishments were medieval: twenty-four hours in a sweatbox so small that the victim could not stand or kneel or lie, although that was going out of fashion because afterwards a man could not work again for another twenty-four hours. There were stocks, in which a man would be suspended in excruciating pain, and the lash, a terrible weapon of heavy, braided leather, hard as a board, which had been forbidden by Georgia lawmakers but was still used in the outlying chain-gang camps.

The Atlanta headlines were etched indelibly in his memory: "HARSH CONVICTED, SENTENCED TO DEATH/Two Atlanta Students Confess They Entered Crime for Thrills."

Fixed just as indelibly was the memory of that nightmarish evening. The streets of Atlanta deserted because of the cold, slicing rain hitting the shop windows—particularly the windows of a large grocery store, the target. Richard waiting outside in the car for the fast getaway. The weight of the Colt .45 suddenly heavy in his hand as he burst through the doors. A voice he did not recognize as his own, shouting, "This is a stickup! Open the till."

Then the wide eyes and mouth of the young kid in the white coat and cap as he shrank backwards. The sight of the other kid suddenly bobbing up from behind a counter about twenty feet farther back, a large black revolver in his hand.

George felt a hot pain in his groin. Instinctively he fired back. He saw the kid's white coat sprout scarlet as he toppled, saw the one nearest the till make a soft slushing noise as he tipped forward onto his face, shot in the back by his own colleague.

Shocked and in agony, clutching his guts, George managed to turn and hobble away. He got through the door, made it to the car, collapsed into the front seat, glimpsed Richard's horrified face as he crashed the gears and screamed the tires, yelling, "Christ! Christ! What do we do now!"

It was the late twenties, but there was no depression in sight yet. In fact, the U.S.A. seemed too prosperous for its own good. Life wasn't quite real, somehow. George's dad had left him half a million dollars in trust. Richard's father owned one of the most powerful newspapers in Atlanta. The boys and their friends were bored with classes, bored with the idea of graduating, bored with chasing girls whose sole ambition seemed to be the preservation of their virginity, bored with driving too fast and drinking moonshine. Couldn't they do something original, dangerous, illegal?

Maybe if that infamous murder case of Leopold and Loeb in Chicago in 1924 hadn't hit the headlines with such shattering effect—a Hollywood movie was even made about it—the idea might never have taken root among the small group. Leopold and Loeb had been, like them, two wealthy university students bored by their academic lives. "Why not commit a perfect murder?" And they do it. A kid of fourteen. Leave his body hidden in a street culvert. The police will find it, but so what? No motive, therefore no clues. Then Loeb discovers he's lost his spectacles at the scene of the crime. . . . George's group wouldn't make a mistake like that: they weren't going to do anything as brutal and stupid as murder. Take a few risks, yeah, but nothing more than that.

Sitting around that table in a roadhouse outside Atlanta and feeling the bourbon slide down as smooth as silk, it seemed so easy, so adult—a bit like Edward G. Robinson discussing his next holdup with his fellow hoodlums. Especially when Frank produced the big black Colt .45 and laid it on the table out of the bartender's sight. "That's the *frightener*, that's all it is. And we don't make elementary goofs like dropping glasses." He looked around and smiled. Frank had a winning smile. "Just make the police look like the dumb bastards they really are. A series of quick, unsolved crimes. Chain-store robberies. Run in with the gun. Stick 'em up! Clean out the till. Into the getaway car. Disappear. No link to established criminals. No clues. One every two weeks. Different neighborhoods. We draw straws. The first two short straws do the first job, then they're through. They've passed the test. All agreed?"

Frank's eyes moved around the table. No one chickened out. And it worked. Three grocery stores robbed. Angry headlines in the press. What were the police doing!

Pressing his hand into his groin to try to stem the flow of blood, George managed to struggle out of the car and into Richard's house; they'd arranged this robbery for a time when his parents would be away. Luckily George's wound was not serious— nothing that disinfectant, bandages, and natural good health couldn't cure. No doctors needed. A few quick phone calls suggesting illusory ailments to explain absences. . . and a week later George was back in class.

George wrote long afterwards: "Then the ghastly reality and the tragic consequences of what we were doing crashed into the awareness of us all. The gun was hidden, the minor crime wave came to an abrupt halt; five young men began to realize that what they'd done in their youth would follow them to their graves."

But their mistake dwarfed the one made by Leopold and Loeb. George had stripped off his bloodstained trousers and jacket and tossed them into a closet in Richard's house—then had forgotten all about them. The suit was found by the maid, who in all innocence sent it off to the cleaners. They saw the bullet hole in the trousers and called the police. George's name tag was sewn inside.

Chief of Detectives Lamar was dry-voiced and hard-eyed as George was led into his office. He emphasized each question by smacking the rubber hose he carried hard into the palm of his own hand. When he did not think George was telling the truth, he aimed the hose at him. George confessed.

A battery of legal talent was assembled to represent both Richard and George. George came to trial first. It took the jury fifteen minutes to pronounce him guilty, with no recommendation for mercy. In those days the penalty for murder in Georgia was death in the electric chair. Judge E. D. Thomas concluded his sentence with the words, "Until you are dead, dead, dead. And may God have mercy on your soul."

George Harsh expected no mercy. He accepted the judgment. Not so his family. They would spend every cent they had. Richard's family were equally determined. There had been no malice aforethought, no determination to murder; agreed, a terrible crime had been committed, but it had stemmed from an idiotic adolescent escapade. There was a long appeal, a mistrial, a great deal of expensive legal wheeling and dealing. Eventually Judge Thomas adjusted his verdict: "I accept the plea of guilty. It is the order of this court that these two young men spend the remainder of their natural lives in a state prison."

It is unlikely that Judge Thomas completely

understood the severity of his sentence; certainly no citizen walking the streets of Atlanta ever would. When George Harsh entered that dark world he disappeared from the sight of normal Georgia citizens forever. If he ever appeared on the streets of Atlanta again it would be as a broken-spirited, worn-out old man. In accordance with the flinty, biblical philosophy of the Deep South in that era, the guilty were punished in Old Testament tradition. There were times during George's incarceration when he was certain the death penalty would have been more merciful.

In the chain gang, a convict lived in an atmosphere of violence, terror, and brutality. Yet during those years of often unendurable hardship, one human consolation remained: friends—friends who would fight and die with a man. Those friendships, heightened by the fact that they existed in a world of fear and hatred, were incorruptible.

George's friends were Nobie, a half–Cherokee Indian, six feet four inches tall, black-haired, stone-faced, monosyllabic, quick with a knife; Bill, a safecracker, gentle and a little crazy, who had spent most of his sixty years behind bars; and most important of all, Hal Heep, a defrocked Jesuit priest, an ex-alcoholic who influenced George Harsh's life to an immense degree.

Heep was an educated man. He knew that education meant more than success; it stretched the world farther than the mind could grasp. Winters brought heavy rains; sometimes workdays were very short, and some days there was no work at all. Heep decided that George's education should continue from where it left off at Oglethorpe University. And this time he would learn about, and from, books. George's mother, brother, and sister made the long journey from Atlanta to deliver them. And George, with Hal Heep's instruction and commentaries, found himself handed an Aladdin's lamp with which to gain infinite riches.

Life suddenly changed on the morning of the escape attempt. Feelings about the chain-gang Boss had been rising like mercury in a hot tube; and then the top blew off. Two convicts seized their guards' shotguns, snatched the Boss's revolver, and blew his brains out. The hammers and chisels for knocking off shackles were in the Boss's truck. The killers got into the pickup, ready to make a run for it. No one wanted to join them. If you killed a cop or a warder in Georgia you were as good as dead. A week later at a police roadblock they were ambushed and shot to death before they could swing open the car door.

Ten convicts were summoned to the grand jury investigation. George Harsh felt that the county solicitor general would have preferred to sweep the matter under the carpet, but one member of the board of inquiry, a Dr. Hemple, would have none of that. For far too long the Georgia chain-gang system had been held up to derision by the world's press. A best-selling book had been published. Hollywood moviemakers, full of dollar-oriented self-righteousness, had leapt in headfirst.

George was called to give his account. As he

later wrote: "What sort of system was this which could mix together on the same gangs older, harder men serving up to life for murder, and young boys serving three months for hobo-ing on freight trains?"

"Is there homosexuality in the gangs?" he was asked.

"Of course there is."

"What is the remedy?"

George looked the inquirers straight in the eye and said bluntly, "Castration for all of us."

The board listened intently as he described the sense of hopelessness and frustration that existed in the gangs. He told them of the humiliation, the intimidation, and the illegal use of the lash. He did not have to explain that if he was sent back to his old camp having sung this song, he might not last more than twenty-four hours. Dr. Hemple sent all ten convicts back to the prison that day accompanied by an armed guard, with orders to collect whatever goods they had and then to move to a new prison in Fulton County, near Atlanta.

George had entered a strange paradise: wooden barracks, flush toilets, hot and cold showers, real food, and, at nearby Bellwood, a fourteen-bed hospital.

Yes, there were still manacles and striped uniforms, but there was a fairness and reason behind the warder's decisions; the prisoners were treated as human beings. And George, Nobie, and Hal were made trusties shortly after their arrival; their manacles were removed.

An opening for a second orderly at the prison hospital occurred some time later, and the senior prison warden recommended George for the job. George's co-orderly, a huge, soft-spoken black man named Randolph, was a lifer in for a particularly brutal murder. In a fit of passionate anger he had not only killed the man who was pursuing his fiancée, but had cut off his head and kicked it around the room. In their years together Harsh could testify that he had never met a kinder, gentler, more scrupulous male nurse in his life. And Randolph had learned a lot from Dr. MacDonald, the skillful, old-fashioned family doctor who ran the Bellwood hospital. George also watched him, and learned from him.

In the early fall of 1940—George was now in his twelfth year of incarceration—heavy rain, slowly turning to ice, marked the arrival of one of Atlanta's periodic ice storms. By early afternoon everything in the city and the surrounding area had ceased to function. Ice coated every road and wire and pipe. Traffic came to a standstill. Telephone communication was cut off. Power failed. The city was dark and dead.

During the storm a sixty-year-old black convict was brought in with severe stomach pains. George looked across at Randolph and said, "Try Doctor MacDonald."

Randolph picked up the phone, listened, shook it as if he were knocking drops of water out of it, and said, "It's been dead for three hours. No way."

George said, "Let's have a drink." A drink consisted of a tumbler full of ginger ale liberally spiked with medical alcohol. "Keeps the hands steady."

Randolph's large dark eyes surveyed him seriously. "George," he said, "we got no phone. We got no lights. We got no power. We got no authority."

George said, "We got spirit lamps. We got hospital equipment. We got a patient who is still trying to raise his right knee, which means the appendix hasn't ruptured yet. And we got responsibility. He'll be dead within two hours unless we operate."

Randolph's eyes were round and wary. He said with the firm emphasis of experience, "If this nigger dies on the operating table, they're going to hang us both."

George said, "Yes. Now we've got no power, so why don't you sterilize the instruments in a pan of alcohol. We'll have to put him out with ether dripped onto a cone. I'll go and scrub up."

Randolph nodded reflectively. "Okay, Doc . . . he's all yours."

George Harsh later recalled, "I got one finger through the muscles around the intestine, and gingerly worked the swollen, pus-filled appendix to the surface. I don't think I breathed as I tied this off, excised it, sutured it, and carefully worked the intestine back into place. Quickly I sutured up the incision, applied the dressing, and Randolph and I gently placed the patient in bed. Without saying anything we both returned to the medical room."

They sat down. George said, "I'll get the ginger ale, you get the medicine. I think it's time for a second drink!"

It was two days before Dr. MacDonald managed to get through to the hospital. By this time they had the patient sitting up and enjoying hospital life. Dr. MacDonald made a careful examination, and then asked George to follow him into his office.

"George," he said. "That incision! Those stitches! Anybody would think you were doing a Caesarean on an elephant. And after all I've taught you." But George realized that he was laughing. And when Dr. MacDonald was laughing he was pleased.

It was about a month before George picked up the phone to hear his sister weeping with happiness.

"George! Mother and Bob and me, we're all in Governor Rivers's office. And he's just told us. Your pardon becomes effective at seven o'clock tomorrow morning. We'll be out to pick you up!"

Dr. MacDonald had written a long letter to the governor; he'd drummed up a load of witnesses from warders and prison inmates; he'd even had a quiet word with the press.

Governor Rivers registered his clemency: "This man has served twelve years in prison for taking a human life. By his recent actions he has restored a human life. To my mind the scales have been balanced."

Randolph was pardoned as well. Both returned to the liberty-filled world of Atlanta. Neither could stand it. Randolph belly-ached about the fact that he'd been in too long: how could he adjust to these cars with fancy gearshifts, pictures with real talking, lights on street corners going red, green, and yellow? Besides, he might even fall in with another girl and something horrible might happen again.

George was unhappy, too. He was offered only one job: as a hit man for numbers racketeers. George had a reputation in the chain gang as a tough guy. They would cut him in for one-third of the profits. In a year he'd be a millionaire. George said no.

It was late 1940. He took a train north to Montreal. There was a war on. England was fighting for its life against injustice and oppression. George thought he was an expert on both subjects. He hoped that without disclosing his background he'd be able to slip in somewhere or other.

In the recruiting office in Montreal, the RAF group captain interviewing George probably sensed that something about him was a little different. George thought the captain was a nice guy—the smart blue uniform, wings and medals above the breast pocket, a thin face and eyes that looked as if they'd squinted through a million or so air miles, the modulated voice—very English.

"Just what branch of aircrew did you wish to volunteer for, old boy?" he asked gently.

The Yanks and Canadians George Harsh had met in the Montreal bars had briefed George on the answer to that question. "Air gunner, sir." If you were American and wanted to get overseas quickly, air gunner was the best bet. A rather unsound bet, mind you: tail-end Charlies were rumored not to have a protracted life expectancy.

The group captain smiled as he glanced through George's application form. "Let's see. Born Milwaukee. Educated Atlanta, Oglethorpe University. Educational tests excellent. I.Q. above average. Physical—first-rate. I say, that's quite a phenomenal night vision. Age . . . hmmm . . . a little over the twenty-eight-year limit, but I think we can forget that." He looked up, eyes suddenly wide and perceptive.

"You do realize that you'll forfeit your United States citizenship?"

"Yes, sir," said George.

So George was accepted. "You'll be sworn in as a member of His Britannic Majesty's Armed Forces in three days' time," said the group captain with a smile. "Just enough time to change your mind if you want to. Then it will be aerial gunnery school in Ontario. Three months' hard work. Turn you from a civilian into an airman. Foot-drill, close-order drill, bayonet practice, military discipline. As tough a time as you've ever had in your life, I expect—"

George did not allow the grim smile in his mind

100

to show. The group captain was a nice guy, plainly a very experienced guy, but one thing he had never done was serve time in a Georgia chain gang.

At the Royal Canadian Air Force Aerial Gunnery School, George, together with thirty other volunteers, faced up to the rigors of foot drill, bayonet practice, and the screaming rhetoric of sergeant majors. What this circus had to do with the education of air gunners Harsh could not figure out, but he stuck with it. He learned the difference between firing banks of Browning machine guns on a plane swooping at three hundred miles an hour, and those glued to a rifle range. He learned about vectors, and parabolas of fire, and arcs of fire, and cones of fire. When the course was over he discovered, to his surprise, that he was first in his class.

Two out of the top six volunteers would be selected for commissions. Each applicant was called before a board, asked a variety of questions, and then required to give a twenty-minute talk on any subject he pleased. With a certain elementary cunning George, deciding that he was now as close to the subject as he would ever be, confined his discourse to the principles and practices of aerial gunnery.

In two days George Harsh leapt five ranks and rose from leading aircraftsman to pilot officer. At the ceremonial parade when he was formally commissioned before the squadron, he listened in some awe to: "We, George the Sixth, King of

101

England, Ireland, Scotland, and the Dominions beyond the Seas, Emperor of India, Defender of the Faith, reposing special faith in our trusty and well-beloved George Harsh, do hereby . . ."

George was sent to Bournemouth, an English seaside resort on the south coast, then was posted to a patched-up squadron and flew six operations with them before being attached to the 102 Squadron of Four Group as squadron gunnery officer. And now George Harsh was in the war. And he discovered the moments that terrified him; the moments that turned him into a cold efficient extension of his own machine guns; and the moments of calculated but intense risk.

It was always vitally important to stay within the bomber stream. At regulated intervals, bomber squadrons rose from the airfields of England to assemble over different locations, at different altitudes, and then drone in one dense aircraft stream towards the target.

Targets were marked a few minutes before the arrival of the repetitive bomber stream by specialist Pathfighter aircraft, which laid a pattern of ground or parachute flares. Thus a thousand aircraft might hit a doomed city or industrial complex in one intense attack, the target vacated as quickly as possible, the casualties minimized.

But should an individual bomber be delayed on takeoff or on its journey and drop out of that stream, its survival was immediately imperiled, as it became a prime target for a concentration of anti-aircraft fire and the attentions of marauding fighters.

For George, however, even in situations of near-desperate crisis, there were moments of intense beauty during those bombing raids. "Flak"—the whistling shrapnel created by the explosions of the anti-aircraft shells—possessed its own lethal beauty. It seemed to rise slowly from the dark earth below and burst in colored balls of purple, orange, green, and gold—pyrotechnics that were intended to rip his aircraft apart. Anti-aircraft fire from the Bofors guns was quite different: it hurtled long necklaces of scarlet fireballs up towards them. To George they were impersonal and unprejudiced; one had to contend with them as a sailor weathers a violent storm.

Night-fighters were different. There was nothing impersonal about them. They were predators out to kill you. Rear gunners and night-fighter pilots were deadly enemies locked in a battle of lethal drama. One would die. The fighter pilot's primary assignment was to destroy the rear gunner. With him out of the way, the bomber was vulnerable. It was simply a matter of experience. And George had got his the only way possible: he had survived an entire tour of thirty missions and had learned many lessons in that arena of no second chances.

He had seen the black shape, blacker than the night, take up station behind him, sliding into position, aligning its guns for attack. George would touch a lever to swing his hydraulically

103

powered turret into position, raise his bank of Browning machine guns so that the golden glowing center of the gunsight enclosed the enemy plane. But until his wingtips touched either side of the circle he was not in range. And firing first was foolish. That would send the ME-109 hurtling to left or right, or suddenly scalding above or below, both wings alight with his return hail of fire. Let him think George had not seen him. Give him first shot. Wait—wait—he, too, would open fire slightly out of range, knowing his vastly superior speed could take him clear. And then it came: needle lines of bright crimson hurtling past George's turret. Now George had a split-second advantage. The bucking from the ME's four cannon and eight machine guns would throw his nose cone—and the nose cone of a fighter was really the end of its gun barrel—off-line. And now he was framed within George's golden circle, and George's finger was on the firing button and a moving hail of heavy machine-gun bullets was sluicing the Messerschmitt cockpit, and suddenly the plane was in flames, sliding sideways and downwards, an airborne funeral pyre.

George knew he could never speculate about the man he had killed. There were more of them out there. Now he had to clear any gun stoppages, ignore the thumping of his heart, and await the next attack. Then once the target had been reached and the bombs had been dropped they'd turn for home.

George later wrote: "Once more you'd cross

over the mud flats of Holland, out over the cold, scalloped Channel, only this time you were heading for home, and in the first gray light of dawn you would pass over Flamborough Head, and you would know you'd made another one. The reaction would set in now, the cold feeling that seemed to settle against your bones. The trembling would start. And you knew that you were passing through that invisible barrier, that your mental gears were reshifting, and that you were rejoining the human race."

George was now on his second tour of operations, and he knew that the odds on his survival were slender. Crew replacements were necessary after every mission. The night of October 5, 1942, he was not scheduled to fly at all. But standing at the end of the runway with an operations officer, signaling the stream of Halifax bombers off the tarmac with his blinking Aldis lamp, he suddenly noticed the pilot of one plane waving his arm frantically. Both officers hurried across; the pilot jabbed his finger towards the rear turret.

They hurried around and bellowed their question at the tail gunner. What was the problem? A huge, fat, plainly not very bright sergeant showed them what was left of his finely adjusted gunsight. It was ruined. The target was Düsseldorf. The flak would be heavy. The sergeant and the entire crew were all replacements; this was their first mission. George, the squadron gunnery officer, ordered the tail gunner out. They needed someone as tail-end Charlie who could hit the target without the aid of a gunsight, and George knew he had had enough practice by now to fill the bill.

Over the intercom he introduced himself to the green crew; they had just arrived from the re-placement depot. After an hour's flying, he thought, "Where's the bomber stream? We should be in the heart of the bomber stream!" Slowly he swung the turret around in a 180-degree sweep. There was shimmering moonlight and an occa-sional fleecy white cloud—great weather for night-fighters. No bomber stream! They were alone.

George let his eyes drop earthwards and groaned. They were not over Düsseldorf. They were over Cologne—he could pick out the twin spires of the great cathedral with ease, and the sweep of the Rhine, silvered in the moonlight. He heard the intercom crackle on, the voice of the pilot saying urgently, "Navigator. Navigator—where are we?" And after a few seconds the well-bred English voice of the puzzled navigator: "I'm damned if I know, old chap."

Just then, the master searchlight of the Cologne defense system locked onto them; they were "coned." The German anti-aircraft gunner had a fat bird sitting in his sights. Pieces of shrapnel began hitting them, sounding like gravel against sheet metal. Then they started taking direct hits, the aircraft jumping and bucking as pieces of the fuselage were torn away. Long flames streamed from the wings and George knew that meant cur-tains.

He pivoted his turret, preparing to launch himself backwards into space. A burst of shrapnel fragments from the flak sprinkled his back with agonizing impact, but nothing could stop his outward plunge. He reached for the parachute handle, hoping to God they hadn't split open his parachute, and forgetting that he had not adjusted the huge amount of parachute harness between his legs. It opened with an immense bang and the pain was intense. He bobbed upwards as if raised on a yo-yo. At the same time he felt in one awful moment his whole rib cage cave in, and passed into merciful oblivion.

George Harsh was jarred back to consciousness when he hit the ground. The searchlight had alerted the anti-aircraft crew and he observed what turned out to be a sergeant and four soldiers trotting across the field towards him. George did not think they were likely to be friendly.

But they were. They seemed to think the entire episode was funny. It seemed he was the first live enemy they had ever encountered. They fetched a litter, shoved a lighted cigarette between his lips, and the sergeant uttered the timeworn phrase, "For you the war is over." Chattering cheerfully, they carried him across to their command post and led him into the hut, where a huge, close-cropped major was sitting. The major roared abuse at them, and they tore back to their posts. An orderly was polishing his jackboots, and he kicked his box up into the air and almost kicked the orderly out the door. Then he turned on George, hands on hips, glancing at George's identity discs, and grinned. "That's how you expect Germans to behave, isn't it, Mr. Harsh? That's the trouble with you bloody English—you think of all Germans as Huns! Now, sit down before you fall down, and I'll get a doctor to look at you before we ferry you off to hospital." The major pulled open a drawer, produced a bottle of cognac and two glasses, sloshed both half full, and handed one to George. "At least invading France meant that the brandy got better," he said. "Skoal!"

George drank several cognacs, but didn't feel much better. He was only vaguely aware of being driven through the rubble-filled streets of Cologne, and for the first twenty-four hours or so had only blurred memories of a hospital: orderlies in white coats, lights above an operating table; a ward where grave-eyed Sisters of Mercy looked down at him; and then slowly the Catholic nuns coming into focus from the periphery of his dreams, whispering around him, fussing over him, chatting to him in German, smoothing his sheets, feeding him soup. George lay back, bewildered.

Then day and night began to separate into their proper component parts, and he became aware that every night meant air raids. Most of the patients, civilian or military, were shuttled down into the basement. George was not part of that assembly. The Nazi colonel in charge, unlike the comradely major, screamed abuse at him. "Not you, *Engländer!* They're your friends up there!

108

See if they can drop a bomb on you, as they drop them on our wives and children!"

The first night that George was aware of being alone in the darkness, the building shaking, the whistles and explosions of bombs all around him, he felt a small hand being slipped into his, and found a small Catholic nun who fit the hand sitting next to his bed. She whispered, "We stay together—yes? Perhaps we could pray together—no?"

George wasn't very good at praying, but she was there every night after that when there was a bombing raid, and George began to get confused about whose side he was supposed to be on.

George's transit from the Cologne hospital to Dulag Luft, the Luftwaffe reception and interrogation center just outside Frankfurt, was not without unusual incident. His ribs were taped up; breathing was difficult, and he was usually in pain. Plainly he was in no condition to run anywhere, so the Wehrmacht who had captured him and were now responsible for handing him over to the Luftwaffe, felt they were safe in entrusting him to the care of a young soldier named, appropriately enough, Adolf.

Adolf was tall, thin, and weedy. His steel helmet was three sizes too large for him, and often slipped down over his eyes. His uniform was intended for a short, fat soldier, so Adolf emerged from tunic and trousers with gangling wrists and scarecrow legs. The journey by train from Cologne to Frankfurt should have taken a few hours; it took Adolf two days. For starters, he caught the train on the wrong side of the platform, and they proceeded for hours in the wrong direction. After getting off at a wayside station, they waited several more hours for the train back.

In the crowded railway station Adolf was suddenly smitten with an attack of diarrhea, and dragged George into the huge lavatory. In haste, he thrust his belt with its attached holster and enormous Luger into George's hands, and bolted for the toilet. The lavatory was swarming with German troops, among them many SS men with swastika armbands on their black tunics. Their looks took on a peculiar intensity as they passed this strange apparition: an RAF officer in a blood-stained tunic holding a large, presumably loaded, revolver.

Adolf returned and managed to find the right train. By now, they had eaten their rations for the journey and both were hungry. Fortunately, their railway carriage was packed with soldiers on leave from the Russian front, carrying sausage, bread, and schnapps. With peasant cunning, Adolf revealed that he was escorting a genuine *englische Flieger*. The combat troops, noting that George was wounded, were both compassionate and curious, and when they found George cooperative and ready to chat, they showed the comradeship of most fighting units, sharing their food and drink with the stranger and his guard. The schnapps was fiery, and George's ribs began to heal remarkably quickly. "Before that journey was over," he later admitted, "I'd learned the chorus of the 'Horst Wessel Lied' by heart and was harmonizing as loudly and drunkenly as any of them."

At Dulag Luft the merriment ended. The Germans had contrived a little ruse that did not contravene the regulations of the Geneva convention. George had been briefed about it back at base during the "escape lectures." All incoming officers were informed that they had to have their uniforms cleaned and their underclothes washed. George was given a hot shower, had his chest retaped, and was ushered into a small cell with a reasonably comfortable cot. For three days he was fed twice a day but was left naked and alone. On the third day, still stark naked, he was marched through a long room full of pretty German secretaries, who took time off from their typing to peep and giggle, and then he was confronted by a board of six officers. It was very hard, George decided, to look like an indomitable flying hero in one's birthday suit; but he answered all the questions with an impervious name, rank, and serial number.

He was grilled for two days, still without clothes, and on the second day a German officer led him back through another room filled with filing cabinets, and then revealed that they knew all about him: squadron number, types of aircraft, commanding officer's name, all the details, ending with, "And look at this, Mr. Harsh . . . ah-ah, I see it is Flight Lieutenant Harsh now, and squadron gunnery officer, too. Mmm . . . it says here that you are an American. Why did you not transfer to the American air force, Mr. Harsh?"

George was impressed—and relieved—when, after a long train journey, he was delivered to North Compound of Sagan, Stalag Luft III, to discover that the British had their own intelligence system.

Chapter Eight

DAVID JONES LEFT THE University of Texas in 1936 and went on duty as second lieutenant, cavalry, at Fort Worth. After a year he enlisted as a flying cadet and was transferred to the USAAF flying school at Randolph Field, then eventually to Riverside, California.

"It was a bombing attack group," he later said, "low-level flying and pretty interesting, considering that you were in the desert with mountains sticking up all over the place. But you could sneak up on some poor guy driving his car happily along some country road in the desert, zoom over his head, and bop, drop a bag of water on him! Scare him to death. We were very young, and we thought that great fun. Also very fast—a hundred and sixty miles an hour!"

Quite happy in his job, David knew very little of the strategic maneuverings that went on at levels above his head. But he did know that when the war in Europe started, things began to look up.

New aircraft began to arrive: Boeing B-17's and Mitchell B-25's. At three hundred miles an hour, they were faster than most of the other American fighters. David Jones was in one of the first squadrons to be equipped with them.

113

But would America join in the conflict?

"We knew there was a chance. If things went the same way as the First World War, then we might be in action. The whole group, sixty-five aircraft, went on maneuvers down in the Carolinas and Mississippi. Six months and we were still on maneuvers. We used to say if it hadn't been for Pearl Harbor we'd *still* be on maneuvers."

After Pearl Harbor, David Jones's vistas began to broaden. Skiddy York, his operations officer, told him that a Colonel Doolittle had approached him about obtaining volunteers for a highly secret and very dangerous mission.

The first bombing raid on Tokyo was on.

"Twenty crew representing four squadrons moved off to Eglin Field in Florida to train," said David. "Jimmy Doolittle really took charge and we were completely sold. You couldn't meet that man without being completely captivated. The plan was simply to cross the Pacific by aircraft carrier and, six hundred and fifty miles from the Japanese mainland, to send off the B-25's to bomb the capital, then fly on to China and find somewhere to land. That was the difficult bit. There were simply no maps with navigation points available. And as there was no hope of getting those babies back aboard the carrier, and we'd arrive over China in the dark, I began to see what Skiddy York meant when he said 'highly secret and very dangerous.'

"We sailed on the aircraft carrier *Hornet* on April 1, 1942. Sixteen B-25's all on one carrier.

One thing really puzzled me about that carrier: They had a billiard table on board! Now what could you do with a billiard table at sea? Even tied up in the home port there was bound to be some movement. But since we used it as a table for shooting craps, it didn't bother us.

"We rendezvoused off north Hawaii, with two carriers, four cruisers, eight destroyers, and two oilers, which represented the bulk of the Pacific Fleet remaining after Pearl Harbor. So if the Japanese succeeded in knocking us off, things would look a bit grim for the West Coast.

"We had planned to proceed to within six hundred and fifty miles of Japan and then launch at dusk. Colonel Doolittle would take off first and drop incendiaries to mark Tokyo. We all had our assigned targets. After releasing our bombs we'd fly to the southeast off the coast, turn southwest, proceed to the tip of Japan, and then west to China where there was a designated airfield waiting to receive us. We decided we'd believe *that* when we saw it. And the unexpected kept popping up all the time.

"We had planned to launch the attack on the evening of April eighteenth. Twenty-four hours before, we left the oilers and the destroyer screen behind, and the carriers and the cruisers proceeded east at a pretty good speed. In fact, the destroyers simply couldn't keep up with us in the heavy weather.

"Then, of course, the unexpected!

"Early on the morning of the eighteenth, we

heard gunfire, and found we'd been sighted by a Japanese picketboat. Guns were trained and it was sunk immediately. But now the decision became hairline. We had to assume that the Japanese naval defenses had been alerted. Therefore an attack upon our small force must be imminent. Should the B-25's go for it? Or should we shove the bombers overboard so that the *Hornet's* fighter planes could be brought up from below to defend the fleet?

"Doolittle solved that little problem with no difficulty. He hadn't come all this far to have his B-25's pushed overboard. He said, 'Okay, we go. Now!'

"It didn't seem to bother him much that we were then eight hundred miles from the Japanese coastline and hadn't a hope in hell of reaching China afterwards. So we started taking off at eight in the morning. We had something less than four-hundred-feet takeoff. But with the strong wind, and the *Hornet* roaring along at thirty knots into the teeth of it, every aircraft made it off the carrier. In fact, one pilot forgot to put his flaps down and more or less fell off the nose of the carrier, but even *he* had gotten enough speed to get his plane up.

"My rear gunner, Joe Maski, was eighteen years old. He was separated from the rest of the crew by an enormous, collapsible bag containing fuel, but he had his intercom. It clicked on, and Joe said quietly, as if he'd been thinking about it, 'Sir, we won't have enough gas.' I paused for a few seconds, then said, 'That's right.' Joe thought about that for a few seconds, then without a word clicked his intercom off. He had gotten the message.

"We hit the mainland after about three hours' flying and naturally we were lost, didn't know where the hell we were. So we turned south, flying low. We were spread out—thirteen planes coming in from different directions to bomb Tokyo—and three others attacking different targets. About the time we were deciding we'd better find something to drop these bombs on, we suddenly spotted the outline of Tokyo Bay and knew where we were. I turned north and pulled up to give the incendiary bombs a spread.

"When the bombs were gone we turned in the general direction of China. We didn't think we had a chance of reaching it, but the general direction would have to do. And then, out of the blue, we picked up a tail wind of thirty-five miles an hour. We'd studied the weather probabilities for this coast, and we didn't expect any wind assistance at all. The navigator was as busy as hell, and after an hour or so he said, 'Hey, looks as if we'll only have to swim about a hundred and fifty miles.' And after another half hour he said, 'Gee, I think we'll have enough juice to make the coast.'

"By now we were staggering along, losing lots of manifold pressure, still using the four engines, fifteen or sixteen rpm's, doing about a hundred and fifty miles an hour, and losing power by the minute, so eventually I'd swear you could almost see the propeller blades turning. We could tell we were getting close to the coast of China because the color of the water changed. But it was getting dark. I pulled up to around four to five thousand feet, and we flew towards what we hoped was our designated airfield. We'd had no navigational fixes for seven hundred miles, no radio contact, no ground aids. As it turned out later, any ground aids we might have used were turned off because the Chinese thought we were Japanese.

"In those days we used to carry big parachute flares. We dropped one overboard and watched it drift down into the gathering darkness. As the flare sank lower we could see we were really in the mountains, and there was no way of making any fancy turns among them. And now as the engines were just puttering, I said, 'Okay, fellas! This is it. Bail out.'

"The gunner and the navigator went out first. Then it was the turn of Hoss, my copilot, and me. In a B-25 behind the cockpit there's a hatch where you enter and exit the aircraft, so we pulled the lever and dropped the hatch, and there we both were, staring down at a big black hole with the wind whistling through. And oh, boy! I've never hated anything more in my whole life. But there was no alternative, so I shouted, 'Okay, Hoss, you're first!' He sat down facing the rear and off he went into the blackness. Then I sat down facing the same way. Legs down and out I went, pulled the ripcord and pretty soon I hit the deck, so I guessed we'd lost quite a lot of altitude. I was carrying the gazette bag with all the details of the mission, and I bruised my arms, but nothing serious.

"So there it was—cold, windy, and black. Nothing on that Chinese mountainside seemed welcoming. And even the sound of the aircraft engine had faded away. I had a few useful things with me. They'd issued us a bottle of whiskey which I was carrying, a canteen of water, a knife . . . I didn't have a pistol. I crawled to the top of the small hill on which I'd landed, draped the parachute over a little bush to make a sort of tent, crawled inside, took a large swig of the whiskey, and shivered all night.

"It started to get light and I could hear a cowbell out in the distance. I concluded I'd better walk west; it was pretty hilly country. I came to a trail in maybe half an hour, and here again I could hear cowbells. Then I came upon a group of Chinese.

"I didn't think our intelligence briefings about this part of China had been all that helpful—you only drink boiled water and eat hard-boiled eggs, that sort of thing—but they'd made one point clear: if you met another human being, and smiled at him, and he smiled back, that would probably be a Chinese. If he didn't smile back it would probably be a Japanese. So I smiled real hard at these people, who looked like farmers, and Intelligence was dead right—they smiled back. So I advanced smiling, got out my cigarettes and handed them around, and they all took one and the smiles continued. I had a little notebook with me, and I knew the names of a couple of towns. The towns didn't do any good, so I drew a map, but they'd obviously never seen a map, and their smiles were now just polite. Then I got real smart and drew a picture of a train, and made as if I was running along a railway line going choo-choo-chooo . . . I got a real laugh out of that. They thought that was wonderful—and probably that I was crazy. So we waved goodbye to each other and I continued heading west.

"Half an hour later I reached a railway line, followed it for a bit, and came to a small station. The stationmaster was a pleasant young man who could print a little English, and then just at that moment who should walk in but Hoss, which was a pleasant reunion, but his Chinese was as negligible as mine. The young stationmaster put us aboard a handcar and pumped it up the track to another, larger station. There we joined an engine and boxcar, and about twenty miles later we arrived at a town called Yushan.

"And there assembled around the station was this huge crowd carrying banners and all smiling, so we knew we were among friends. A man in a Western suit stepped forward, and said in good English, "How do you do? Welcome to Yushan. I am Danny Wang, mayor of Yushan, and this reception is in your honor as American heroes!"

Hoss and I stopped smiling and looked at each other in disbelief. Twenty-four hours after we'd taken off from the carrier, and we were being welcomed by a crowd of five thousand people somewhere in the backwoods of China! Of course it was all due to the magic of radio. As soon as we hit Tokyo, the navy released the news, and flashed the report to the Chinese so they knew about it almost before we parachuted out."

As a result of the Tokyo raid, David Jones received the quickest promotion of his entire career—captain to major in one month!—and soon found himself commanding a squadron heading for England. But "heading for" and "getting to" were far different situations. Aircraft then could not fly three thousand miles nonstop across the north Atlantic. One mostly island-hopped: from Bangor, Maine, to Labrador, to Greenland, to Iceland, to England. And that was no picnic either.

"We got to Bangor, ready to cross to Goose Bay, and there were aircraft flocking through to get across the ocean. Well, the first guy got off the ground, and splash, he went in; the next guy took off, same thing happened. So Command called a halt and said, 'Perhaps we'd better think this thing over.' Now we came under control of Ferry Command. They said, 'Okay, you B-26's. Take all your armor plate out. Take all your guns out. And get three of your crew members out!' We did all that. They said, 'Now go!'

"We got off to Goose Bay and then made Greenland, and then we finally made it to England. From there I led a dozen fighters to take part in the invasion of North Africa. We landed in Tunisia in November 1942.

"The airfield was really beat-up—shell holes and burnt-out French planes everywhere. Nobody there. No organization. We just sat on the ground for days. No way of refueling or moving. Then supplies started showing up from the invasion forces which came ashore about a hundred miles west of us. Gradually things got better and our group moved across to Algiers.

"Going over England, the group commander had been lost: he'd found himself over Cherbourg and got shot down. So I'm now the boss. And our job is to bomb Germans. A new lieutenant colonel had arrived the day before, and said, 'What's up?' So I told him we had these missions, and he said, 'Well, hell, I'd better go along.'

"So it was nine in the morning, and we were making a low-level attack, fifteen hundred feet, when bang! flak hit the port engine and knocked it out. No way of staying airborne. I just picked out a little straight stretch between these hillocks and put her down. The hillocks knocked the wings off and slowed us, and she slid on her belly across the desert. That first impact threw the lieutenant colonel out through the nose, and as we accelerated after impact the wing scraped over him, so the poor guy got further injuries.

"We managed to scramble out of our wreck and began to stagger off, looking for assistance. We hadn't gone more than a mile when we saw a line of German soldiers approaching; they'd seen us crash. So they didn't have to tell us that our war was over. They took us to a first-aid station and patched us up.

"They brought me to their fighter headquarters, where the man in charge was a blond guy with an Iron Cross, sweater, desert boots, and so on. The debonair fighter pilot. Nice guy. He spoke a little English, and gave me a deck chair in the fighter operations room. I suppose by now it was about five in the afternoon. So I sat there watching the German fighters landing and refueling, and taking off again. At the end of the day they came in to file their reports, and I was sort of included in the circle—a lot of cheerful banter, in fact. 'Why are you teamed up with the Russians?' to which I replied, 'Why are you fighting with the Japanese?' Schoolboy stuff, really. Daft conversation, all very congenial. In fact, after a few moments you wondered what the hell all the fighting was about.

"I got to Sagan, Stalag Luft III, on January 16, the day before my birthday. I thought, 'Oh, well, now I might get some rest.' Not a hope. Bub Clark was the senior American officer. 'Ah, I'm glad to have you here, Major. I've got a little job for you. We're moving this entire wooden partition a foot out. The Germans won't notice and we'll have a terrific hiding place for all our escape tools.'

"Then, of course, when we moved to North Compound, I was rounded up to join Wally Floody's underground commandos. What a strike force thirty feet down!"

Chapter Nine

WHEN ROYAL CANADIAN AIR Force fighter pilot Wally Floody took off in his Spitfire for his maiden excursion into aerial combat, his knowledge of the art was limited. He had never heard the wise words of German ace Adolf Galland: "The first rule of all air combat is to see the opponent first. Like the hunter who stalks his prey and who maneuvers himself unnoticed into the most favorable position for the kill, the fighter in the opening of a dogfight must detect the opponent as early as possible in order to attain a superior position for the attack."

Nor had he heard the words of a disgruntled RAF squadron leader who observed, "We came into the war being great at patrolling in tight formations, line abreast, wingtip to wingtip. Bloody spectacular for air shows over Croydon. Bloody useless for combat because you were so bloody busy seeing that you didn't nip a piece out of the other chap's wing, that you never even noticed the Hun diving out of the sun to knock half your squadron out of the sky."

Flying Officer Wallace Floody was twenty-three years old. Six feet two, thin but muscular, with heavy brows, dark thoughtful eyes, and dark hair, he was his own man. He'd roughed it around

America in his late teens, and spent four years working the richest gold mine ever discovered in Canada. It was owned by Harry Oakes, who became a multimillionaire, was knighted by the queen, and was murdered in unsavory circumstances in the Bahamas in 1941.

"A tough place to work," Wally admitted. "Turn your back and there was always someone ready to take a poke at you."

Wally was Canadian, and proud of it. He'd married the prettiest, most intelligent girl he'd ever met. When he joined 401 Squadron—the number-one squadron of the Royal Canadian Air Force— Betty insisted on moving around to every camp to which he was posted.

When Wally reached England, his Spitfire squadron began their training by doing sweeps up and down the British east coast. Then they were posted to the famous Biggin Hill fighter station to the south of London for operational duties.

One October morning, three Royal Canadian squadrons—thirty Spitfires in all—set off from Biggin Hill for the French town of St. Omer, looking for trouble. They found it. At that time the fighter arm of the Luftwaffe had never been more powerful and more effective. They jumped 401 Squadron with over two hundred Messerschmitt 109's. Wally Floody, who realized that he had never before in his life had his sights aligned on a Messerschmitt and never fired his guns in combat before, suddenly found those sights full of Messerschmitts gyrating crazily around the skies. The next thing he knew was that his plane was disintegrating around him. Pieces were falling off, and smoke and flame were enveloping him. Without delay he flipped over and bailed out. He was to learn later that seven out of the ten aircraft in his flight had been destroyed.

Wally realized that, borne by a strong wind, he was floating down towards the autumnal fields of France, and that a small village, about ten houses on either side of the road, stood directly in his way. Oscillating madly, he came in towards the stone sidewall of a small cottage, using his feet and arms to try to push it away.

"The next thing I knew," reported Wally, "I was flat on my ass on the paved road, winded and confused. I turned my head and saw a group of soldiers running towards me. They were about two hundred yards away, wearing gray uniforms, and I guessed they were German. At that moment the door of the cottage I'd tried to knock down suddenly opened and a little old lady in a black bombazine dress scooted out, carrying a bottle in one hand and a glass in the other. Quite deadpan, as if she were serving a client in a restaurant, she looked down, filled the glass, and handed it to me. It was cognac. I drank it. The Germans had now broken the hundred-yard barrier, and were shouting rude words at my angel of mercy. This time she smiled at me and refilled the glass. I gulped that down, too. The Germans now surrounded us, trying to push the old lady away, but she screamed abuse at them, and they left her alone. She carefully took the glass from my hand, walked back to her cottage, and closed the door behind her. I thought, 'Welcome to France!'"

That Wally was going to become arguably the best escape tunneler of World War Two did not concern him. For the moment he had other things to worry about. Such as arriving at Dulag Luft, the Luftwaffe transit camp on the outskirts of Frankfurt am Main.

When Lieutenant Colonel Bub Clark left Dulag Luft for Stalag Luft III, he was dressed in a manner befitting neither his rank nor his length of service. Despite his fresh features and red hair he looked more like a member of a rather rundown Russian folk group than the second-in-command of the first authentic USAAF fighter squadrons to arrive in the British Isles. His six-foot-two-and-a-half-inch frame was concealed by a pair of British Army khaki trousers, several inches too short, and a Russian-type blouse given him by his German captors. All he needed was a violin!

Johnny Dodge put that right immediately, as a welcome to his fellow American. "He grabbed me by the arm," said Bub Clark, "gave me a pair of flannel pajamas which were priceless in Sagan at that time, and a decent shirt, and made me look respectable until I got my uniform back. The Germans decided that my American officer's uniform—leather jacket, light-colored shirt and slacks, and low-cut shoes—looked more civilian than military."

They were probably right about that, but it happened to be what Bub Clark had been wearing as he grabbed his flying helmet and headed for his Spitfire on that morning in July.

In order to familiarize American fighter squadrons with RAF planes and tactics, seven officers, including Bub Clark, had been temporarily transferred to a British fighter wing and taught how to fly a Spitfire. That day, three squadrons of twelve Spitfires each took off from Tangmere in Kent.

Bub Clark flew number two, on the tail of Flight Lieutenant Freddie Green. They crossed the Channel at zero altitude, observing complete radio silence, intending to rise immediately to eighteen thousand feet when German radar picked them up; they would then receive instructions from their own radar intelligence.

The theory was that, since the Germans had declared war on the Soviet Union, practically every squadron of the Luftwaffe had moved to the eastern front. Not true. On his headphones Bub Clark heard their wing commander break radio silence and call back to British radar, "What's the form?" and heard the radar officer's voice delivering the bad news: "There are fifty to sixty bandits above you, and more taking off from their local airfields. We will continue to give you instructions as to their location."

The instructions seemed to be slightly superfluous, because as they made a 180-degree turn over Abbeville, they could see far down below little German Messerschmitts and Focke-Wulfs busy rising to meet them. Bub Clark knew that the general idea of these sweeps was to provoke the Germans into coming up at you, exchange a few bursts of fire as they closed, and then head for home before your fuel ran out.

Today, Freddie Green had other ideas. He called his cohort of four Spitfires to follow him down, with a second section to give them cover. Bub Clark hurtled down after Freddie, uncertain where the others were. Two aircraft flashed into his sights as he sped above them and he opened fire, but whether he hit or missed he never knew. He was beginning to understand that Freddie's Spitfire was faster than his, and that he was losing Freddie as they headed for the coast.

Both planes were close to the ground when Bub heard Freddie call, "I'm going through the gate," which meant he was opening the throttles and using maximum power. "I took the same action," said Bub. "Freddie had a wax job on his Spitfire, and mine was a rather beat-up bird which had just come out of maintenance. And when a big hole appeared in my left wing—which was normal when you had four Focke-Wulfs on your tail—I signaled him to change direction. Plainly Freddie never got that signal as he bored a hole back to Britain.

"I made a hard right turn to starboard and zoomed around over the French coast again, where to my surprise all the antiflak batteries went mad, using me as a live target for practice. Then the four F-W's got into the act again and I found myself approaching two, head-on. I could tell they were firing at me from the flashes in their wings, but then we'd skimmed past each other again and I was steering for home—at wave-top level. That gave the F-W's, still on my tail and anxious to get their Iron Cross, a bit of trouble, because when you're trying to squirt someone down with your guns and hold your aircraft a few feet above the waves, one mistake can be lethal. But they were doing their best, as I could see by the waterspouts their cannon fire made all around me. Then by the sound of my engine I knew something had happened—a bullet had entered it, perhaps. My airspeed indicator stopped at around three-twenty. I decided I wasn't going to sit there forever and just get shot down. I had used up all my ammunition, and my fuel situation wasn't going to be all that good, so I made another hard break and saw that the F-W's were now far away out to sea—they were probably at the limit of their gas or ammunition and had decided to call it a day—but I had a little work to do yet.

"My engine was slowly packing up. I was approximately sixty miles or so from the coast of Britain—France was close enough to see. And there was the ditching problem. We'd had lots of drill about it back at base, but no pilot I ever met was very thrilled about the idea. The Spitfire was difficult to ditch into the sea.

"First step: jettison your canopy. If you hit the water with it *closed* you were making it hard for yourself. I tugged it back. It wouldn't move. I tugged it harder. It still wouldn't budge. I wrestled with it, and gave up. I already had my feet on the dashboard against the shock of hitting the waves. I'd been warned about that: there was a big radiator situated under the central portion of the cockpit. On impact the deceleration shoved it up through the floor, and your legs were trapped. Very nasty if the canopy won't open and your legs are trapped. It seemed for a few seconds that the history of Lieutenant Colonel Clark was about to end. I steered for the coast of France, so low now that I was leaving a wake behind. But the engine was still turning over quite valiantly, although there was a certain putt-putt-putt quality about it.

"And suddenly there was the beach, and I was skimming across, and the cliffs were not too high for me to coax her up and over. Then there was a wheat field, and I pancaked down onto it and slid to a halt. And the canopy opened! I couldn't believe it. As I got out onto the wing I tried to find out what had gone wrong. Had the catch stuck? And then I suddenly understood that the force of the slipstream had kept it closed. Once the slipstream stopped, the canopy could open.

"I did not have time to brood over this. I had landed more or less under an unusual, tall concrete structure, which was practically embedded in antiflak batteries . . . now I understood why I had been so unwelcome when I did my previous turn over the coast. It was heavily camouflaged with nets. I thought it was either some sort of radar or a range finder for the big German guns which were lobbing shells over the channel from time to time.

"I was wrong on both counts. Later I learned that it was part of the *Knickebein*—the "crooked leg" system of intersecting radio pulses—which the Germans used to guide their bombers to their targets.

"Just then I saw anti-aircraft crews converging on me from all sides."

The anti-aircraft gunners who swarmed around Bub's plane were quite pleasant, and when he was finally driven to the officers' club in Boulogne he was treated as a popular live trophy, with the German pilots in friendly argument about who could take the credit for shooting him down.

Bub felt it was not his place to join in this celebration, but he smiled and accepted a glass of wine with them. When he finally arrived at Dulag Luft, he fended off their main question: what was an American colonel doing flying a British plane in a British raid?

They kept him at Dulag Luft for almost a month, and when any American crew member arrived they immediately asked him what he knew about this mysterious Colonel Clark. The answers were always the same: "The only Colonel Clark we know is dead." That was the official verdict. Back at base they thought he was dead. His wife thought he was dead.

When Bub Clark arrived at Sagan, Stalag Luft III, he found that, for a dead man, he had to work pretty hard.

Captain John Bennett was flying with Ninety-seven Group, the first squadron of B-17's to arrive in Britain.

"I was flying my Fortress in the rear slot of a flight of B-17's attacking the submarine pens at Brest on the north coast of France. It was a strange kind of mission, and I had a feeling that my squadron was in the wrong part of it.

"The plan was, the first group of B-17's would attack the target escorted by Spitfires. Then we —the second group—would go in *without* an escort, the theory being that the first group will have attracted all the fighters, and they'll have used up all their ammunition and fuel. So we'll be safe. Then the third group can go in under escort again. Great idea! In theory."

John Bennett had signed up for the Civilian Pilot Training Scheme before Pearl Harbor, then had gone to Pendleton as a second lieutenant. Since he was only a second pilot, he was delighted when he was reassigned to a B-17 squadron as first pilot and told to fly on the northern circuit across to England.

"I was escorting four P-38's, the twin-engine fighter planes. We were brand-new pilots and none of us had ever flown in Atlantic weather with just instruments before. It scared the bejesus out of you. You had a P-38 stuck on the tip of either wing flying as close as he dared because it was pretty certain he'd be lost if he dropped out of formation, and that Atlantic Ocean down below was no place for putting your landing wheels down.

"When we reached Stornoway in Scotland we flew south to Turnberry. I'd collected four more P-38's and we were losing altitude to land, when suddenly out of the mist came this great rock, Ailsa Craig! All eight P-38's just said goodbye and soared straight up into the overcast. People forget that in those days our navigational aids were pretty fundamental; there was no radar equipment aboard. The British had to send up some specially equipped aircraft to round up the P-38's and bring them safely down on the airfield.

"We flew on to our British base near Peterborough and had to speak in an English accent, and use British landing instructions. That was absolutely necessary. The Germans could intercept all our aircraft radio signals, and no one wanted them to know that American aircraft were landing and how many there were. So instead of saying, 'Request permission to land,' or something on that order, we had to say in our very best English accents, 'May I pancake—may I pancake?'

"In those early days the going was tough. I lasted eight missions. Then came that daylight raid on Brest.

"We had to bomb those submarine pens at a height of fourteen thousand feet. We were closing on the French coast and climbing in tight formation, when the Focke-Wulf 190's hit us. We were just red meat for those German fighters. As I say, I was in the rear slot and three of them came at me, shearing up at my belly like sharks through clear water. And they had it worked out; they were very clever attacks. They knew exactly where our weak points were. They dove down below our formation and then came up underneath at an oblique angle, so that the top-turret gunner didn't see them at all as they flashed up past him; the rear-turret gunner couldn't depress his guns sufficiently to open fire; only the ball-turret gunner in the belly had a chance to align his sights, but that was difficult.

"Those first attacks just sluiced us with cannon-shell and machine-gun fire. The flare rack on the back of my seat caught fire immediately—a vicious fire on the flight deck. And I had no controls, absolutely nothing. I could pull and wrench and nothing happened. My autopilot was also knocked out. I couldn't even talk to my crew; every radio connection had gone. I could shout, "Bail out!" But only my copilot and perhaps the navigator could hear me. My copilot stood up to move back and grab his chute without being burned by the flare rack. He was wearing a British detachable-type chute. I'd decided against that. I said to myself, 'Hey, baby, you may not have time to grab that sort of chute and clip it on,' so I was sitting on mine.

"I have this eternal mental picture of him standing there—I was never going to see him again— when there was this awful, violent, noisy snapping sound and bang, everything was gone. I was obviously thrown forward, and narrowly missed losing both eyes. Don't know what I hit but I had two deep punctures on either side of my nose and just below the eyes. Then I came to and thought, 'This is it!' Then a second flash thought, 'No, it's not; they're not going to get away with this!' And then the fundamental realization, 'Oh, my God. You're not even in the aircraft! You're somewhere in midair, and you're stuck in something!' The 'something' was a big piece of metal wreckage, and I had my right foot firmly fixed in it. My right boot was laced up pretty tightly but somehow or other I wrenched my foot out of it, and made a snatch for my chute handle. Fortunately I missed it, because my second reflexive thought was, 'Fool! If you'd pulled your chute, it would have snagged on the debris.'

"So I held on for a few more seconds, and when I seemed to be in the clear I tugged, and talk about pain! The straps between my legs snapped up into my groin and I felt as if I'd been kicked by a horse. But I'm now swinging in some agony and trying to reach up and grab the parachute risers, when I hear this funny noise, this whoosh-whoosh-whoosh sound, and I glance up and there's an enormous piece of the Flying Fort—looked like one whole side of it—coming down like an enormous falling leaf scything from side to side, and bound to hit me and my parachute. I'll never know how it missed us, but it did. So I could now turn my attention to other details. I could feel the wind blowing at about thirty knots, *not* the ideal landing speed for a first parachute landing. And the earth is flying up at me, and I'm swooping into a field. And there in the middle of the field is this great big, solid, wooden wagon, and I'm heading right for it!

"And in this chute and the wind I'm oscillating like a kid on a swing, and on the downward swing I'm going to hit the cart. I draw my knees right up under my chin to try and fend it off, and I streak over it, missing it by inches, and then—wham! The parachute has snagged on it and whacks me down on the ground, and I'm almost jerked apart for a second time. But there's no time to lie there. I remember those RAF briefings: first thing you do is hide your parachute. So where am I going to hide my parachute? And I'm conscious that both ankles are hurting like hell, and I'm stumbling around, trying to stuff the chute into the cart. The country around me seems to be full of hedges and banks and little fields. I hobble across the field like a crippled crab, and there's a small lane running somewhere or other, and a fairly high bank on either side with thickish hedges growing along it. I thought if I could get up that bank and squiggle down under the hedge, half bury myself in the loose twigs and leaves, I might get some rest and check my bearings. So I get into that position. I realize that I'll have to move pretty quickly, because there'll be German search parties around looking for the likes of us. Then I remember my RAF escape kit. It contained a few good things, like halazone for purifying water, and stay-awake tablets which I think must have been Benzedrine. I needed to stay awake so I swallowed a couple of those.

"Next thing I know I open my eyes, and realize that it's almost dark—I must have been fast asleep for hours. Maybe they'd mixed up the sleeping tablets with the Benzedrine, because I had slept like a baby. Then I heard shouting down below me, quite close, and another voice shouting back from farther away, and I also realized that they were shouting in German. And I presumed they were looking for me, because when I peered out there was a truck about fifty yards away down the lane and soldiers climbing aboard, and the engine started and off they went. Maybe they'd found the parachute, but they hadn't found me.

"The sound of the engine died away and I decided I must get moving. The sooner I leave this area the better. I wriggled back onto the bank and decided to put the escape kit back in my pocket. Then I discovered my flying suit has been almost torn off, and all I had left were the pockets. Fortunately there were lots of sturdy pieces of wood around in that hedge, and I found one branch that I could use as a crutch, because my right ankle was giving me hell, and the left was just about bearable. So, by using the sole of my left foot, and taking most of my weight on that and using the crutch for the right, I made some progress down the lane. But I can tell you I wasn't making an awful lot of speed, that's for sure. I also had one of these little button compasses issued by the RAF, and I decided I would head for Spain—

south—that was the way to go. I really had no idea it was about five or six hundred miles away; I guess I wasn't thinking all that clearly. I thought I'd jump a train or steal a bicycle. But I can tell you I spent, I suppose, six of the most miserable days of my life during that period.

"I tried to contact the French, and I was a little bitter at the time that no one would help me. But later I understood just how frightened they were. The Germans had smashed them into the ground. The penalties for sheltering Allied airmen and escaped POWs were savage—often a concentration camp or a firing squad. The Resistance had not had time to get started. The Americans hadn't even invaded North Africa yet, and the French were plumb scared of me. And when I saw myself eventually in a mirror, I'd have been damned scared of me, too. The two punctures below my eyes had poured blood down my unshaven face, so that it was half blood and half mud, and the two black eyes helped that picture no end. My uniform was now in bloody, muddy rags, and I was hopping along rather like the hunchback of Notre Dame, or an escaper from a leper colony.

"I remember passing through one tiny hamlet and seeing these two youths on the street, about sixteen years old. I'd got out my escape map and I wanted to ask them where I was. I was trying to communicate with them when an older youth walked by and said something to them, and baby, they looked scared to death . . . just jumped on their bikes and raced off down the street. The Germans had them scared all right.

"As far as I know, all I had to eat during those six days were the two tubes of condensed milk in my escape kit. I tried sugar beet in the fields and couldn't eat that, and I tried half-rotten apples lying in the orchards, but they were awful. I also realized that if I didn't get some medication I wouldn't be going anywhere.

"I saw a small cafe on a lonely country crossroad. I'd reached the point where I couldn't go any farther. I'd gotten a whole load of shrapnel splinters in one thigh, and a larger piece of shrapnel had gone deep into my right buttock and was festering badly. Both ankles were giving me hell. So what with all that and near-emasculation from the parachute straps, I was in poor shape.

"I opened the door of the cafe and staggered in. There was this nice woman in her mid-thirties with a small girl of about five hanging on to her apron, and I think she almost dropped dead at the sight of me. After that first look of horror I got across to her in some sort of language that I was an American airman, and she gave me bread and soup with wine in it. I couldn't stand the wine, but it all probably did me a lot of good. And, of course, more than anything else I wanted to sleep. She understood that and took me out to her chicken coop. There were no chickens in it, and it was dry and warm, and she gave me a coat to cover myself with, and I just lay down in the straw—and slept very heavily. I woke up hearing this peculiar noise, and then understood it was the noise of a chain being dragged across wood. The woman had locked the coop up by putting this chain around it, and now it was being pulled loose. The door opened and there stood two French gendarmes with automatic weapons pointed at me. An automatic is a very dangerous weapon, especially if it's cocked, and both of these were. And the younger of the two gendarmes looked very jittery with his.

"The end of that story is that they took me down to the local village and the police station. They were pretty good to me. They let me wash, then share their lunch, and I have a terrible feeling that I ate most of it. Then the schoolmistress of the local school was called in and she spoke reasonable English. She told me that the Luftwaffe were coming to get me, and should be there shortly. But who shows up? A group of German civilians, who didn't look hospitable at all, and as it turned out were certainly some branch of the Gestapo. They took me to what was a nice country house, but I didn't see the inside of that. I was lodged outside in the stables, which had been converted into a jail, and I have an idea that some pretty nasty things went on there, which could have accounted for the fear which seemed widespread around there.

"I was given no medical attention at all. Every day they interrogated me. Every day they threatened to shoot me. They thought I was a spy infiltrated in from the U.S.A.

"These people weren't amateurs. And they weren't kidding. Since I'd been shot down out of an exploding aircraft, everyone would think I was dead. So they had nothing to lose by shooting me. I was a nonperson. When the Luftwaffe did come to pick me up, no one was more grateful than I. They took me straight back to their fighter base, and before I knew what was happening I was undressed and stuffed into a glorious hot bath with an orderly shaving me. Then a doctor arrived, my broken ankle was bound up, and the shrapnel splinters were extracted from my thigh.

"Then, when I was cleaned up and feeling better, I was taken down to the officers' club. That was strange because it was, oddly enough, a heartwarming experience. They were a bunch of fliers, just like me. Same problems. Same experiences. They were on duty, flying for their country, getting killed if necessary, but there was no personal hatred for the RAF or USAAF aircrews. A lot of them spoke English, offered me wine—I drank a glass—and then as I was being gently escorted out, I was almost at the door when I heard this noise behind me, and I turned. They'd all come to attention and everyone was saluting me with the full arm-stretch of the Nazi regime. And dammit, I had the hardest time not returning that same Nazi salute. Fortunately I managed to compromise with the usual military salute. But there was a chivalry about that episode—something hard to explain."

At the outbreak of war, Jimmy James was twenty-three years old. Three years earlier his father had died, and Jimmy had decided it was time to see the world. He worked his passage on an American freighter from his native England to Panama, and continued northwards through the States until he reached a small town in British Columbia, where he got a job as bank clerk in the local branch of the Bank of Commerce.

He stayed there for a couple of years without making his fortune. If he'd joined Wally Floody working in a gold mine not far away, he wouldn't have made any money either. Those were hard times. In fact, he was so broke that when he read about the RAF offering short service commissions to suitable applicants, he wrote to England to apply for one. Accepted and commissioned, he now saw a future through Walter Mitty glasses: the debonair young fighter pilot, white silk scarf flying in the wind, bushy moustache, lovely girls trying to kiss him between sips of ale in the local pub. At the selection board that would decide which branch of the RAF he should join, the selection officer was cheery and brisk: "Well, James, what do you want to fly?"

James was just clearing his throat, preparing to answer, when the selection officer seized on one point: "By Jove, James, I see you got eighty-three percent in navigation! Jolly good show."

"Thank you, sir, I was just thinking—"

"We want chaps like you in our new bomber squadrons. Lots of fun. Big new engines. Bags of throttle to push forward. . . ." He scribbled a note on his pad and called, "Next!"

Jimmy James had completed his training and was flying a mission as second pilot to Squadron Leader George Peacock, when he suddenly found himself coned by searchlights.

"We were somewhere over Holland, and every gun down there seemed to have us in its sights. Lit up like a Christmas tree. Flak came soaring up at us, rattling against us like hail on a corrugated iron shed. And for some reason known only to old George, instead of making the usual maneuver—a bloody quick, vertical nosedive towards terra firma in order to try and break out of the searchlight cone—George continued to plug on heavenwards.

"We never reached it. Bang! The port engine cascaded flame. That was one engine gone and we'd only got two. And with a full bomb-load and a lot of merry flames about, the situation was split-second hazardous. And George Peacock had caught on, yelling, 'Bail out! Bail out!' We had this tail gunner, a guy named Webster. I think he won the first-out prize: one swing of his turret and he'd gone. Out went the rest of us—at speed.

"Poor old George Peacock hung on for a few more seconds, and poof—the whole plane exploded, raining pieces of metal down past us. Our navigator also left it too late and trailed down with his parachute in flames. They were pretty grim seconds, I can tell you.

"As I sailed down in the darkness, I could see the outline of the sea and various fires, and I was thinking, 'If I can reach the North Sea with all this confusion going on, I might manage to borrow a boat and get to England.' It wasn't until quite a while afterwards that I understood that when your aircraft blows up, and you hop out into space with seconds to spare, you're not in any condition to make detailed plans about escape.

"I hit the ground pretty hard; I sprained one ankle a bit. It was muddy and horrible and I saw dark forms moving towards me and I thought, 'Hell, the Germans are pretty quick at this sort of thing.' Then one of the forms said, 'Moo-oo,' and I realized it was the wrong sort of animal. I buried my parachute in the mud, found a gate, and began to limp in a westerly direction. All I had to do now was find the sea, grab a boat, and sail through the dawn towards England.

"I walked west for the whole of the night, jumping into these deep dikes which drained the road whenever I heard a vehicle approach."

Jimmy was still wearing his flying clothes and flying boots, but he reassured himself that any member of the Dutch civilian population would think he was a German airman out for an early morning walk. He would not have been quite so reassured had he known that he had an enormous black eye, blood all over his face, and mud plastering his clothing. As the light grew, a Dutch

145

civilian invited Jimmy to his house and gave him coffee and food. But he had a brother who was frightened of what the Germans might do and slipped out of the house. Within an hour the Dutch police had arrived, and for Jimmy James the long road to Sagan—and experiences that would test his courage and resolution to the limit—had begun.

Part Three

Under a
Dark Moon

Chapter Ten

ON JANUARY 10, 1944, Roger Bushell gave the order to reopen Harry.

The American contingent had been marched away to their new South Compound in the late fall, shortly after Tom had been discovered. Winter was approaching when Roger decided to close down both Dick and Harry until the New Year. Roger also knew that under the leadership of Colonel Rojo Goodrich, Bub Clark, and many others, the Americans were perfectly capable of digging their own tunnels, and they had certainly needed no instruction in making the lives of their captors as difficult as possible. As the two compounds existed side by side, with only barbed-wire fences dividing them, a regular system of semaphore signals was set up to relay messages and exchange general war information gathered from smuggled radios.

Wally Floody, Flight Lieutenant Henry Crump, and Harry Marshall assembled in Hut 104—all lookouts on full alert—and began the task of reopening Harry. It was a cold day, and the stove was very hot—a pleasantly warm environment in which to start chipping away at the cement that sealed the cracks in the tiled concrete block on which it stood. It had been sealed so well that it took two hours to get it open.

Wally peered down the shaft with more than just professional zeal. For almost a year his life had revolved around Harry. Sand from Harry could be found in his hair, his ears, and his mouth, and often he felt that Harry was in the food he ate. Harry had made several attempts to kill him, but he bore Harry no ill feelings. Harry was the road to freedom.

"Well, you bastard," he said cheerfully, "what are you going to do to us this time?"

Harry had a habit of springing surprises when least expected. After that first experience with David Jones in Tom's thirty-foot-deep shaft, Wally had surveyed Harry with renewed respect —a respect that had increased just over a week later when Wally and his assistant were finishing the second of the two workshops opening off the bottom of the shaft. Again they had heard the almost inaudible "crack" and had taken off like greased cats. They had been installing the very last ceiling board, which would have completed the job. Who would have anticipated a second fall? But one could expect anything of Harry. When they had gone back down, they'd discovered both workshops obliterated and the shaft half full of sand.

Earlier, however, one event occurred that had cheered them all up. A friend of Wally's, a Canadian ex-fighter pilot named Red Noble, had solved all of Harry's lighting problems with one bold stroke. Red, a pleasant, argumentative, flamboyant character, had just spent another ten days in the cooler. Released and strolling back to his barrack block, he spied a large coil of electric cable leaning against a tall telegraph pole. As every prisoner of war knows, the magpie instinct for theft goes hand in hand with the will to survive.

Red Noble glanced up at the German electrician working industriously at the very top of the pole. There was no way he could get to earth in less than sixty seconds.

"I'm sure you don't need this," said Red Noble affably, and, seizing the coil, he bolted for the nearest barrack doorway. The workman shouted and threatened for at least ten seconds, by which time the coil—eight hundred feet of top-quality, waterproofed electric cable—had disappeared from German eyes forever. Red had sped through one barrack block, doubled along to another, and passed through a third. Willing hands had grabbed the coil and stowed it away behind partition walls with the speed of conjurers. The unfortunate workman, knowing that the culprit could never be traced and that he would be held responsible, had not reported the loss.

Previously the tunnelers had managed to "liberate" only enough electric wire to light the shafts and the first few feet of Dick and Harry; the remainder of the tunnels had to be excavated by the hot, oxygen-consuming light of the fat-lamps. Now, plugged into the German power supply, Harry was glorious. Power was switched off by

151

the Germans in the daytime, but at night they worked in a blaze of electricity.

Looking down into Harry's shaft, Wally Floody decided it all looked pretty good. Harry Marshall began pumping experimentally, and on hearing unusual noises explored and said, "This needs some repair."

"Right," agreed Wally. "Now we'll move cautiously along the entire length, examine and test every support. We're bound to find a few falls. Mark every suspect support with white chalk and we'll replace it." They came back up after scrutinizing the tunnel from one end to the other, and Roger Bushell was anxious to hear how Harry had survived the winter.

"We had completed one hundred and fifteen feet by the time we stopped," reported Wally. "Now we've got half a dozen frames to replace, and the air pipes are choked in various places. That's a big nuisance because there's a lot of weight pressing down on our shoring, and it's practically impossible to lever up the floorboards. We can get round it but it's going to take a little time."

It took four days.

"How many feet do we have to go to get under the perimeter fence and into the trees?" demanded Roger.

"Around two hundred and twenty feet," answered Wally. "But we've got to dig two more halting places, and then the vertical shaft up to the exit trap will be around twenty-five feet."

"And the sand problem's eternally with us," said Roger. He looked across at Hornblower. "You can't do much with snow on the ground, can you, Peter?"

Peter Fanshawe was, as usual, composed, casual, and to the point. "Crump and I have been examining various possiblilites and we've come up with a reasonable alternative. There's no way of safely dispersing sand with snow or frost on the ground. But we do have a theater. . . ."

There was a long, openmouthed pause. No one had thought about the theater.

"Beneath the rising tiers of the theater's seats," Hornblower went on, "there is quite a large area of space. It was sealed off when the theater was finished, but it would be quite easy to build a swing-door trap under one of the seats. There we should be able to store *all* the sand we take out of Harry."

Later, trudging around the perimeter track, and trying to ignore the bitter wind that blew in from somewhere near the arctic ice cap, Hornblower knew he needed strong and enthusiastic workers to lend a hand.

Jimmy James passed him going in the opposite direction.

"Morning, Jimmy," he said breezily. "How would you like a job?"

"What had you got in mind?" said Jimmy.

"You've had a lot of experience in sand dispersal. I'd like you to take charge of a team."

"With snow on the ground?" questioned Jimmy. "Isn't that a bit risky?"

"Very risky," agreed Hornblower, "but we're not going to spill any."

As Harry's length increased, so did the problems. They started at the face with the digging. A man lay on one side in a two-foot-square hole scraping at the sand with a knife or trowel, and then scraping the sand back past his body to the number-two man, who loaded it onto the wheeled trolley. Sometimes the men wore long johns; often they were naked. When the trolley was full, one tugged on the rope and watched it disappear back down the tunnel. Shortly afterwards one would feel a tug at the rope from the "halting place" and would haul the trolley back laden with bed boards, shoring timbers, and milk cans for the air pipe, ready to drive the tunnel farther.

At the entrance shaft, the large metal water jugs that the Germans used for kitchen purposes were filled with sand and hauled up into the barrack block. There it was spread on a blanket and hauled off to the dispersal point, where "penguins," or sand distributors, were loaded with heavy bags— thirty-five pounds of sand in sacks that they carried on their shoulders around the back of their necks.

"You'll need tall men for that duty," said Hornblower. "They can wear long overcoats and conceal the bags easier. Underneath the theater auditorium you'll need the smallest chaps you can find—there isn't much headroom."

"We're not doing this in daylight?" asked Jimmy.

"No, it gets dark early, and we've got the run of the compound until ten o'clock. That will give us four hours of work every evening. And we've got to work out various routes to and from the theater. We can't have a long procession of dark figures going back and forth."

"At least it's all out of the full glare of the perimeter lights. What about all our thespians?"

"They're moaning like hell, but Wings Day has calmed them down. Escape is more important than Shakespeare or 'What the Butler Saw on His Night Off.'"

Every night from then on Jimmy and coworker Ian Cross of the RAF supervised the activity under the auditorium. The entrance trap was fashioned by Johnny Travis under Seat 13. "Perverted sense of humor," said Ian.

"Thirteen is supposed to be lucky in some countries," said Jimmy James.

"I hope it's lucky for us," said Ian.

Kommandant von Lindeiner was very proud of the theater in North Compound, possibly because he was invited to all opening nights and big occasions—Wings Day's hair almost turned white after one Christmas pantomime when the jokes were so filthy that they might have shocked a gang of stevedores. Kommandant von Lindeiner, however, laughed in all the right places—although it was plain that his command of English was not such that he could actually grasp what was going on. But mainly Kommandant von Lindeiner was proud because he was an educated man and he recognized theater as a symbol of continuing civilization in a Europe disintegrating into anarchy.

Three hundred and fifty seats had been constructed from Red Cross crates. Workshops produced backdrops, stage furniture, and wigs. Historical costumes too difficult to reproduce in the workshop were rented from firms in Berlin, Dresden, or Görlitz. Many classical productions were staged, including *Saint Joan, Hamlet, A Midsummer Night's Dream, As You Like It,* and *The Importance of Being Earnest,* as well as lighter works such as *Design for Living, Blithe Spirit,* and *The Man Who Came to Dinner.* Stalag Luft III also boasted five orchestras—including symphony, dance, and jazz groups—all of high professional standards.

February arrived with a bright moon high and clear above the tops of the pines, and air of almost crystalline and icy purity. Clocks struck and church bells rang across the snow from the ancient spires of Sagan, and the passing of the two-hundred-foot mark in Harry was celebrated with cups of hot tea. Ferrets, smelling activity, were on the rampage.

George Harsh stared out of his lookout window in Hut 104 that morning and exclaimed, "Jesus

Christ!" under his breath. He had watched the large posse of Wehrmacht form up outside the Main Gate without too much suspicion, lulled by their Germanic enthusiasm for numbering off, and suddenly the suspicion turned to a violent alarm bell as he saw them leap into activity.

The Main Gate was thrown open. They broke ranks and raced like Olympic runners for the barrack blocks. And which barrack block? Hut 104!

George was at the door yelling, "Ferrets! Ferrets!" They were racing along the corridor, every soldier swinging open a different door and charging in. George thought in agony, "Christ, how many seconds to close Harry?"

Nothing to do but hope now. He grabbed his book, stuck his feet on the table and showed his teeth in a mirthless grin as his own door was smashed open and an eager young Wehrmacht soldier came racing through.

"Do come in," said George. "So nice of you to knock."

The lad smiled and said, "*Bitte?*" And George said, "I agree with you entirely. Have you read Sophocles? He was one of the three great tragic Greek poets born some five centuries before Christ." His ears waited for the shriek of German triumph that would cascade along the corridor if they hadn't closed Harry in time. Not a sound. George closed the book. "I'll lend it to you sometime, if you feel like a good read," he went on, knowing his breathing belonged to a human being again.

Wally Floody was too far away in Harry's subterranean bowels to have any knowledge of what had happened until he returned to the bottom of the shaft. He later told George, "Your yell warned them. See what I mean when I say you need good men guarding your ass? Pat Langford—" an RCAF flight lieutenant—"set the record with his little team. Down with concrete slab, level with the floor. Up with red-hot stove and down on top of slab. Quick sweep of broom brushing floor dirt into crack. Total time—twenty seconds. Naturally Rubberneck was leading the charge." Rubberneck was one of the most watchful and therefore most disliked ferrets. He was tall, thin, and miserable. No one bothered to discover his real name: having him around was bad enough.

Roger Bushell held an inquest. "It's bound to happen. They know we're up to something. They're increasing every aspect of security."

Wally said, "Rubberneck's our chief danger. He's the craftiest bastard of the lot."

"One bit of good news," said Bushell. "He's going on a two-week furlough on March first. Now, can we get the tunnel finished before he returns?"

"It's a tall order," answered Wally, "but we'll give it a damn good try."

"Great," said Roger with a smile. "Let's hope that bugger Rubberneck hasn't got any other little tricks up his sleeve."

On March 1 they discovered he had.

Morning roll call. Cold and clear. Everyone

158

knew that something was up. For one thing, a squad of armed Wehrmacht guards with stern expressions on their faces had been assembled and formed into a hollow square.

A sheet of paper in his hands, the German adjutant began to make his statement: "When the names of the following prisoners are called, they will break ranks, and stand over there." A finger stabbed towards the space between the soldiers' ranks. "Wing Commander Robert Tuck . . . Flight Lieutenant Wallace Floody . . . Flight Lieutenant George Harsh . . . Lieutenant Commander Peter Fanshawe . . ."

The names were called out. Twenty in all, among them four of the most important members of the Escape Committee. Was it a coincidence? Had the Germans discovered a link to Harry?

The parade was dismissed. The twenty chosen men were marched into—of all places—Hut 104! Wally caught George's eye. This was getting very serious. And then the relief.

"You are all being transferred to Belaria Compound, nearby. You will not return to your barrack blocks. Your belongings are now being assembled and will be brought to you here. You will then be searched before you move to the other camp."

"A random selection of kriegies they suspect might be involved in any escape plan," said Roger Bushell as the depleted Escape Committee assembled to discuss their future plans. "But they've picked up four of our key players."

Tom Ker-Ramsay, who had now taken over as chief tunnel engineer, said, "Roger, how they missed finding you out, I'll never understand."

Roger said, "Plainly all the smoke screens have worked. Lying low, the acting job." He smiled grimly. "But at least dear Bub Clark won't know for quite a time how I double-crossed him."

Roger Bushell was neither headstrong nor a fool. He planned every move that he and the Escape Committee would make with the astuteness of an experienced general. He knew that he was a prime target of the Gestapo, and he knew that somehow he had to divert suspicion that he was engaged in escape activities. All that winter he lay low. Then he made a move. The orchestras and the theatrical company were the mainstays of the camp's artistic life. Roger had a resonant voice, and as an accomplished barrister was a good actor. He approached the actors about a part. They were delighted. They would soon be going into rehearsals for George Bernard Shaw's *Pygmalion*. What about the male lead—Professor Higgins? His second ploy was more devious. For weeks now the "contacts"—the kriegies in touch with various guards and ferrets—had been briefed to spread the word that Roger Bushell was no longer in the escape business. "Much more interested in the theater these days." An odd sentence here, an enigmatic look there, tiny strands of information to be swallowed by ferrets and passed on to higher-ups.

Roger Bushell would have been very pleased to

know about the meeting called early in 1944 by Kommandant von Lindeiner, and reported at a much later date by Oberfeldwebel Glemnitz. All his senior officers and NCOs had been summoned. All knew that the escape season was approaching, and that a large breakout would be a catastrophe for the stalag staff. The Gestapo would hold them responsible.

There was one question Kommandant von Lindeiner needed to have answered: When it came to escaping, who was the most dangerous man in Stalag Luft III? He asked his most experienced and sensible NCO first.

Glemnitz creased his leathery face. "Without any doubt, sir, Colonel Clark."

"Not Squadron Leader Bushell?"

"Once I believed it was Squadron Leader Bushell, but he has quieted down, Kommandant. More interested in the theater these days."

Kommandant von Lindeiner questioned them all in turn. Bushell was definitely off the list of suspects. Escape plans were much more to the fore in South Compound, among the Americans; Colonel Bub Clark was the man to watch.

Kommandant von Lindeiner respected Clark; he had solved the hygiene problem when he first arrived and had been a leader in escape plans after that. And there seemed to be a definite link between Colonel Clark and escape security.

"Captain Broili," said Lindeiner sternly, "I want you to see that an English-speaking tracker is within sight and sound of Colonel Clark twenty-four hours a day until further notice."

For the rest of his sojourn in South Compound, Bub Clark was quite surprised to find that the Germans thought him so important.

It was undeniably the forcible removal of Hornblower, Wally Floody, George Harsh, and Bob Tuck that added a new dimension of determination to the underground tunnelers. On March 3, Harry Marshall's beaming face appeared around the corner of Roger Bushell's door. He held up both hands, with fingers spread.

"Ten feet," said Roger Bushell, pulling him inside. "That's great."

Harry held up two more fingers.

"Twelve!" exclaimed Roger. "That's unbelievable!"

On March 4 they beat that distance by two feet. Fourteen feet of Harry dug, air pipes laid, timber supports firmly planted, all sand dispersed. It was their record distance ever. In ten days, working with a sweaty, gritty, backbreaking intensity, they moved Harry out another hundred and ten feet.

"We've got four days left before that bastard Rubberneck returns," announced Harry Marshall as he gave Roger Bushell the latest figures.

"Can you do it?" asked Roger.

"I think so. At this minute we're working on the second half-way house, Leicester Square. The exit shaft is going to be the problem—going to be hell, in fact. Try digging a hole in a sand ceiling directly above your head. The sand falls down and smothers you. Twenty cubic feet of sand on top of you and you're buried alive."

"So?" questioned Roger anxiously.

"The carpenters have invented a shield for us," Harry explained. "Made of three removable struts. You hold it above your head against the sand ceiling, you slip out the first strut and start digging the sand away in the open space. It falls down past your face—"

"But the weight on your holding arm must be bloody awful," said Roger.

"Bloody awful," agreed Harry. "Then you slip out the second strut and dig out that section. Then the next man takes over."

"Can you finish it in the four days remaining?" Roger demanded.

Harry Marshall nodded. "Yes, Roger, we can."

Roger said slowly, "I wish Wally, Hornblower, George Harsh, and the others knew."

Underneath the theater auditorium, Jimmy James and Ian Cross watched the golden streams of sand pouring through Seat 13's trapdoor and on to the receiving area below. They had already dug deep trenches away from that area, stashing the excavated soil into any corner of the arena they could, leaving themselves corridors where they and their workers toiled.

The newly mined sand with its peculiar odor had long been the subject of "smell" precautions. Tobacco would camouflage its scent and pipe smokers were welcome. In addition, tins of smoldering tobacco were laid in secluded corners to help, until Hut 104 and parts of the theater resembled a smoker's paradise.

In peaceful moments Jimmy and Ian discussed their escape futures. Ian had already risked life and limb in one solo attempt from North Compound.

It had happened in the first days after their arrival from East Compound. North was still being cleared by Russian workmen and German trucks. Ian had noticed that a truck laden with pine trunks and branches was about to leave. In one quick movement, he had slithered underneath and found himself a position where he could hang on—hopefully until the truck passed through the Main Gate and delivered him to freedom.

Unfortunately Oberfeldwebel Glemnitz had spotted him. Glemnitz had walked across and had a quick word with the German truck driver. The truck roared off, belching noise and smoke, careening over humps and bumps and tree stumps on a wild circuit, before returning to the waiting figure of Glemnitz. He had bent down and said in a gentle voice, "I hope you enjoyed your ride, Squadron Leader, and came to no harm. But I think a safer place for you is in the cooler."

Now Ian said thoughtfully, "What do you think of all these warnings we're getting about the Gestapo? Roger Bushell's pretty hot on that."

"It is the duty of all officers to escape or attempt to escape," replied Jimmy with a grin. "Listen to

Wings Day if you want chapter and verse on that subject. The Geneva convention makes it clear that escaped prisoners of war like us are a protected species as long as we don't break laws, attack civilians, do all those damn-fool things you see in Hollywood movies, like strangling sentries. If apprehended, we give up in a peaceful fashion, and should be conveyed back to our POW camp and popped in the cooler."

"I hope you're right," said Ian Cross.

During that final day of Harry's construction the nineteen-foot ladder was safely rigged against the wooden framework of the exit shaft. And tunnelers Johnny Bull and Harry Marshall climbed it to check the thickness of soil still left to break through.

Harry was now 336 feet long, the entrance shaft 28 feet deep, the exit 20 feet high.

At the top of the ladder, careful not to tread on Marshall's hands a few rungs below him, Flight Lieutenant Lester "Johnny" Bull gently inserted a sharpened wire into the earth above his head and pushed it through. It met little resistance. Freedom was only nine inches away. Johnny Bull was an enthusiastic and courageous young officer who had taken up the task of tunneling with cheerful optimism; now he knew he was close to freedom.

In some excitement he told Marshall of his discovery, displayed the length of wire, and added, "Hell, if a passing German sentry trod on this bit of grass, he'd fall straight through into the tunnel!"

Harry Marshall was already on his way down. "A fact we've got to remedy with the speed of light," he hissed. "Let's get moving."

A new wooden frame with a timber base was firmly fixed into position and packed with sand, and the two were trolleyed back to Hut 104 to report their findings to Roger Bushell. He immediately called the most important members of the Escape Committee to a meeting to consider their future and immediate plans.

"Harry is finished," he announced to the elated circle. "The final exit trap is in place and ready to be broken. The entrance is sealed until we decide the breakout night. Now let's go over it all again. It's no longer in theory; this is for real!"

There were a hundred things to discuss. "One of the most important," said Roger, "is the fact that we've got two hundred escapers on our hands and practically none of them have ever been through a tunnel as long and as confining as Harry. Some might panic. We've got to be ready for that."

Tom Ker-Ramsay intervened at that point. "What say we place an experienced tunneler between every twenty escapers? So if things go wrong—no, let me rephrase that—when things go wrong, he will be able to prevent panic, and get things moving again."

The proposal carried unanimously. Then Roger said to Ker-Ramsay, "Tom, you're in charge of briefing the escapers. Say, ten groups of twenty each. Discuss every aspect of getting to the assembly point, descending to the tunnel, and getting through it and out the other side. I leave it to you to have them rehearsed like the corps of the Ballets Russes." He paused, and in complete silence stared around the small group that carried the responsibility for the success or failure of the breakout.

"Now the point at issue. What night do we choose? You all know that the next 'moonless' period is in roughly two weeks. Thursday the twenty-third, Friday the twenty-fourth, and Saturday the twenty-fifth. The night of a completely 'moonless' period is Friday. I favor Friday night because Saturday is a big day in terms of railway journeys—they start puffing to all corners of the Reich on Friday evening and go right through to Saturday evening. Sunday is a dead day in terms of train travel." He looked up. "Questions?"

There were both questions and objections, the main one voiced by several of the group: "Roger, aren't we going too early? Why not leave the mass escape for another month? It's still bloody cold now. There's snow on the ground. It will probably snow again before the end of March and during that weekend. Our footsteps will show up, drawing maps to wherever we are hiding. Ninety percent of the hard-arsers trying to cross-country will never make it. April and it's spring, it's warm, you've got a chance to sleep out and not freeze to death! My vote goes for leaving it for one month."

Many of the Escape Committee felt the same way. Roger nodded, and said, "Let's hear what the tunnelers have to say."

The tunnelers, however, had a different view. In the middle of March the ground was frozen solid. In spring the rains would come; who knew what would happen to Harry then? Yes, it had survived the winter remarkably well, but there had been falls and signs of wear and tear even though the frozen conditions had helped to preserve it. They could not guarantee that Harry, finished and sealed, would last another month. Delay now, and who knew what would happen? Certainly the German security measures could only increase: that had happened at the time of Tom, and Tom had been discovered. The tunnelers were firm and articulate. Harry was ready and waiting. Don't risk a year's work by delay. Use it!

The vote was conclusive—"Go" on the night of Friday, March 24. With one proviso: the final decision had to be made by Roger Bushell, by 11:30 A.M. on that Friday. A "Stop" would be ordered only if the weather was completely abominable or some other unforeseen and formidable obstacle arose.

All escape sections went into full production. Nearly two hundred pounds of "fudge" (a hard, glutinous mixture of various camp provisions) was packed into flat, four-ounce cocoa tins—four allocated to each train traveler, six to each hard-arser. All escape clothes had to be examined, checked, and rechecked; maps were issued, compasses handed out; passes, papers, and documents were checked against each individual alias and returned to Tim Walenn's department for the vital date stamps of March 24. All languages, aliases, and cover stories had to be rehearsed to the satisfaction of Escape Committee members. And Tom Ker-Ramsay began his routine lectures on the exact procedures to his separate groups of twenty.

"As you probably know or might have guessed," he said, "six hundred kriegies have been working on Tom, Dick, and Harry since April of last year. You're the lucky ones—you are part of the two hundred chosen, hopefully, to escape.

"The first thirty places have been awarded by the Escape Committee to those characters who they think are most likely to make a successful escape . . . able to travel by train and get away with it, fluent in German and other languages. Their names have been put in a hat and they go out in the order they've been drawn. Then the names of the most prominent workers were put in and twenty drawn out. After that the names of the thirty most important administrative workers: stooges, penguins, workers above ground in clothing, compasses, maps—you know the form—and twenty drawn. Finally all the remaining names were shoved in and drawn out until we'd got two hundred. We thought that was the fairest way we could arrange things.

"Now let's start at the beginning. On Friday

night, March twenty-fourth, you'll all have a time and a number. On that night all journeys around the compound will be controlled: we don't want a queue of two hundred standing patiently outside Hut One-oh-four for their turn. There'll be marshals everywhere to keep you moving. At your specific time you will leave your barrack hut and make your way on a route given to you to Hut One-oh-nine or One-ten. From there you will be rerouted to Hut One-oh-four.

"The inhabitants of Hut One-oh-four who are not amongst the escapers will have already moved to other huts. You will be assigned a space in which to wait."

Ker-Ramsay eyed the group of twenty would-be escapers with fierce attention. He had heard all the rumors of how tough the Germans were going to be with escapers from now on, and tried to believe it was all bluff. But he also knew that the Gestapo did not bluff about anything.

"I'll start with a bit of good news. Last week —purely by chance—we had a bonus delivered by the YMCA, who had no idea they were being so helpful: five hundred feet of finest-quality manila rope, intended for use in boxing rings and for other athletic purposes. As this is not included amongst the 'parole items' barred by the Geneva convention, you will be pleased to know it is a godsend to us: marvelous for trolley-pulling, and the chance of ropes breaking is now negligible."

There was applause from the ranks. Some comedian began to make a joke and Ker-Ramsay stamped on it ferociously. "Shut up! This is not funny. Your life and probably the lives of others will depend upon your doing exactly as you are told."

There was total silence.

"You will be taken in pairs to the bottom of Harry's shaft for a rehearsal of what will happen. You will be shown how to lie on a trolley. You have got to balance upon it. If your weight is too far forward you'll tip it up, too far back and the same thing will happen. Remember Harry is only two feet square. You do not—repeat—you do *not* look up, for you might hit your head against the roof and create a sand fall. If a large fall occurs you will be buried alive, and more importantly, you may have ruined the entire escape timetable."

Silence continued.

"Harry—give or take a foot or two—is three hundred and forty feet long. There are two wide chambers—Piccadilly Circus and Leicester Square —along its length. In each chamber a 'puller' will be stationed. This strong-armed kriegie will haul the first twenty through in numbered order; he will then be replaced by another 'puller' and take up his own place in the escape line. And so on.

"At the exit itself a ladder will lead twenty feet upwards. Two members of Harry's engineering team will have cut through the last nine inches of soil, but there will be no cheers and no noise. All signals will be made in absolute silence by tugs on the right ropes."

A voice at the back asked, "Will there be a marshal there to give us a 'Go'?"

"Yes. You will receive a tug when the coast is clear and the patrolling guard has passed—guided by the rope, you will crawl on your bellies into the trees. If you feel a tug on the rope, you will lie still and wait for the next tug to tell you to proceed. A marshal will be waiting in the cover of the trees. He will keep you waiting there until you and your party assemble. You will be in the woods. It will be dark. It will be bloody cold and you will be bloody silent.

"You'll need a bit of luck, and I hope you all get it."

Zero hour crept closer, and the discussions and arguments were sometimes closer to fights.

"Of course it's ambitious," snarled Roger Bushell. "What else is there to be but bloody ambitious? What time have we got? At the very best, nine P.M. Friday until five-thirty A.M. Saturday. Eight and a half hours, five hundred and ten minutes . . .

"From past experience with other tunnels we know that with a good practiced team we can pass a man through every two to three minutes. But half of these kriegies are children by comparison. So we'll hope for one every four minutes. I don't care if we get them all out or not, but we must use every minute. So we want two hundred men fully briefed, fully equipped, and ready to go!"

Chapter Eleven

Friday, March 24, 1944. 9:00 p.m.

THE FAINT GLOW FROM the fat-lamp caught the glint of sweat on Johnny Bull's forehead as he wrenched desperately at the wooden frame of the exit trap. He had to be quiet—who knew what he would see when he broke free?

"Bloody thing won't move," he hissed. "Must have swollen in the damp and then frozen."

Flight Lieutenant Harry Marshall, second traffic controller, and designated to be first out and away, was staring up at him. "For Christ's sake, Johnny, you're doing all the hard work," he whispered urgently. "Come down! Let me have a go."

Crowded together at the bottom of the shaft were Czech Flight Lieutenant Ernst Valenta, Marshall's escape partner; Roger Bushell and Bernard Scheidhauer; Lieutenant Rupert Stevens, a South African; and tough Sydney Dowse. Rope in hand, Dowse crouched behind them waiting to pull the first escaper through from Leicester Square—pull the first twenty through and then escape himself.

Every face was tense, but nothing was said. There was no point in trying to get into the act,

173

no room for anyone to interfere with the efforts of Marshall and Bull.

Since 11:30 that morning, when the final decision to break out had been made, the atmosphere in North Compound had been electric, an excitement so tangible that Roger Bushell feared the Germans might smell it in the air. But everything went as planned. Every escaper was issued civilian clothes, forged documents, money, food, maps, and compasses. The first thirty carried attaché cases or small suitcases, small maps of the frontier areas they were aiming to cross, an identity ration card, letters from German firms identifying their business, and authority to travel by train. They carried no Red Cross food or large maps because in case of an arrest those things would certainly give them away. The next forty escapers were traveling by workmen's trains for the first part of their journeys, and hard-arsing across country afterwards.

By 9:00 P.M. the two hundred kriegies were crowded into every room and sitting in the corridor. A lookout was posted at every window to watch for prowling ferrets. Extra light bulbs had been fitted into waiting sockets and Harry was lit up like a Christmas tree. Zero hour was 9:30, and as the seconds ticked away, conversation dwindled and eyes began to look questioningly at wristwatches.

Nine-thirty passed and nothing happened. Now faces were concerned. This was supposed to be a

174

split-second operation, and nothing was happening. What the hell had gone wrong?

At the bottom of Harry's entrance shaft, chief tunnel dispatcher Tom Ker-Ramsay glared first at his watch and then at the prone figure, suitcase held neatly in front of him on the trolley. His assistant marshaling the queue at the top of the shaft whispered down, "Tom! What's going on?"

"Nothing," said Tom Ker-Ramsay in sheer exasperation. "Absolutely nothing!"

There was no way for him to contact his nearest trolley-hauler a hundred feet away in the tunnel; sound simply did not reach that far. A tug on the rope was the only contact possible, and they had not considered a Morse code signal for "Why the bloody holdup?"

Ten o'clock came, and now there was a tenseness in the air that was as palpable as the excitement they had felt all day.

At the exit shaft, Johnny Bull suddenly said, "It's loosening—it's loosening." He was back having another stint at the top of the ladder. "I'll let this edge down first, and let the sand pour out. Watch out down below."

The retaining wooden shield gone, he began to poke at the nine-inch layer of grass and dirt. It broke away easily, dropping in soft plumps down the shaft. Cautiously Johnny Bull raised his head through the hole, lifting it with the slow concentration of a sniper about to take aim. He was facing the perimeter fence, which, as usual, was bathed in the brilliance of the full searchlight swath. The exit trap was in the darkness, and the sentry on his lonely beat outside the perimeter wire was fortunately trudging the other way, with his back towards Johnny. The watchtower, a high, black, matchstick construction, was silhouetted against the sky, no more than thirty yards away. He did a slow, periscope turn with his head. Damn, damn, damn! They had surfaced as expected inside the first fringe of firs, but no trees protected them from being seen from the watchtower or the perimeter sentry trail. Escapers would have to crawl fifteen to twenty feet across the snow, leaving a trail behind them. Bull climbed back down the ladder and reported to Roger Bushell, who did not hesitate. "Okay, change the plan. Johnny Bull operates at the exit. He ties a rope to the top rung of the ladder. Harry Marshall—you follow him out, crawl past him with the rope into the trees. Tie the other end to a tree and signal back to Johnny. Two tugs means it's safe to crawl across." He lifted his voice slightly to whisper to Sydney Dowse. "Got those instructions, Sydney? Every man passes the new arrangements to the man behind him. Move now!"

Johnny Bull climbed the ladder, poked his head out to let his eyes grow accustomed to the darkness, and saw that the patrolling sentry still had his back towards him. He climbed out and lay facedown in the snow at the side of the tunnel. His arm reached down, his hand tapped Harry Marshall on the head, and Harry was out and past him, carrying the end of the rope as he crawled

176

for the shelter of the trees. There he tied it to a trunk, confirmed that the sentry was still patrolling in a safe direction, and tugged the rope twice. Fifteen seconds later Valenta was by his side, followed in rapid succession by Bushell and Scheidhauer.

Roger Bushell grasped Marshall's hand, whispered, "Good luck!" and watched Valenta and him disappear into the darkness. Marshall was dressed in a black civilian suit and a skiing cap, had papers forged in the name of Petr Kovalkov, a glassworker; he had maps, a compass, two hundred reichsmarks, and food. Their intention was to reach Mittelwalde on the Czech border, and contact a secret organization about which his partner, Valenta, knew a great deal. If that failed they would head south into Yugoslavia and try to join up with Tito's partisans.

Crouching in the trees, Bushell and Scheidhauer watched the sentry complete his patrol and return along the wire in the opposite direction. To their relief, he did not even turn his head as he passed the tunnel exit. When his back was far enough away, Bushell gave two sharp tugs on the rope. Lieutenant Stevens's head appeared above ground and he crawled rapidly across to join them. The chain of escape was established. Alerted by Stevens's disappearance, Sydney Dowse pulled in the first man from Leicester Square; the hauler there, seeing the trolley go, pulled in his escaper from Piccadilly Circus, and the Piccadilly hauler tugged his laden trolley from the entrance shaft.

Tom Ker-Ramsay blinked. Suddenly the trolley and its occupant took off, whisked along the tunnel as if on elastic. Tom felt a great wave of emotion, a surge of elation. In a loud whisper he called up the shaft, "We're off! We're off! We're moving!"

Fifteen minutes earlier they had all felt the sudden flow of cold air pouring towards them through Harry, and known that Johnny Bull had broken through the last nine inches of topsoil. The message was passed back to Hut 104, and now the old excitement was back with them again.

Within seconds the rope attached to the back of the trolley stopped spinning loose from its coil as the escaper reached Piccadilly Circus. Tom tugged it back, and turned to the next man waiting to go. For a second he did not recognize him. "Tim Walenn!" he exclaimed. "Where's the great moustache gone?"

"Shaved it off," replied Tim cheerfully. "No point in starting a new fashion in Germany." He followed Ker-Ramsay's eyes down to the suitcase he was carrying. "I know it's a bit bigger than . . ."

"Tim," said Ker-Ramsay accusingly, "that's not the suitcase I inspected for size last Monday."

Tim smiled. "Found I had too much stuff to fit into the other, Tom. I'll get it through, all right."

Tim Walenn's forgery department had done as much for the escapers as any department in the camp. They had worked long hours by bad light; they had ruined their eyesight; it had sometimes taken weeks and weeks of industrious calligraphy to produce one perfect hand-inscribed document. Tom Ker-Ramsay took Tim's case and fastened it to the trolley. "That goes through first—alone. You follow it alone. Collect it at the exit." He shook Tim's hand and gave him a slap on the back as he sped away. Tim Walenn had five days to live.

11:45 P.M.

The twentieth man scheduled to leave, Wings Day, was sitting on the side of Harry's shaft, his long legs perched on the first rungs of the ladder. There was a smile on his deeply lined face; for the first time in his life he was actually enjoying an escape. Then suddenly the lights went out. The brilliant electric glow was gone. The effect was paralyzing. It was like being plunged under inky black water. They knew what had happened. Approaching bombers! Air raid! The Germans switched off all power at the source.

Wings's first reaction was fury. God, what a time for their own RAF to mount a raid. Then the irony struck him: here they were—one set of aircrews escaping from the Sagan prisoner-of-war camp, and another bunch of British airmen parachuting down from the scarlet skies over that city to replace them.

Beneath his feet in the darkness Wings Day saw the glimmer of fat-lamps being lit by Tom Ker-Ramsay. The traffic controller at the top of the shaft tapped Wings's shoulder, grunted, "Good luck, sir," and watched him go.

Wings accepted a box of matches from Tom and began to help him light the reserve of fat-lamps. Tom said, "Looks as if the hauler at Piccadilly has quit. He's pulling nothing through."

"Forget it," grunted Wings. "Keep the pace up! Better one more out than none at all. Tell you what, I'll pull myself along to Piccadilly, and start the train moving again. There's bound to be Sydney Dowse waiting at the far end; he knows I'm Number Twenty. I'm his signal to exit."

There was only one hauler missing, and Wings pulled his escape partner, Flying Officer Pawel Tobolski, through to join him, then went on to the exit where Sydney greeted him with a wide grin before he set off up the ladder. Order was restored. Indeed, although half an hour had been lost in the general confusion, the escape rate had actually improved: without the perimeter searchlights, escapers found it easier to slide across towards the trees. The lookouts at the windows had seen the doubling of guards and the entrance of the *Hundführers* with their trained and vicious dogs, but none of them had perceived the activity in 104. No kriegie underrated the ruthlessness of the trigger-happy guards. Shortly before Christmas, only three months before, Canadian Flight Lieutenant McCloskey in the cooler had decided to make a dash for the door, and had been shot twice at point-blank range by the guard. A week or so later Squadron Leader Grant, after lockup time and influenced by a Christmas party in Hut 101, was creeping back to his own Hut 103, when a *Hundführer* spotted him and released his dog. Backed against a hut and trying to evade the dog, Grant had been shot five times in the stomach. He had recovered, but every escaper sliding across towards the woods knew the chance he was taking.

1:00 A.M.

All the suitcase carriers—those who were posing as civilians—were through the tunnel and had left for the Sagan railway station or other destinations. It was now the turn of the blanket brigade, the ones who would chance it on foot, and several of these had also bent regulations and overloaded. One reached Ker-Ramsay's side with a blanket rolled into a fat sausage-shape so large that Tom said angrily, "You must be out of your mind. That will exactly fill the tunnel like a bloody cork. Take half of that stuff out *now!*" Another who narrowly passed scrutiny got stuck three times before he reached Piccadilly. Ker-Ramsay threatened to send him to the end of the queue, and on the next try he passed through with eel-like speed—although without half his supplies.

The rate of passage, now that the electric lights were back on and sentries were patrolling along the perimeter wire, had slowed. Blanket holders were still causing delays, and the time per man was down to one every fourteen minutes. Ker-Ramsay knew that the chances of getting two hundred men out were slim.

Jimmy James, thirty-ninth in line, clambered swiftly down the ladder and peered along Harry. It was one of the most glorious sights he had ever seen—an avenue of light! He positioned himself on the trolley, pack in front of his face, head well down, and away he went, rattling along like an express train. In a flash he arrived at Piccadilly Circus, scrambled past the hauler and rearranged himself on the next trolley. One tug of the rope and he was off again towards Leicester Square. Another few seconds, another changeover, and he was speeding towards the tunnel exit 130 feet away.

The pace slowed slightly as he passed through the curtain of blankets designed to muffle sound and keep light away from the shaft exit. The traffic controller's dim figure took his arm and pointed to the ladder leading upwards. Jimmy saw the gaping hole, the bright clear stars, and like a great number of escapers that night immediately remembered the RAF's Latin motto, *Per ardua ad astra* ("Through adversities to the stars"). No doubt the coiner of the tag line must have meant it for just this moment.

He felt the quick tap on the top of his head, the quick tug on the rope as he scrambled out, and felt suddenly silhouetted like a fly on a white ceiling: snow all around, the brilliant lights of the arc lamps on the maze of barbed wire, the watchtower looming overhead, and the sentry—fortunately far away on his beat. Every movement he made seemed enormous as he crawled along the dark track towards the heap of brushwood that had previously formed one of the ferret observation posts.

Waiting behind the brushwood hideout he saw the face of George McGill, who had taken over as traffic controller, grinning at him and giving him a thumbs-up. Jimmy scrambled past him, returning the gesture, and headed for his own rendezvous.

1:30 A.M.

The traffic suddenly stopped. Ker-Ramsay, hauling back what should have been an empty trolley, realized he still had live cargo aboard. Still clutching his blanket, the disappointed kriegie looked up with a despondent face. Ker-Ramsay asked in some exasperation, "What's up?"

Glumly the escaper climbed off his perch. "There's a sand fall between Piccadilly and Leicester Square. Cookie Long's crawled forward to try and clear it. Some job! I admire his guts."

Ker-Ramsay had been working hard all night. He was past cursing now.

"Okay, take a rest and have a smoke. We'll get

a tug on the rope if Cookie manages to dig it out. He knows what he's got to do."

Tom Ker-Ramsay found himself a seat in the sand and considered the implications. If it was a big fall the escape was finished. Flight Lieutenant James "Cookie" Long had to scrabble through to the fall, load the sand onto the trolley, push his way back, unload it, then go forward again and replace shoring timbers.

The two men puffed away at their cigarettes and did not say very much. Thirty minutes later the rope strained against the tethered trolley and Ker-Ramsay grabbed it, exclaiming, "By God, he's cleared it. Thirty minutes! Bloody good! Give him a pat on the back for me as you go through."

"Sure will," said the departing kriegie as his shoes disappeared from sight.

Fifteen minutes later the same thing happened. A blanket carrier had looked up or twisted around or dropped his package, and caused another fall. This time Cookie Long cleared it in twenty minutes, but Tom Ker-Ramsay as chief tunnel traffic officer knew he had to make a harsh decision. The blanket boys were gumming up the flow.

He called up to his assistant at the top of the shaft: "Bill, no more blankets. They're causing too many holdups. Sorry for the hard-arsers, but that's it."

There was no great protest. Everyone obeyed his edict. The urge to escape was greater than the desire for blanket warmth. They left their blankets at the top of the shaft and the rate of progression improved to one man every ten minutes.

2:30 A.M.

Ker-Ramsay had to make another hard decision.

"Bill, no use deceiving ourselves. If we manage to put a hundred through Harry it will be a miracle. Tell Numbers One-oh-one to Two Hundred they've got to abandon. With a bit of luck we've got haulers standing by who will try and seal up Harry so that we can reopen tomorrow or in a few days. Snow might cover up our tracks. Tell them to stow their documents inside the wall hidey-holes, and eat what they can of their escape rations, and do whatever they can with their escape clothes. Say 'Sorry, chaps.'"

3:30 A.M.

It was still dark, no glimmer of dawn in the sky, and the blanket carriers, now down to overcoats and stuffed pockets, were filtering through at a reasonable rate; the interchange of haulers and traffic controllers at the exit point was working very well, and although a jagged black trail against the snow marked the trail to the trees, the sentries patrolling close against the perimeter wire looked always inwards, and the guards on the watchtowers had similar tunnel vision.

The guards were changed at regular intervals throughout the night. They suspected nothing.

4:30 A.M.

George Mc Gill, acting as traffic controller under the trees, almost had a heart attack! With the sentry now walking with his back towards them a hundred yards away, it seemed perfectly safe to tug the rope and bring the next escaper out of the exit trap. Suddenly a movement in the watchtower looming against the searchlight glare made him pause. A guard was coming down the watchtower steps. Christ! Had he seen the exit and the dark path that led to the trees? The guard reached the bottom of the steps, and with the stride of a man who knew exactly what he was doing moved directly towards the exit hole. Three more strides and he'd fall through the goddam trap! The traffic controller froze as he watched the action. Unhurriedly the guard opened his fly and relieved himself. If he'd taken aim he could have pissed straight down the hole. He yawned, stretched his arms above his head, and walked back the way he came, climbing the steps and disappearing into the darkness of his watchtower. How had he missed the black escape path? The traffic controller, realizing he still had his mouth open, gave the rope a sharp tug. The next escaper crawled into the shelter of the trees.

"Okay, number eighty-seven," said Ker-Ramsay, glancing at his watch for what felt like the millionth time and realizing that the escape queue was backing up, "you are the last to go through. It will be getting gray by the time you get to the exit trap, so get a move on. Good luck!"

Tom Ker-Ramsay watched the eighty-seventh pair of feet disappear down the tunnel and yawned in a great stretch of fatigue. At 5:00 A.M., all being well, the trap-closing team would go into action, drawing the guide rope back into the tunnel, trying as best they could to cover the escape trail and the ground above the exit.

Then he heard the sound they had all feared. Sharp and clear—the sound of a rifle shot. He hoped to God it had not killed anybody. The game was up!

On one knee Ker-Ramsay yelled up the tunnel, "Come back! Do you hear me! Come back!"

The escaper could not hear him, or if he did hear he had no intention of returning. Freedom lay at the end of Tunnel Harry, and that's where he was going. Frustrated, Ker-Ramsay grabbed the rope, and felt the manila burn his fingers. With his feet braced on either side of the tunnel entrance, he managed to halt the trolley. But the escaper, believing that the rope must have jammed, fought tenaciously to continue. Whether he managed to untie the rear rope or it just broke free Ker-Ramsay would never know; all he did know was that he was hauling a length of rope back to the bottom of the shaft. Number 87 was on his own.

Tom Ker-Ramsay raced up the ladder. Yes, everybody had heard the shot. What was the procedure now?

"Tell every window watcher to keep his eyes peeled for any action out in the compound, and report back to me. Continue to hide everything in the hidey-holes—food, documents, money, escape clothing. I'm going back down the shaft—I expect there'll be a few survivors coming back!"

Up above outside in the woods, it was Flight Lieutenant Langlois's turn to be traffic controller. He was crouching behind one of the brushwood piles. His eyes were wide with apprehension, and for very good reason: the bloody patrolling sentry approaching the nearby guard tower, instead of following the well-worn perimeter track outside the wire, had elected to skirt around the edge of the woods on a track that would take him directly to the exit trap!

Langlois had already brought two men into the woods: Squadron Leader Revell-Carter, Number 75, and Flight Lieutenant Ogilvie, 76. Flight Lieutenant Shand, Number 77, was having a very unhappy time. Seeing the sentry's route, Langlois had tugged the rope in a series of frantic jerks that indicated "Stop!" Shand had stopped midway between the hole and the woods; as the light was now shading from gray to bright, his concern increased with every second that passed.

Squadron Leader Revell-Carter was also watching this situation from behind a tree. He had also noted the sentry's deviation from the usual beat and realized with mounting horror that if the sentry continued in that direction he would fall down the exit trap. He did not seem to have noticed or understood the significance of the trail that led from the trap to the trees, but he was certainly interested in the steam that rose from the hole . . . so interested that he unslung his rifle and brought it to the ready. At that moment Flight Lieutenant Shand decided that there was no point in lying still and getting shot—better make a mad dash for the trees and die like a martyr. He leapt to his feet and ran for it. Both Langlois and Revell-Carter had the same thought: the sentry would shoot Shand. Instinctively Revell-Carter stepped out of his hiding place, his hands high, shouting, "*Nicht schiessen! Nicht schiessen!* Don't shoot!" Langlois also appeared with hands up.

The surprised guard halted for one second, then fired a shot into the air. Immediately the guards in the watchtowers and in the compound were alerted. Guns were trained from above on the small group near the exit shaft. Squadron Leader McBride emerged from the exit with his hands up.

Flight Lieutenant Shand, ignorant of all the anxiety on his behalf, did not stop to wonder who was going to shoot whom. Unaware that Squadron

Leader Revell-Carter was standing with his hands up, ready to draw fire if necessary, he made his mad dash for the trees, and kept on running—more or less—for the next four days, hiding in the woods every night to catch his breath and rest. (He was hiding near the station at Kohfurt many miles away, waiting to steal a ride on a freight train, when he was surprised and apprehended by railway officials. He was returned to Sagan on April 6. Flight Lieutenant Ogilvie also made the most of his opportunity and raced away, but he also was caught soon afterwards.)

At the bottom of Harry's entrance shaft the impasse between Number 87 and Ker-Ramsay continued. With no one to haul him in either direction, 87 decided to propel the trolley backwards. This was difficult, and he got the trolley off the rails. Then he saw another figure—that of the hauler who had been stationed at Piccadilly and had gone forward to investigate the holdup—crawling towards him. Number 87 wriggled backwards to Ker-Ramsay, followed by the hauler.

Ker-Ramsay told them to go back to Hut 104 and do what the others were doing, and ask one of the window watchers to report back on what was happening. Meanwhile he would wait to see if any other escapers reappeared. Another did, sweating profusely in his heavy clothing, scrambling out of the tunnel in a panic, exclaiming, "There's a ferret right behind me!"

That was alarming, all the more so because it

might not be a ferret but a guard with an automatic weapon to spray bullets along Harry.

Three minutes later Ker-Ramsay heard the panting of another man crawling through. A ferret was after him too! Four more escapers returned, convinced that a ferret was snapping at their heels. The seventh had been in the exit shaft when the shot was fired; he knew he was not being pursued by a ferret.

All relevant personnel accounted for, Tom Ker-Ramsay climbed the ladder and superintended the closing of Harry. Then he began to sort out the problems in Hut 104. Several of the would-be escapers had already squeezed out through windows and returned to their own huts. Others had decided that the only realistic way of destroying forged documents was by burning them in the corridor, and the place was full of smoke. The window watchers had observed four or five escapers marched into the guard hut next to the Main Gate at gunpoint.

One other point also became clear: the Germans had no idea from which hut Harry had been tunneled. They had searched Hut 104 so thoroughly on so many occasions that they did not suspect that the tunnel originated there. So they sent a *Hundführer* and his dog into *every* hut. At 5:30 A.M. a very tired guard with an even wearier German shepherd came into Hut 104. The guard glanced around and appeared to be more interested in the large number of overcoats hanging in the corridor than anything else. He decided to

191

make use of them and piled them into a large heap. The dog seemed to interpret this as an act of kindness by his master, curled up on top and went to sleep. His handler decided that this made sense and settled on the floor next to him.

An hour later, having worked out the puzzle, the German guards surrounded Hut 104 with armed men and machine guns. The hut doors were opened, and all prisoners were ordered out, lined up into two ranks, and made to strip. It began to snow. Kommandant von Lindeiner arrived, plainly very unhappy and very angry. If any POW played the fool or disobeyed instructions he would personally shoot two of them himself. He had done his best to treat his prisoners with military respect and done the best he could in providing facilities. And this is how they had repaid him! He would be court-martialed, his career ended; he would probably be lucky to avoid prison.

No North Compound ferret was anxious to explore Harry backwards from the exit shaft, so Charlie was summoned from East Compound. He disappeared and after an hour or so the German adjutant became so sure that Charlie would suffocate that he went off to get the British adjutant out of bed to order the trap opened and save Charlie's life. They were too late: the kriegies had heard Charlie banging around under Harry's stove and shouting for help, taken pity on him, and let him out. Charlie could not speak highly enough of such a superb tunnel!

But there was little levity that night. Back in

Stalag Luft III headquarters, administrative officers were shrieking the news into telephones, and getting angry responses. How many had escaped? They didn't know. . . . Didn't know! Why not? Because the breakout had only just been discovered. The commandant and his staff were at that moment busy checking the records and photographs of every officer in North Compound. They would pass that information on as quickly as possible. Meanwhile this should be treated as a *Kriegfahndung*, a manhunt of national proportions. It was Obersturmbannführer Max Wielen, chief of the nearest Kriminalpolizei headquarters in Breslau,⋆ who raised the emergency to a *Grossfahndung*—a national alert!

⋆The Kriminalpolizei, or Kripo, were the German civilian police, not to be confused with the dreaded Geheime Staatspolizei, or Gestapo. Although Kripo and Gestapo occasionally worked together, their relations were more often marked by mutual distrust, even dislike.

Chapter Twelve

WINGS DAY, SIDE BY side with Tobolski in his Feldwebel uniform, tramped through the woods on their way to the Sagan railway station. Briefings back at camp had alerted them to what they could expect to see and the right directions to take. Nevertheless, in the dark it was not easy, and blackout curtains and shutters, which were now obligatory in this part of the Reich, made it even more difficult.

They fumbled their way to the tunnel that led under the main station to the big hall, and as they mounted the steps on the far side they could glimpse chinks of light and hear a buzz of conversation. Their nerves had been fully stretched in the woods, alert for the sounds of shots or a warning siren; the streets of Sagan had been silent, dark, and deserted. But this—pushing through a heavy curtain and finding themselves in a railway hall brilliant with light and sound and the smell of tobacco smoke—was a traumatic shock. They paused, blinking, suddenly feeling their disguises absurd and their presence here ridiculous.

The air raid had plainly thrown train arrivals and departures into confusion. Men, women, and children stood or sat by their bundles and suitcases with resigned looks on their faces. The usual sausages were being munched by the hungry. There were lots of soldiers about and a sprinkling of prison guards. From time to time a loudspeaker blared news of trains. A glance through the glass windows of the refreshment room revealed that it was packed with jostling people—many singing and waving beer glasses, a few drunk. Wings decided that was a good sign. Then, with a slight sense of incredulity, he began to recognize his fellow escapers. In Wings's terms, "they stood out like raisins in a cake." There was Squadron Leader Tom Kirby-Green, large and brown-skinned, with teeth flashing, looking more like a Spaniard than the Englishman he really was. Now he really did look like a Spanish onion seller, and his companion, Flying Officer Gordon Kidder, looked a bit like a character out of musical comedy. Perhaps they'd overdone it?

After a few more seconds spent appraising the situation, Wings slid up next to Kirby-Green and whispered out of the side of his mouth, "What's the word?"

The dark eyes flashed across to him. "The raid was on Berlin. All trains disorganized and running late. Expecting Breslau train at any moment."

"Any guards from the camp?"

"One or two in the refreshment room getting drunk. You can see them through the windows."

Wings moved away and surveyed the refreshment room. He vaguely recognized the two guards, but they did not have much contact with the kriegies. Both had girls on their arms and their thoughts did not seem to be on security. Wings spotted Tobolski, who had gone to buy the tickets. Again he moved into a darker corner and Tobolski approached and stood for a few seconds by his side. Wings felt the ticket slipped into his pocket as Tob said quietly, "Berlin train due in about half an hour."

A few minutes later, amid a barrage of loud-speaker announcements, the Breslau train hissed and puffed its way noisily into the station. Wings stationed himself near the platform barrier. More of his good friends were going on that train than were taking any other route of escape. That seemed to be the quickest and safest way out; they were all hoping to make it by various routes across the Alps or into Czechoslovakia or Yugoslavia.

Silently he wished them good luck as he watched them file past. He was confident enough now to give each one a nod, a wink, a smile. He had no premonition that he was saying a final farewell to so many friends he had known so well during these long years of captivity.

Flight Lieutenant Bram van der Stok had managed to get out of Holland when the Nazis invaded, and had flown with the RAF during those first months of the war. Because of his zeal for escaping, his intelligence, his familiarity with the countryside, and his gift for languages, the Escape Committee had rated his chances of making a home run very highly, and he was among the first twenty through the tunnel.

He was traveling alone.

Cautiously he made his way through the woods, and almost bumped into a dark figure. It was a German civilian who said sharply, "What are you doing in these woods at this time of night?"

Bram van der Stok had rehearsed his reply to that question.

"I'm a Dutch worker. I'm afraid the police might arrest me for being out-of-doors during an air raid. Do you speak Dutch? I'm a bit scared."

The German did not speak Dutch, but Bram van der Stok's cover was perfect; the civilian took him under his wing. "I know the way to the station. You stick with me and you'll be all right."

At the station he left Bram to his own devices, and the first thing Bram discovered was that the heavy raid on Berlin had delayed his train by three hours. Bram wished someone could have told the chief of Bomber Command what trouble he was causing his fellow air force men.

He then observed one of the German censors at the camp. He knew her slightly by sight; he hoped to God she didn't know *him*. But she was suspicious of one of the men on the platform, whom Bram recognized as Kirby-Green. If the police picked him up they would be alerted at once. He hardly dared look around—the station was full of Stalag Luft III escapers. And—oh, hell—she was telling an officer of the German military police to go across, accost Kirby-Green, and demand to see his papers. Then he became conscious that the bright female eyes were fixed on him. Bram van der Stok moved closer, not away. The only way to counter suspicion was to face it. One thing the Escape Committee had not taken into consideration was a female Sherlock Holmes sitting in the Sagan station. Her question was abrupt: "You are traveling tonight?"

At least he was comfortable with his German. "Yes, I'm Dutch—you can probably tell from my accent."

"You know the trains are running late?"

"Yes, I understand that is so." Bram took a quick glance at Kirby-Green. He was putting his papers away. The military policeman was satisfied. Thank God for that.

"There are many strangers around these days," said Bram equably. That seemed to satisfy her. She had done her duty as a good German woman.

The train for Breslau arrived at 3:30 A.M. Bram van der Stok traveled second-class. He saw eight fellow escapers from Sagan, among them Roger Bushell and Lieutenant Scheidhauer, but not even by the flutter of an eyebrow did he offer a sign of recognition. They chugged into Breslau station at 5:00 A.M. There was no bustle of security, no groups of Gestapo or military police with hard watchful eyes. The tunnel hadn't been discovered . . . yet!

Sergeant Peter Bergsland was Norwegian. When the Germans invaded his country he fled to England. There he joined the RAF, was shot down, and duly arrived at Stalag Luft III. He had already made one near-successful attempt at escape. He had managed to "acquire" a set of blue overalls used by the ferrets. He approached the Escape Committee with his idea and they approved it. A pass was issued describing him as a Danish worker who was being transferred to Flensburg. The run of ordinary guards around the camp were not particularly alert; many of them came from flak batteries on the eastern front and the guard duty at Sagan was ostensibly a rest period.

The one on duty when Sergeant Bergsland approached the gate was not very bright. He examined the pass and said, "But there's no photograph of you here."

Sergeant Bergsland's German was perfect, with just enough of a Danish inflection to increase his credibility. "Look, I've just arrived, and I'm immediately being transferred to Flensburg . . . you can see what it says on the pass. I'll get my photograph taken there. Do let me through, my friend, I'm in a bit of a hurry."

The guard tutted, and shrugged his shoulders, and opened the gate. Sergeant Bergsland proceeded along the road towards the Kommandantur and the guards' barracks, and then became conscious of footsteps hurrying behind him. It was a German Feldwebel. He had seen what was going on. He knew all about passes without photographs. Sergeant Bergsland was returned through the gates at gunpoint.

Sergeant Bergsland and his partner, fellow countryman Lieutenant Jens Muller, also RAF, decided to team up for the Sagan escape. They headed for Stettin, where Swedish ships regularly docked and departed. Both spoke perfect Swedish.

They came out of the tunnel as Numbers 43 and 44, and Muller was surprised at the ease of passage through Harry. His report to Intelligence explained what had happened:

"It took me three minutes to get through the tunnel. Above ground I crawled along holding the rope for several feet: it was tied to a tree. Sergeant Bergsland joined me; we arranged our clothes and walked to the Sagan railway station.

"Bergsland was wearing a civilian suit he had made for himself from a Royal Marine uniform, with an RAF overcoat slightly altered with brown leather sewn over the buttons. A black RAF tie, no hat. He carried a small suitcase which had been sent from Norway. In it were Norwegian toothpaste and soap, sandwiches, and one hundred and sixty-three reichsmarks given to him by the Escape Committee.

"We caught the 2:04 train to Frankfurt an der Oder. Our papers stated that we were Norwegian electricians from the *Arbeitslager* in Frankfurt working in the vicinity of Sagan. For the journey from Frankfurt to Stettin we had other papers ordering us to change our place of work from Frankfurt to Stettin, and to report to the Bürgermeister of Stettin."

The Longest Tunnel

Inside Harry. The tunnel measured two feet
by two feet. The Trolley shown here was
used to haul sand back from the digging face.
A lower trolley, operating on the same
tracks, conveyed prisoners during the mass
escape of March 24, 1944.

What captivity does to a man: a thinner, more haggard Roger Bushell with British fighter ace Bob Tuck (*left*).

Left to right: George Harsh, in charge of tunnel security: Wing Commander Bob Tuck, RAF; and Bill Webster, USAAF.

Jimmy James, reunited with his fiancée, Madge, at the end of the war.

Wing Commander Harry "Wings" Day.

Major Jack
Churchill
in 1941.

The journey was uneventful. They traveled in a third-class carriage full of civilians and looked like any ordinary travelers. They arrived at Frankfurt at 6:00 in the morning, and caught a connecting train to Kurstrin at 8:00 A.M. They had a beer in the station cafe, and while they were sipping, the first inspection took place. A wandering German Feldwebel of the military police approached them. He looked at the cheerful, fresh-faced young men who spoke excellent German with a Norwegian accent, gave their papers a cursory examination, touched his cap, and departed. Bergsland and Muller clinked mugs, smiled, and drank up. They caught the 10:00 A.M. train from Kurstrin to Stettin and arrived at lunchtime.

"We walked around the town, visited a cinema and a beer hall, and after dusk went to an address given to us by the Escape Committee.

"It was a French brothel bearing the inscription '*Nur fur Ausländers Deutschen verboten.*' We knocked on the door. As we did so a Pole who was standing on the street approached us and asked us if we had any black-market wares for sale. We asked him if he knew any Swedish sailors. He fetched one out of the brothel. We made our identity known, talking in Swedish, and he told us that his ship was leaving that night and to meet us at twenty hundred hours outside the brothel."

The Swede was as good as his word, and was waiting for them when they returned. He led them to the docks, and told them to duck under a chain while he reported to the Control Office. He would then go aboard, wait for an all clear, and then whistle them to come aboard.

They waited in vain. No signal was given. Seamen cast off the ropes and they watched the ship set sail down the channel. They could hazard a guess that he probably tried to enlist help to get them aboard, and was probably told by his friends that one was likely to end up in a Nazi concentration camp if caught. They were now inside the docks, and they had to get out. The best meeting place in town was obviously the brothel, if they could get through. They decided to take a chance; the officer at Control hardly bothered to glance at their papers. But disappointingly the brothel was a no-nonsense establishment, and closed its doors at 2:00 A.M. The area itself, however, was certainly populated by seamen; and they looked like seamen. Small cafes were open; small, sordid hotels did business. They had a meal and paid for a room in one of the hotels. They had taken part in one of the most momentous escapes in history; they'd taken their chances and gotten away with it. They were already asleep as their heads fell towards the pillows, and did not awake until four o'clock the following afternoon. Muller looked across at Bergsland and grinned. "Another visit to Seventeen Klein Oder Strasse, I think."

They arrived at the brothel at six, and met two more Swedish sailors coming out through the door. They were affable when the two Norwegians explained their difficulties.

"*Ja*," they said. "You come, catch the tram

with us and we go back to our docks. Four miles out near Parnitz." By that time it was eight-thirty and getting dark. The Swedish sailors slouched up to the German soldier on guard, showing their papers, the two Norwegians close behind. The guard was helpful. "All part of the same crew?" he inquired, and they nodded vigorously. He stood aside to let them pass, not even asking for papers.

Safely on deck, the Swedes slapped them on the back, and said, "Not bad, eh? Now we've got to hide you because the ship doesn't sail until seven tomorrow morning, and there's bound to be a German search before we sail."

Their hiding place was the anchor locker holding the great coiled chain. In one corner was a pile of netting and sacks. The sailors heaved it aside and formed a sort of inner nest. "Now you can sleep. But don't be snoring when the Germans arrive tomorrow morning. Usually they don't have dogs. Dogs don't like climbing up and down thin steel companion ladders."

Hours later Bergsland and Muller heard the Germans tramping towards them; the hatch was thrown open and closed again; the search was perfunctory. The feet stamped away. Half an hour later the propellers began to thrash water and they felt the ship begin to move. Their two friends came down with food and drink, and the smell of the sea coming in through the hawseholes in the bow was like an elixir of freedom.

When they reached Sweden they shook hands

and gave a whoop of joy, for it was a small victory for all of them. Then they went to find the British consulate. Two out of seventy-six had reached freedom.

Bram van der Stok sat on a bench in the Breslau railway station and pretended to doze. He believed that "he travels fastest who travels alone." He was wearing civilian clothes—at least they looked like that, although they were in fact an Australian air force overcoat and a converted naval jacket and trousers, RAF shoes and a beret.

He bought a second-class ticket to Alkmaar, boarded the train, and at 10:00 A.M. arrived in Dresden, where he had a long layover. He dozed in two cinemas until 8:00 P.M., then went back to the station to catch a train to the Dutch border at Bentheim. He realized that the tunnel had been discovered, and the hunt was on, because his papers were carefully scrutinized on four occasions. At the frontier post his papers were examined again, but now it was easier. His Dutch was, naturally, perfect, and his papers were in order. He traveled by train to Oldenzaal, then on to Utrecht. Here the Escape Committee had given him the address of an underground resistance worker. The man welcomed him, gave him fake identity papers and ration cards, and kept him safe in his home for three days. But there was no victory yet. Holland was part of Germany's conquered Europe; informers and spies were everywhere. Bram van der Stok still had to move fast. He traveled by bicycle to another safe house in Belgium, where he was given Belgian identity papers, then on by train through Brussels to Paris. More false papers and south again to Toulouse, and now he was installed in the Maquis resistance chain. He met up with two American lieutenants, two RAF pilots, a French officer, a Russian, and a French girl who acted as a guide. Together they crossed the Pyrenees and arrived in Lérida. The Spanish were neutral, but not necessarily friendly. The British consul took them over in Lérida, and Bram van der Stok arrived in Gibraltar on July 8. His escape journey had taken almost three and a half months. He was back in England within a few days, the third to make a home run.

Twenty minutes after the Breslau train left carrying Bram van der Stok on his adventurous journey, and Bushell and Scheidhauer on theirs, the Berlin train steamed into the station. It was packed. Wings Day managed to squeeze into a corridor, hemmed in by soldiers and civilians. Everyone was tired, irritated by the delays, and no one wanted to chat. Wings and Tobolski had decided to travel separately during this journey and link up again in the Berlin station.

As a compromise Wings had been allowed by the Escape Committee to use the paper identifying him as Hungarian for the first part of the journey; he had never seen a more convincing and beautifully forged document in his life. This was to pass him through the ticket barrier in Berlin. After he rejoined Tobolski he would revert to the Colonel Browne identity, Unteroffizier Tobolski covering for Wings's lack of German.

Wings stood with his back against a window and closed his eyes. He didn't think he could sleep standing up, but he must have managed a bit of it because when he opened them again the gray light of dawn was seeping across a flat Silesian landscape made up of dark patches of fir trees and sweeping areas of snow. He thought fleetingly of how much he'd love a cup of tea. He wouldn't get one of those before he made the wearisome and dangerous passage through the ticket barrier. At 8:00 A.M. they hissed noisily into Berlin's cavernous station. Wings allowed himself to be borne along on the tide of hurrying humanity. To his surprise and with a vague sense of sadness, he realized that no one had even examined that beautiful Hungarian identity document as he was swept through the barrier.

Wings explored a couple of exits before he found Tobolski and they moved off into the devastated landscape of Germany's capital city. They had accomplished the first part of their journey, and if all went well they would separate in Berlin and set off on their own: Wings to proceed to Stettin; Tobolski—not far from his own country and able to speak German like a native—with half a dozen alternatives to consider.

Now they had to check two likely contacts. Tobolski had a sister who was married to a German and living in a Berlin suburb. But she had children, and would have to be approached with maximum caution for both her own good and theirs.

The other contact was much more intriguing: A flight lieutenant in Sagan, who had previously spent many weeks in Berlin pretending to be amenable to broadcasting Nazi propaganda in English, had told Wings he knew some possibly trustworthy contacts in the German capital. One in particular, a middle-aged German couple named Kunis, had seemed quite willing to shelter RAF escapers for a night or two. They also had a Danish lodger named Eric, who had once boasted that he might be able to arrange to get prisoners into Denmark, where escape possibilities back to Britain were much more promising. They lived in a bombed-out apartment block in a suburb. Wings and Tobolski decided that they would sound out this contact first.

Wings had memorized the directions the flight lieutenant had given him from the station to the Kunis's apartment, but memory and actuality collided as they walked through the streets of Berlin on that gloomy March morning. The previous night seven hundred British bombers—the armada that had halted the Sagan escape—had dropped thousands of tons of bombs, and the city was still smoldering. From continual nightly bombing, ninety-five percent of the houses were gutted; entire streets lay desolate and empty. Wings knew this did not augur well for the chances of finding the Kunises in their apartment.

The streets were still packed and littered with

rubble. Some were totally impassable. Others had a narrow, single-track corridor bulldozed through for traffic to pass. There wasn't much traffic. There weren't many civilians either, and those there were were middle-aged or elderly.

Tobolski, with his perfect German and the camouflage of his reassuring uniform, could ask passersby the way through this maze. Wings stood to one side and reflected gloomily on his chosen profession. A span of time equal to less than half a man's lifetime had passed since the invention of the flying machine, and in that time man seemed to have used the machine mainly to destroy himself.

They found the street where Herr and Frau Kunis lived. Their building didn't look much different from the others, but it still had a roof, and stairs that went up from a door that was more or less whole. They climbed up and pressed the bell outside the door. Frau Kunis answered. She was a short, plump woman of about forty-five, gray-haired and friendly. Wings thought, with hope, that she didn't seem very put out at the idea of a German Luftwaffe Unteroffizier and a tall, skinny scarecrow knocking at her front door.

She and Tobolski did all the talking. Did she remember a friend of theirs, in the RAF, whom she had met a few months ago? Of course she did. How was he? Back in his prisoner-of-war camp. Oh good, that must be nice for him. Wouldn't they come in?

They entered a surprisingly large room, quite

well furnished. Frau Kunis apologized for the general condition of the apartment, explaining that most of the other rooms were open to the cold March air and were boarded up. She introduced her husband. Herr Kunis was probably fifteen years older than she, well-dressed, soft-spoken. He explained that, being an artist by trade and inclination, he owned a small factory in the vicinity of Breslau where he manufactured carpets and tapestries of his own design.

Frau Kunis said she would like to offer them coffee, but it wasn't particularly good coffee. Ah, said Wings, we can remedy that. Opening his cardboard briefcase, he produced a jar of coffee that made Frau Kunis's eyes sparkle. Would she please accept this as a small gift?

Frau Kunis flew off to the kitchen. Wings Day let Tobolski explain their murky relationship— the German Unteroffizier giving this Irish colonel a tour of Berlin. As if the Gestapo would ever believe that! On the other hand, how could he believe that he himself—not much more than twelve hours ago—had been sitting in a prisoner-of-war camp, and was now being received very politely in the living room of a German couple who were ostensibly the enemy? Didn't quite make sense. What did these days?

Herr Kunis chattered away, and Wings discovered he spoke excellent English. "Before the war I traveled quite extensively in both Britain and America selling my carpets," he said. He had made many friends there. He also made it clear that he disliked persecution, especially that endured by the Jews over the past years. He had many good Jewish friends, though he had no idea what had happened to them. With any luck this damned war would be over soon.

Frau Kunis came back with coffee and cake, and said, "This is just a snack. You must stay for lunch." She chatted away happily. And Wings thought he began to understand their attitude. It was clear that they did not want to be oppressed by any sinister truth and were quite prepared to accept him and Tobolski at face value. Maybe it was something to do with the bombing, Wings thought. Maybe a state of mind had evolved that made a moment over coffee and cake, discussing inanities a thousand times more pleasant than reality.

Lunch was excellent. Schnapps first, then a bottle of wine. Over it Wings explained the real reason for their visit. "You have a young Danish lodger here, I understand?"

"Ah, yes, a nice boy—Eric Engels." Frau Kunis's motherly intuition took over. "We have a small servant's room here, with only a single bed, I am afraid. But if you would like to rest there for a few hours and then rejoin us for dinner tonight, you could meet Eric."

They lay on the bed head-to-toe; they were unconscious within seconds.

Chapter Thirteen

BEYOND THE PLATE-GLASS windows the peaks of the
Bavarian Alps lifted against the darkening sky:
immense sculptured mountains of sheer, sym-
metrical beauty, a vast panorama of snow-covered
plateau and tumbling glacier. Only a madman
would have christened this tranquil, privileged
human eyrie the "Wolf's Nest."

The madman was inside striding jerkily around
the huge lounge. He was almost incoherent with
rage, the voice pitched to the screaming point.
The terror-fliers who had escaped last night would
be shot and cremated! All of them! No mercy! No
interrogation! They would be taught a lesson
they—and the other terror-fliers in Germany's
POW camps—would never forget! Himmler and
the Gestapo would carry out these orders, since it
was clear he could not trust either Reichsmarschall
Goering or Feldmarschall Wilhelm Keitel to ex-
pedite this matter. But they would cooperate.
Teleprints must be dispatched at once!

Those three men, all present now, had engaged
in their own screaming match, Himmler cursing
Keitel as commander in chief with overall power
over all prisoners of war for allowing the escape
to happen, and lambasting Goering for allowing

211

his Luftwaffe to treat the terror-fliers as human beings.

Goering, grasping to retain some of his waning power, tried to mollify Hitler: "But, Führer, if we dispose of every one of these escaped airmen we shall never be able to conceal such an episode. A hundred escaped prisoners shot? The British and Americans hold hundreds, thousands of German airmen and soldiers. There will be reprisals against them."

In the eleven years since Hitler had first come to absolute power (ironically, March 24, the day the Sagan mass escape took place, was the anniversary) no one had survived for long after questioning his decisions. No votes had ever been taken in the Reichstag; no bill or statute had ever been debated or discussed. But Goering's words gave him pause.

"Then fifty will be shot!" he screamed. "Fifty of the terror-fliers will be executed. And since the Luftwaffe cannot be trusted"—he shot a venomous glance at his once favorite colleague—"the Gestapo will handle the matter." The nod towards Himmler fixed that decision irrevocably.

The next morning Keitel met Major General Graevenitz, retiring head of the *Kriegsgefangenenwesen*—the office that administered POWs—and his successor, Major General Adolf Westhoff, in military headquarters, Berchtesgaden. He came straight to the point: "This is a bad business. I tell you these escapes must stop. The purpose of these very severe measures is to set an example.

Men who have escaped will be shot and cremated. Many of them are doubtlessly already dead. Others will be executed as they are recaptured."

Both major generals were senior officers, and the idea was anathema to them. Shooting prisoners of war! God knows where such actions would end! It could extend to major generals!

Graevenitz strongly objected, but Keitel had spent too much time the night before arguing the issue, and did not intend to take any more. "I don't give a damn," he shouted. "It has been discussed in the Führer's presence, and that is his decision. The matter has been handed over to the Gestapo, and there is to be no interference in their handling of the matter."

The German High Command might not interfere, but they intended to distance themselves from this atrocity as quickly as possible. Westhoff returned to his headquarters and wrote a report on the interview, which he sent to Keitel, pointing out that both he and Major General Graevenitz had protested emphatically: shooting and cremating escaping POWs was totally against the Geneva conventions. He wanted written confirmation of this protest if such happenings occurred—this despite Keitel's order that nothing in writing should ever refer to the matter. Keitel returned Westhoff's memo with one amendment: "I did not say the officers should be 'shot'—but 'handed over to the Gestapo.'"

Giving evidence long afterwards, Westhoff repeated that his true feelings were that "an intention to kill emanated from the very center of the German Reich, and radiated through all Hitler's subordinates who hurried to execute his orders." Even Keitel was tarred with that brush. It was he who instructed: "As an intimidating example, the names of those shot are to be posted in camp so that everyone can see them. The urns are to be returned to the camp and buried there. I forbid that anything be recorded in writing concerning the shootings or that any talks concerning this matter take place with any other department, not even the Foreign Office. I hope, however, that prisoners of war will get such a shock that in future they will not attempt to escape."

Himmler moved into action as soon as he left that meeting with Hitler. He immediately got on the phone to Obergruppen-führer Ernst Kaltenbrunner, his second-in-command in the Gestapo hierarchy, in Berlin. Kaltenbrunner would prepare the text of a top-secret teleprint message dispatched to all Gestapo headquarters where the escaped officers were recaptured. They were to be taken by road back somewhere towards Sagan and shot, ostensibly while "attempting to escape." Kaltenbrunner had two deputies: SS Major Erich Brunner of the Gestapo, and high-ranking General Artur Nebe, head of the Kripo. Himmler suggested that General Nebe be handed the task of selecting the fifty to die. All records and photos of captured officer aircrew were made available to him.

After the war, Dr. Hans Merton, a senior official in Berlin, reported General Nebe's reactions: "Nebe was blowing his top, screaming to know if he was expected to run the Sagan case entirely by himself. Owing to the Berlin raids and illness, none of his aides had arrived in the Berlin headquarters that morning. 'Take the teleprints which report the individual recaptures,' Nebe shouted. 'Write down the names of the recaptured men, and the places where they are now. Then bring me the cards of the recaptured men. You have heard about the Führer's order. Then you know what to do. [S.S. Gruppenführer] Müller, Kaltenbrunner, and I are lunching together. I will take Kaltenbrunner another list of the men to be shot when I see him at lunchtime.'

"I gave Nebe the personal file cards of those reported captured since the list was made up. Each card contained a photograph and personal details of the officer concerned. Nebe was very excited. In my view his agitated behavior was due to the fact that he was very keenly aware of the monstrous thing he was about to do.

"When I gave Nebe the cards, he threw several in front of me, saying, 'Have a look at whether they have wives or children.' We put the cards in two piles. Then he took my cards. I briefly gave him the personal details of the officers he had put aside. I remember Nebe said of one of them, '*He* will be shot!' And he put the card on the pile in front of him. He looked at the photograph of another officer and said, 'He is so young. No.' He took another card and looked at it, and said,

'Children—no!' And he put the card on the second stack.

"He looked at the two piles, suddenly changed a card from one stack to the other, and handed me a pile with the order, 'Make a list of those. Quickly!' "

Teleprint instructions concerning the shootings and the names were in the hands of the regional Gestapo heads within a matter of hours. The operation was known as *Aktion Kugel*: "Operation Bullet." The instructions had a footnote attached: "Burn after reading!"

Attached too were the names of five other escapers among the Sagan contingent who came under the *Aktion Kugel* provisions; they were to be sent to Gestapo headquarters for "special treatment."

Jimmy James had planned a picturesque escape route—why not see some of Europe while he had the chance? Down through the Danube Valley— that region of immortal musical dreams—and on into Greece. That should be the easy bit, because his traveling companion was Sotiris Skanzikas, known as Skan, a cheerful Greek fighter pilot who had fought with the RAF. They would cross the northern plains of Greece and slip into neutral Turkey, probably even have time for a short tour of the fabulous mosques in Istanbul. Jimmy had dreamed about such things as he'd lain in his bunk at night. But now, with his escaping experience behind him, he knew it would be no more than a dream.

To start with, they were traveling in a group of twelve, all ostensibly foreign workers—there were millions of foreign workers in Germany, so why should they be noticed? Leading the party as a perfect German speaker was Jerzy Mondschein, a Pole, and his three pals: Squadron Leader Willy Williams, Flight Lieutenant Reginald "Rusty" Kierath (both from Australia), and Johnny Bull.

Major Johnny Dodge represented the United States; his traveling partner, Flight Lieutenant Jimmy Wernham, had been born in Scotland and raised in Canada. The group was rounded out by two more Polish officers; Doug Poynter of the Royal Navy's Fleet Air Arm; and fifty-seven-year-old Pop Green, a First World War recipient of the Military Cross, who had faked his age and wangled his way into the rear turret of a slow Witley bomber, where he had hardly had time to align his nest of machine guns before being removed from the sky by a ME-109.

They had gathered together in the forest and set off across country at around 1:30 A.M., heading southwest for the small country station of Tschiebsdorf, on a branch line, a couple of hours' march from Sagan.

They arrived at the station well before 5:00 A.M., when their local train was due to arrive. There was only one man on duty in the ticket office, and his mouth dropped open when Jerzy

217

Mondschein popped his head in and said, "Twelve tickets to Boberohrsdorf."

"Twelve!" The ticket clerk went away, thought about it, came back, and said disbelievingly, "Twelve!"

"*Ja*," said Jerzy Mondschein belligerently, and thrust the money through the window.

He got the tickets. Boberohrsdorf lay about fifty miles to the south, near the town of Hirschberg. From there, it was only about forty miles across country to the Czech border. They would part there and take their separate chances.

They all crowded into the small waiting room. Shortly before 5:00 A.M., a middle-aged man and woman who looked as if they belonged to the farming community peered in. Their faces contracted and their eyeballs squinted as they stared in disbelief at the mysterious twelve.

The train chugged in, pulling six old-fashioned coaches. It appeared to be empty. The twelve filled one compartment, leaving no room for anyone else to sit. At every station a few people clambered aboard. Then gradually the train filled up with school-children bound for Hirschberg. An elderly female ticket collector arrived and looked angrily around the group. All appeared to be asleep or dozing, except Jerzy Mondschein. They kept their eyes closed as they heard her irritated chatter and Jerzy's placating reply as he handed over the tickets to be clipped.

Startled eyes opened when she left. What was the matter?

"You bloody fools," said Jerzy cheerfully. "You've all been puffing away in a nonsmoking compartment."

"And, gentlemen," added Johnny Dodge politely, "it is now snowing. Heavily."

They arrived at Boberohrsdorf at 9:00 A.M. It was still snowing. No one got on at that station. There was no porter at the barrier. They filed out through a gap in the fence and separated in a white world of whirling snowflakes.

Johnny Bull, Jerzy Mondschein, Willy Williams, and Rusty Kierath stuck together and, like Jimmy James and Skan, took to the open, snow-covered mountains. What was the forty-mile distance to the coveted Czech border to them? They were a bit thin and undernourished, but they were still young and healthy!

But they found the journey—in bitter cold, often struggling through waist-deep snow, and floundering down steep slopes—an almost unendurable ordeal. And there was no place to rest. On the afternoon of the second day they saw a military patrol, on skis, traveling swiftly towards them. The Germans had rifles over their shoulders. The four airmen were stuck in snow as securely as flies on flypaper.

In the nearest small town, Reichenberg, they were interrogated harshly, one by one. Here they were joined three days later by Flying Officer Johnny Stower—who had come very close to freedom on a previous escape attempt, actually reaching Swiss territory and then inadvertently walking out of it again—and Czech fighter pilot Flight Lieutenant I. P. Tonder. They too had been heading for Czechoslovakia, and had come out of Harry as Numbers 21 and 22. Believing that the lateness of the exit and the airraid alarm would create chaos at the station, they had decided to walk south. After three days and nights, hoping that the heat of pursuit was off, they had decided to risk a train. The heat was not off—the *Grossfahndung* had intensified it—and every train was searched rigorously.

In the Reichenberg jail they had a chance to talk together. Tonder—the only one of the six who would survive—knew that all five of his comrades were depressed by the Gestapo's death threats. Willy Williams admitted privately to Tonder that he had been informed he would be shot. The Gestapo had got their list and were ticking off names.

Johnny Bull, Rusty Kierath, Jerzy Mondschein, and Willy Williams were taken from their cell at 4:00 A.M. on the fifth day after the escape. Their urns were returned to Sagan, bearing the date March 29, 1944, and the name of the small town of Brüx. Johnny Stower was taken away at 8:00 A.M. on March 31. An urn bearing his name but no place of execution reached Sagan. Tonder lived only because he was Czech, and the Nazis, suspecting some organized plan (since so many Sagan escapers had headed for that country), thought they could obtain information from him. Tonder was interrogated for months and passed from jail to jail until the end of 1944. He lived to tell his story.

Flight Lieutenant George McGill, Flying Officer Henry Birkland, Flight Lieutenant Pat Langford—who could snap Harry's entrance tunnel with the finality of a slammed door—Flight Lieutenant Mike Casey, Flight Lieutenant George Wiley, Flight Lieutenant Thomas Leigh, Flying Officer John Pohe, Flight Lieutenant Cyril Swain, Flight Lieutenant Charles Hall, Flight Lieutenant Brian Evans, Flying Officer Wlodzimierz Kolanowski, and Flying Officer Bob Stewart: all were carried away in black cars on March 30 and 31, never to be seen alive again.

Within five days of the breakout, those who were recaptured close to Sagan—thirty-five men —had been collected at the Görlitz jail. All but four of them would die, including Harry Marshall, who dug with the energy of a Yorkshire miner, and whom Wally Floody would remember with such admiration for all the tussles they had had over the vagaries of Tunnel Harry. Marshall and Ernst Valenta had been first out of the tunnel and first away. They'd given up the idea of trains and decided to walk to Czechoslovakia. Then there was Ian Cross, Jimmy James's coconspirator under the theater; and Al Hake, John Bennett's tutor in the delicate art of compass making. Al could scarcely hobble out to the three huge black Capitan cars because of the frostbitten condition of his feet. The guards wore black leather overcoats and deadpan faces—Gestapo killers, influenced by Hollywood crime films, tended to act like stereotyped movie gangsters, and even used the word "gangster" to describe anyone opposing them.

Jimmy James and Skan Skanzikas walked through the village of Boberohrsdorf, aware that the snow piled on the eaves of the cottages, and the snow on the mountains rearing up behind those chimneys, was going to make their journey perilous. They struck off across the fields towards the lower slopes. The hillside tilted up at a steep angle, and before long they were tugging themselves upwards, hand over hand, using bushes and branches. Exhausted and puffing, they reached a small plateau, and now conditions were even worse as they found themselves waist-deep in soft snow. By late afternoon they had advanced a few miles, but now they were conscious of the lack of sleep the night before; they were soaking wet; their thin clothing was hopeless against this kind of weather; they had to take a rest. They found an open deeryard and managed to light a small fire from sticks. A manger full of hay stood against one side and they took turns watching the fire, the other trying to snatch a little sleep in the hay. Neither gave them comfort, and they knew they had to find better shelter than this before night fell.

They labored on to another, higher ridge and saw down below them the spires and roofs of Hirschberg. The high mountains still loomed ahead of them. Skanzikas was shivering and blue with cold. Jimmy James, with his experience in below-zero conditions in Canada, knew that hypothermia was a real danger if they attempted a crossing of those high peaks. He caught the look in Skan's eyes and said, "Tell you what. There's a railway station in Hirschberg. I think we should try and catch a local train there and move right down to the Czech border. After all, nobody took the slightest notice of us on our journey this morning."

Skan nodded. They wouldn't stay alive traveling like this. They dropped down into a valley and followed the snow-covered road into town. It was beginning to get dark. None of the passersby paid any attention to them, and their spirits began to rise. Their spirits rose even higher when they entered the railway station. It was crowded, and there were queues at the ticket kiosk. Surely they could get lost among this many people. Then, without warning, they found themselves confronted by a helmeted policeman and a tough-looking civilian in a black-belted leather coat who demanded their papers. They hardly glanced at them. Then they examined their packs. "You will come with us," was the order as their arms were taken in a strong grasp. News of the Sagan escape had been flashed to all stations and broadcast over the radio.

Johnny Dodge and his companion, Jimmy Wernham, met with similar experiences. They followed the riverbank to Hirschberg and tried to buy railway tickets at a small railway station on the outskirts. They were refused. They walked northwest along the main road, but trying to tramp through two-foot-deep snow was too slow. They returned to Hirschberg. This time Johnny Dodge managed to buy railway tickets to a small town near the Czech border. They were sitting in the railway carriage when a civilian entered—perhaps the same man who had apprehended Jimmy James and Skan Skanzikas—demanding to see their documents and to know what they were doing. Neither Johnny Dodge's nor Jimmy Wernham's German was good enough to stand this sort of interrogation. They were arrested and handed over to the station police. Jimmy Wernham's name was on the death list. Johnny Dodge's was on the *Aktion Kugel* list; he was one of five prisoners to be handed over to the Gestapo for "special treatment."

Chapter Fourteen

DESPITE THE NARROW BED in the Kunis's small back room, Wings Day and Pawel Tobolski slept well and awoke refreshed that afternoon. They decided that it was far too dangerous for their hosts if they stayed much longer. Nevertheless, they warmly thanked the couple and promised to return that evening to meet Eric Engels. After that they would disappear.

They walked back into town and entered a tavern. Inside four soldiers from the nearby anti-aircraft battery got into conversation with Tobolski, while Wings Day kept his nose in his beer mug. They left after about an hour to walk the streets, and Tobolski explained the conversation: "They'd all served on the Russian front. All had been wounded and were on light duty before returning there. They said it was hell. They also told me about a troop transit center at the station where all soldiers on leave report in and are given food and a night's lodgings when necessary. That might be useful if I can get myself registered there. Thousands must pass through."

"Didn't they think I was a bit dumb, not saying a word?" asked Wings.

"I told them you were Hungarian, and a bit soft

in the head, but a very good mechanic who was being transferred to my hometown where I was now going on leave, and acting as your escort."

Wings grinned. "I don't mind the Hungarian mechanic part, but don't overplay the 'soft in the head' bit—that's beyond my artistic capacity."

Eric Engels was a tall, good-looking young Dane, with what Wings Day thought was a weak face. He spoke excellent German, and his English wasn't bad. Yes, he remembered their flight lieutenant friend and hoped he was well. Like the Kunises, he didn't seem to find it strange that an oddly dressed Irish colonel accompanied by a Luftwaffe corporal should be dropping in for dinner; perhaps the presence of so many foreign workers in Germany had deadened local curiosity.

Wings felt immediately that Eric was unreliable. That opinion was reinforced after meeting his girlfriend, who arrived halfway through the meal. She was slender, dark, attractive, and not much more than eighteen. Eric explained that she was a ballerina with the Berlin opera company. Wings looked at her enviously. She was the first pretty female he had seen in nearly five years, with a sharp mind to go with her trim form. Clearly she did not trust him or Tobolski. Wings wondered if she had once been a member of the Hitler Youth movement.

The radio was left on both during and after supper, and Wings watched the hostility growing in her eyes as reports of enemy aircraft crossing the coastline were broadcast. When the announcer reported that the air raid would arrive at Berlin in fifteen minutes' time, Eric and his girlfriend decided to leave. Herr and Frau Kunis took Wings and Tobolski down to the basement for the half hour it lasted. None of the other people sheltering there took the slightest notice of them.

They agreed to stay for the night, and the next morning worked out their plans. Wings felt certain that Eric Engels was a dud. He also felt a deep sense of responsibility towards both the Kunises and Tobolski. They would leave the apartment now and never return. If the ballerina betrayed them, Herr and Frau Kunis could get away with the story that an authentic Luftwaffe corporal was accompanying this strange visitor, and they had come to visit the lodger, not them. As for Tobolski, he could exist in Berlin society, probably find shelter in the troop transit center, probably move west and escape because he had a genuine German corporal's paybook, which he had obtained through some bribery and blackmail back in Sagan. Wings explained his anxieties to Tob.

Tobolski said yes, he would go and examine the possibilities of the troop transit center, but he was not abandoning Wings until they had visited his sister in Stettin, and checked out the possibilities there.

Reluctantly Wings agreed. They said goodbye to the Kunises and promised to contact them after the war. Wings walked towards the city with Tobolski and they chose a place to meet at noon the following day. Wings went to the station to find out about trains to Stettin. There seemed to be regular service, and although civilians went through a different barrier than the military, apparently there were no special checks. It soon began to get dark, so Wings decided he'd better find a bar and consider where he might find shelter for the night. He fell asleep over his glass of beer, and when he jolted awake decided that the sooner he left there the better, as the other customers were glancing at him with curiosity.

There were hundreds of half-gutted houses around. What about one of them? That was a mistake. Stealing around inky-black hallways, broken rooms, and shaky staircases with only a match to light one's way was a chilling experience.

Wings went back to the streets—and ran into an air raid. He followed the crowd to below-ground shelter. Blackout doors led through a wide corridor to a long room with cell-like spaces opening on either side. It was crowded, and just as in the London Underground, regulars had staked out their places. Wings was chased off a few times by indignant hausfraus, but managed to find a space between two German families. It was warm and foggy. The raid consisted of a series of distant rumblings and occasional earthquakelike convulsions. Wings lay awake thinking, "What the hell am I doing here! If I'm to be in *any* air-raid shelter, it should be one in London." He fell asleep trying to be philosophic about the fortunes of war.

228

The next morning he made for the station, where he could wash and shave and order coffee. He was feeling reasonably human, therefore, when he met Tobolski, who was also in good spirits. The troop transit center had been helpful: they'd accepted his paybook without question and given him hot food and a mattress on the floor, and now he was duly registered with them. Tobolski bought two tickets to Stettin, but again they decided to travel separately.

Wings was walking down the platform towards the coaches when a chill entered his heart. A man in a black leather overcoat and peaked cap was striding along beside him. He also wore jackboots, and he was showing Wings a medallion he had produced from his pocket. An eagle and a swastika were cut into its surface. He had authority.

Wings stopped at once, and hoped that his look of slight bewilderment was sufficient. He showed his papers: he had an excellent forged *Ausweis*, which gave him permission to travel between Berlin and Stettin, and he had his beautiful Hungarian passport. Would it hold up?

The official scrutinized the Hungarian document for probably ninety seconds, reading every page and going back to examine some for a second time. Plainly he was well aware of the escapers from Sagan, but who in his right mind would ever want to impersonate a Hungarian? Except a Hungarian. Obviously there was no way of interrogating this strange fellow, and plainly he did not look anything like these young airmen he was after. Wings climbed into a crowded carriage, his conviction about his Hungarian origins now justified, and feeling a little sad at not being able to say, "I told you so."

At Stettin they found a bar for Wings to wait in, and Tobolski went to look for his sister. He returned with a solemn face. His sister was completely uncooperative; she would not help him even if he were alone. She was married to a German. She had two kids. The risks were too awesome even to contemplate. The husband would certainly be shot; she could also be executed, but if not she would be sent to a concentration camp. Wings breathed in deeply, thought fleetingly of the courage of the Kunises, and said he understood.

Tob said there was one small bright aspect. His sister owned a small piece of property half a mile from her house. There was a shed on it. They could spend the night there; she would not be implicated. They found it without difficulty. It was quite large, warm, and weatherproof; there was a lot of burlap sacking and a big pile of hay. There were also boiled eggs, black bread, and a jug of milk. Wings smiled and said, "Good girl!" And Tob smiled back.

They left at dawn, deciding to examine the shipping situation. It was not good. The docks were extensive but surrounded by steel fencing twelve feet high; the only hopeful sign was the dozens of French POWs who were working on the docks and who seemed to be transported to and from work by trucks morning and evening. Later that day, Wings, carrying a piece of lumber over his shoulder and hopeful that he looked like a dock laborer, managed to get into conversation with a couple of the workers. Though he had studied French before, his facility improved enormously after a year of sharing a POW camp with only Frenchmen. Conversationally he was quite good. The two Frenchmen not only warmed to him, but said they were proud to be chosen by him as some-one he could trust. Certainly they could help. They arranged a rendezvous at a nearby bridge at nine o'clock that night, and although they temporarily froze with fright when they found Wings accompanied by a German soldier, they were soon very impressed with the Polish pilot's bravery in doing the impersonation. They insisted that Wings and Tobolski come back to their billet, an old redbrick building that held around eighty of their fellow workers. They would be quite safe, and among friends. It seemed so.

When Wings awoke next morning, it was still dark outside, but the lights were on and there seemed to be a certain amount of consternation. Tob was already up and working on his uniform. And a loud voice was shouting in English, "Englishmen! We know you are here! Stand up or it will be worse for everyone here!" Half a dozen uniformed police blocked the entrance, and approaching them were more men in black leather coats and peaked caps.

Later, in the police station, Wings found himself being interrogated by a middle-aged officer, who told him that the French POWs were trustworthy, but that their captors had managed to plant a French informer among them. Wings said he would like to wring his neck. The officer smiled and said that someone was bound to, sooner or later, because no one—not even those who made use of him—liked an informer, and after he had served his purpose he would be betrayed to his own countrymen. Doubtless he would be found floating in the harbor.

Tob and Wings were then moved to another building and thrust into a cell. They were there for four days. At about three in the morning of the last day the light was suddenly switched on, and they were marched to a large room where eight barbers were working busily shaving beards and clipping hair. Wings did not like the implications behind this activity. Then they were taken to another office and told they were leaving "under escort." Wings did not like the escort either: four leather-coated policemen wearing heavy-caliber revolvers. Wings and Tobolski were not handcuffed, but were informed that if they attempted escape they would be shot. At the station two cars were waiting, one to transport Tob, the other Wings. Wings protested strongly but the policemen reiterated that they had no say in this matter. Tob was being taken to another railway station. Wings said anxiously, "Is he being taken back to Sagan?" The reply was, "Possibly, but we do not know." As Wings had no knowledge of what had happened to the POWs who had escaped from Sagan, and as the Luftwaffe in the past had treated escaped prisoners honorably, he did not feel overly worried. He managed a wave to Tob, who saluted in return and went off to his execution with the same bravery as he had faced life.

Alone, Wings began to feel concern about his own future. From the policemen's attitude, he knew that he was being handed over to the Gestapo. At their headquarters in Prinz-Albert-Strasse, he was led along wide corridors and up an imposing marble staircase, to a large office partitioned off into many smaller cubicles. He was told to sit down near a large door, while a senior policeman kept an eye on him.

An hour later a tall, thin, worried-looking officer, whom Wings recognized from his insignia as a general, marched in and proceeded straight through to his office. He did not glance at Wings Day. The general's face was gray and he looked ill. Had Wings known at that moment that this was the General Nebe who a few days before had chosen which of his friends would die, it is unlikely that he would have retained his military correctness. But he did not know. He did not know either, nor could he foresee, that within a few more months General Nebe would die horribly, hanged in a piano-wire noose for having conspired to assassinate Adolf Hitler.

A few minutes later Wings was led before the general, and Wings examined the officer's face with much interest. It was a thin face, with a beaky nose and intelligent eyes—more a scholar's face than that of a merciless police general. The words that he uttered, however, did not match the image. In slow and distinct German, which Wings understood quite well, he said, "You have made yourself a great nuisance to the Reich. You have been a leader in three mass escapes. The Luftwaffe cannot hold you. You are, therefore, going to a place from which you will never escape again. It is an impossibility. That is all."

Wings decided that was *not* all. He replied, "Herr General, escape is my duty. I am an officer."

General Nebe ignored him, waving a dismissive hand. "Take him away. That is all."

Wings felt his arms gripped by strong hands. Two men dressed like his earlier escorts had now taken charge. Realizing that Wings was offering no resistance, they released their hold and took him down to the courtyard outside. A car was waiting. They sat on either side of him. Wings saw immediately that he was not being driven to some other part of Berlin, but out of town. He thought, "Well, it won't be long now. Brace yourself. In one of these woods lining the road, you'll be invited to get out to relieve yourself. No good saying you feel very comfortable, thank you. You'll be dragged out."

The car drove on. It skirted a high wall and stopped at a small wicket gate. Wings's escort got out and indicated he should go through. He took a deep breath. What was this going to be: a hangman's noose or a firing squad? He walked through, and as soon as he got inside he knew he was in some sort of prison. A small enclosure, barbed wire, tall watchtowers. He was taken to a small hut at one end where an SS officer took possession of him. He then led Wings into another compound, where stood another man with an outstretched hand. It was Johnny Dodge, as usual beaming, and inevitably courteous:

"Hello, Wings. Welcome to Sonderlager A of Sachsenhausen concentration camp. So far, I'm afraid, I'm the only member of the welcoming committee."

Later Sydney Dowse arrived, having undergone Gestapo interrogation at Prinz-Albert-Strasse. Sydney had intended to take a train from Sagan to Berlin with Polish pilot Danny Krol, then make for Danzig and—they hoped—a ship to Sweden. The sudden air-raid alarm had ruined all those plans, and the two men had decided to make a run for the Polish border. They walked and hid for twelve days, until they reached the small town of Oels, only a mile or two away from the border. Unfortunately they were spotted there by a Hitler Youth, who informed the Home Guard. Sydney and Danny were pried from their hiding place with shotgun barrels and handed over to the police. Within a short time the Breslau Gestapo arrived and proceeded to interrogate them. They told Sydney that he would be escorted to Berlin for further interrogation.

Sydney said, "What about my friend? What's

going to happen to him? You're not thinking of shooting him, are you?"

They smiled. "You have our solemn word that he will be sent back to Sagan."

They were placed in separate cells. Messages between them were relayed by a friendly Frenchman, who took Sydney's news around to Danny.

But next morning, not certain whether his message had been delivered, as soon as the prison warder opened the door, Sydney swiftly sidestepped him and ran around to Danny's cell. "Danny, they're taking me to Berlin, but you're going back to Sagan. It's okay! Good luck!"

The warder handed Sydney over to the waiting Gestapo. It was April 12. They had been out for nineteen days. Sydney never saw Danny again. But the Gestapo kept their promise: Danny was sent back to Sagan, in a small cremation urn marked Breslau. No date of death. And there was one more thing that Sydney did not know: he was one of the five on the *Aktion Kugel* list.

Sydney and Wings Day were joined in Sachsenhausen by Jimmy James, who asked, with a kind of gallows humor, "Is this Colditz?" Colditz was an old German castle where recalcitrant officer aircrews invariably ended up—still scheming escape plots.

Wings Day read Jimmy's thoughts. By now he had asked some questions about Sachsenhausen and knew the full horror of the place. Grimly he pointed to the high, thin stack of Sachsenhausen's crematorium, its ovens as usual providing the human fuel that sent a constant thin eddy of smoke across the landscape.

"That, Jimmy, is the only way of escape from here. Up the chimney!"

Chapter Fifteen

TOWARDS THE END OF March 1944, Kriminalkommissar Walter Herberg was on leave at his parents' home in Mainz when over the radio he heard the news of the terror-fliers' escape from Sagan, Stalag Luft III, and the *Grossfahndung* calling all security to the alert. So he was not surprised, when he got back to his apartment in Karlsruhe, to find his telephone ringing insistently. The most important call was from Gestapo headquarters, ordering him to report for duty at once.

Walter Herberg was a slim, dark man in his mid-thirties. He had studied law, then had been a sports journalist. Fascinated by the Führer's flamboyant and patriotic rhetoric, and attracted to the opportunities afforded by Nazi party membership, he had joined in 1934 and had been placed in an administrative department in an editorial capacity to deal with anticommunist and antisabotage matters.

At Gestapo headquarters, he was slightly puzzled to find his department head, Dr. Faber, telling him that he had been assigned a special task and that he was to report to the head of the Karlsruhe Gestapo, Oberregierungsrat Josef Gmeiner.

"Ah," said Gmeiner as he came in, "Herberg.

We need your help." He held out a teleprinter message. "Read this, and commit it to memory. It has to be destroyed."

Walter Herberg did not like what he read:

REICH TOP SECRET. RSHA [Reichssicherheitshauptamt—Reich Main Security Office] to Chief of the Gestapo Office, Karlsruhe, or his deputy. By order of the Führer the Reichsführer SS [Himmler] has ordered that the British airman [Dennis] Cochran who escaped from Sagan and is now held by the Kripo at Karlsruhe, will be taken over by officials from your office and during transport in the direction of Breslau will be shot while trying to escape. The shooting will be done in such a way that the prisoner concerned will be unaware of what is going to happen. The corpse will remain on the spot until inspected by the local gendarmerie and a death certificate has been issued. The body is to be cremated in the nearest crematorium. The urn is to be kept by the Gestapo office. Further instructions about the urn to be issued at a given time.

The death certificate is to be returned to me with a description of the spot where the shooting took place. Only persons strictly concerned with this matter will be allowed to know of this teleprint. These persons must be pledged to special secrecy. The teleprint must be destroyed after the order is carried out. I must be notified by teleprint of the destruction of the teleprint. The Kripo, Karlsruhe, have been given relevant instructions.

(Signed) Müller
SS Gruppenführer and
Lieutenant General of Police

Looking up, Herberg noticed that Gmeiner's cold eyes were fixed on him. "I now deputize you to carry out this order."

Herberg's mind froze. He could not believe what he was being ordered to do. "Shoot—shoot . . . this man? I can't do that. You must give it to somebody else."

"I am giving you the order, Herberg. You are now pledged under the oath of Gestapo secrecy. Besides, you do not have to do the actual shooting. Kriminalsekretärs Boschert and Preiss will carry out the execution. But neither has any brains. Someone must smooth out matters with the state authorities and the cremation people."

"Herr Oberregierungsrat," protested Herberg, "I know a little about the law and I know that no state attorney will issue a death certificate without knowing the name, and all about the man who has been"—"murdered" was the word that rose in his mouth, but he altered it—"shot. Besides, there is no crematorium on the road between Karlsruhe and Breslau."

Gmeiner held up a silencing hand. "I am a trained lawyer, Herberg, and I know what I am doing. There is a crematorium at the concentration camp of Natzweiler, to the west of Breslau.

240

You will have no difficulty with a death certificate or a cremation there. And this is how you will arrange the execution. You will stop on the road and suggest to the prisoner that you all get out to urinate. Naturally you will watch him to see that he does not try to escape. Boschert and Preiss will then take over."

Gmeiner was now smiling in a self-congratulatory manner. "Now we shall bring in Boschert and Preiss and give them their orders."

The next morning, Herberg, accompanied by Heinrich Boschert and Otto Preiss, picked up the prisoner from the Kripo cells in Karlsruhe. He had almost made it into Switzerland—had been arrested, in fact, with only the river between him and Basel. He was a tall, good-looking young man, wearing an RAF uniform that had been dyed a darker color. Operating as a displaced person doing casual labor, and speaking excellent German, he had had a good cover story. They placed him, handcuffed, in the back of their Mercedes, and Walter Herberg engaged him in polite conversation.

"What was your rank in the Royal Air Force, Herr Cochran?"

"I was a flying officer."

"What is the equivalent of that in the American air force?"

Dennis Cochran plainly had no suspicions. He was relaxed and talkative.

Herberg suddenly became aware that, despite

241

his air of indifference the day before, Boschert was so preoccupied and nervous that he had driven right up to the gates of Natzweiler concentration camp.

"For God's sake," said Herberg angrily, aware by this time that Cochran's German was quite good, "this is not where we hand over our prisoner. It's in Breslau itself. Get back on the road immediately."

The concentration camp sentry now approached, inquiring what they wanted. Herberg put him off, saying they'd taken the wrong road.

The nerves of all three executioners were now taut as bowstrings. The job had to be done quickly. A side road led off the main road; it was narrow and heavily wooded. Herberg said, "Let's all make a rest stop. You'd better take the opportunity, Herr Cochran."

Dennis Cochran was handcuffed in front. They went into the woods. Herberg lagged behind. He heard the sound of two shots. He went forward and saw Cochran's body lying facedown on the grass. They wrapped the body in a blanket but had great difficulty fitting it into the back of the Mercedes. They had to slide back the roof and open the windows. Then they drove back to Natzweiler. Adjutant Otto Ganninger received them. He did not seem surprised when Herberg told him that their captive had tried to escape and they'd had to shoot him.

Ganninger nodded and told him the camp had received instructions. Did he need a death certificate? When Herberg said he did, Ganninger took him across to another building, but the Kripo camp registrar refused to comply with the demand. The death had taken place outside the camp; he had no authority to issue a death certificate in such a case. Flustered, Ganninger called in the camp doctor.

"This is with the authority of Reichsführer Himmler," Herberg insisted.

"You have no written document to that effect," said the doctor. "Therefore we cannot comply with your demand."

Concerned now, Ganninger and Herberg returned to Ganninger's office. The body had been taken to the crematorium. Herberg did not ask what had happened to it. The nightmare had begun.

Two weeks later, he was called into Gmeiner's office. "Herberg, I have just received a teleprint from the RSHA in Berlin. They complain that the Karlsruhe report is incomplete. No death certificate, no cremation certificate. I am going to give you a blank sheet of our notepaper signed by myself, and you are going to Müller's office in Berlin to fill in the relevant details." Oberregierungsrat Gmeiner was not pleased.

SS Gruppenführer Müller was not pleased either. Herberg waited outside his office with other Gestapo officials summoned from places as far apart as Munich, Strasbourg, and Vienna, apparently for the same purpose.

Müller was livid. "What is the matter with all

you people? Have you no imagination? We ask you to perform an important secret task—the execution and disposal of a terror-flier's body in a way which will make the action of little concern to any authorities who may wish to investigate it. And what do you do?"

Müller brandished a sheaf of papers. "Every Gestapo office sent in the same idiotic report: 'We allowed the prisoner to step outside the car in which we were transporting him to relieve himself. He ran away and we shot him.'"

Herberg did not like to remind the Gruppenführer that this was exactly what the first secret teleprinter message had demanded.

"Couldn't you have stopped for car repairs? Couldn't he have gotten free of his handcuffs and attacked you in the car? I want details of the local scene at Karlsruhe!" Müller was now bellowing. "I want an original—believable—report. Go back to Karlsruhe, write the report, and then send it by special courier to this office."

Even as the train took him back to Karlsruhe, even as he climbed into bed that night, Herberg knew that he was doomed.

Roger Bushell and Bernard Scheidhauer had revealed little of their escape plans to anyone, but they had leaked the fact that they were going to catch the first train from Sagan to Breslau, possibly hide there for a bit, and then move on. They had to move fast—put as much distance between them and Sagan, Stalag Luft III, as they could.

In both of Roger's previous escape attempts, that understanding had been at the heart of his near-success.

The third and fourth men out through Harry, they walked briskly to the station. The Breslau train was on time, and it was not until they reached Breslau that they heard of the air raid on Berlin, which had delayed every train within a hundred-mile radius of the capital. They paced the platform impatiently. When they nearly walked right into French Flight Lieutenant Van Wymeersch, the escapers abruptly and studiously avoided each other.

The express to Saarbrücken was delayed, but once it chuffed out of the station they felt more relaxed. Roger Bushell's memory was drawn back to the past and those two other escapes. He smiled at the memory of Billy the Goat, at Dulag Luft —the transit camp—in 1940. In those early slap-happy days, if you wanted to dig a tunnel, you collected a few similar-minded friends who owned knives and bent forks, selected a dark corner, and went to work. Wings Day and Johnny Dodge had been behind the plan. "We're going to tunnel our way out of this bloody place," Wings declared.

The prisoners were beginners at the trade. They zigzagged up and down, veered to left or right according to the geographical propensities of the man scraping away at the face, resulting in a tunnel that was pitch-black, wet, muddy, and pitted with sharp rocks. Wings Day, doing his stint at digging, cut his knee quite badly on a sharp flint—

an injury that was to plague him from that moment onwards.

The tunnel was finished in May 1941, and they set the escape for early June: eighteen kriegies would make the attempt.

Roger Bushell grinned at the memory of Wings's face when he said to him, "Wings, I want a twenty-four-hour start. Alone."

Wings had a fit. "You are out of your mind. You want a twenty-four-hour start on the others by using the tunnel before them?"

"I don't want to use the tunnel," said Roger. "I want to use Billy the Goat's shed. If I'm caught, I'll admit how I escaped. You'll go ahead through the tunnel as planned."

Billy the Goat lived on the camp exercise field outside the barbed-wire fences. The kriegies were allowed out under guard for exercise—escorted out and back again. Only a single strand of wire fenced off the exercise field from the outside world. Billy was kept there by the Germans as a primitive animal lawn mower. The kriegies made him their mascot. They admired his belligerence: nothing moved into his line of vision without instantly being attacked. Mocking and dodging kriegies were assailed from front or rear.

Roger explained: "Over the past week, concealed by the football enthusiasts, I've been in Billy's shed scraping a shallow depression in the ground big enough to hold me. The night before the tunnel escape, my friends will cover me with a cardboard cover and heap Billy's straw and droppings on top. They'll then tramp back to the camp—the guards are very lackadaisical about the count—and you can easily cover for me at roll call. As soon as it's dark I'm on my way to catch a tram to Frankfurt, a night train to somewhere near the Swiss border, and within twenty-four hours, *before* the tunnel breakout, I'm eating croissants in the best Swiss hotel."

"Not a bad scheme," Wings admitted.

Wings also knew that, of all the many would-be escapers, Roger Bushell was the best equipped and most likely to succeed. If he did make the run home, he would be damn useful to the British with his information.

"Okay," said Wings. "I'll back you."

They stowed Roger away in late afternoon when they vacated the field, deciding that if he could spend five or six hours cooped up with smelly Billy he could cope with anything. They covered his absence from the returning squads and at roll call without difficulty.

Alone in his shallow hiding place, covered as planned by thin boards, straw, and droppings, Roger Bushell lay still and listened to Billy's chumpings and rustlings. When it was dark enough and, Roger thought, safe enough to lever up the lid of his covering, he found the goat regarding him with dark, satanic eyes. But he was still chewing the goodies Roger's friends had left behind to keep him happy, and made no move to interfere as Roger unlatched the door and stepped out into the darkness. He brushed the bits of straw and dirt off his new civilian suit, which he had bribed a guard to slip to him. He had German money, he had papers that should pass muster, and his command of the language was excellent. He was a German-Swiss gentleman, resident in Switzerland and enjoying a short holiday. And he knew where he was going. He crossed the field, slipped under the single strand of wire, and was outside the main camp. There were a few lights here and there, a star-filled sky, the new-mown-grass smell of June. He walked along paths to Oberursel's main street, and caught the streetcar to the Frankfurt station.

When the train arrived, Roger climbed into a half-empty compartment and hid behind his newspaper. The train started off, trundling through the darkness, sweeping past the rows of lights, heading south. An express, it stopped only at the main stations: Darmstadt first, then on to Mannheim, and from there to Heidelberg, a few miles to the southeast.

But could escape be this easy? It seemed so normal to be sitting here in this train jogging through the night, that he had difficulty repressing his exultation. He wanted to tap people on the knee, talk to them, smile at them, tell them that there were no words to express the ecstasy of these moments. The feeling was so heady that Roger had to will himself to be cautious.

The train stopped at Karlsruhe. After every stop ticket inspectors had appeared and used their hole punches. No trouble at all. No suspicious looks. Karlsruhe was no different, and on they rattled towards the dawn and Roger's changing station, Tuttlingen, from where he would catch a branch-line train to Bondorf, fifteen miles away. From Bondorf he would walk ten miles to the German-Swiss border.

He sat in the waiting room at Tuttlingen, waiting for the early morning "workman's connection," going through the *Völkischer Beobachter* for the second time. The sun was up by the time he arrived in Bondorf, but it was a bit early to be on the streets of a small town, so again it was the waiting room and the newspaper. As people began to stream onto the platform to catch their connections, he walked towards the center of the pretty southern Baden town. He stopped at a cafe for coffee and cake. He found a bookshop that sold guidebooks and maps and purchased one of each. Carrying these in his hand, he felt entirely the part of the visiting Swiss tourist. He supposed that some Germans and Swiss still took vacations. By noon he was on the road heading towards the border town of Stühlingen. The sun was shining, the birds singing, and Roger knew he was getting close to the tricky part. A mile from the village, he turned off on a wooded hillside and sat down with his back against a tree. He was well aware that the main danger now was overconfidence. Switzerland lay across the valley, peaceful, beautiful, free. Roger sat there through that sunny afternoon trying to make up his mind. The break back at Dulag Luft would not take place before nightfall. Once that was discovered the alarms at every border post would ring. Should he wait for nightfall to edge towards the border, or should he make a bold exit through the normal route—the main village street of Stühlingen? Around this fist of Swiss territory pushing into Germany's Baden, known as the Schaffhausen, border crossings were said to be less closely watched than elsewhere in Germany. Should he trust those rumors? He had only two or three hours to decide.

With doubts still lingering in his mind, Roger walked slowly down the hillside and along the wooded paths that led to the main village street. The sun was still shining brightly; it was a glorious June afternoon. There were only a few people on the street. No one took the slightest notice of him. He even paused to glance with interest into a few shop windows. Looking ahead he could see a sign that he decided must indicate the line of the German-Swiss border, but no sign of a customs barrier. So what? Such things happened in many parts of Europe, especially when you were so far off the beaten track.

He realized he must be within a few yards of freedom. The barked shout of "Halt!" brought him to a standstill. A burly officer in the uniform of the German border guards had emerged from a house to his right. In one hand he had a large pistol, which he pointed directly at Roger; the other hand was held out for Roger's papers. Roger smiled and began to explain the precise nature of his visit. With railway guards, with all sorts of minor officials, he would have gotten away with it. But this man was trained, watchful, suspicious, and knew that there was a war on.

There was no hope. Roger was under arrest.

Later he discovered that if he had made his attempt two or three hundred yards away on either side of the village he could have crossed without interference—indeed, he could have taken a troop of Boy Scouts across with him!

Roger learned from that experience. His second escape, made a year later, avoided most of the first escape's pitfalls. He planned it with his usual thoroughness.

During the guarded transport of kriegies by cattle car, the chances of escape were pretty good. This time Roger chose his companion carefully: Jack Zaphok, a brave and resourceful Czech fighter pilot. And Czechoslovakia was Roger's target. He wangled a way for them both to join a transport conveying POWs between Lübeck and Barth. The train moved slowly, and it often stopped for hours at a time during the nighttime journey. With help from the other POWs it was comparatively easy to pry up a few timbers in the car floor and slip through. Jack and he crossed country, knowing the branch-line station for which they were aiming. Their escape—so far— had gone unnoticed. No one was alerted. Their local train ride to the Czech border was uneventful. They had worn civilian clothes under their uniforms. Tim Walenn's forged documents were

251

excellent; Jack Zaphok's Czech was fluent. As two traveling businessmen they passed through border and customs controls without difficulty and took a train to Prague. Zaphok contacted the Czech underground, which provided ration cards and more forged papers. They were holed up in an apartment with a married couple. With care they could even wander around the city in that magical spring, with the war seemingly far away, the spires of the old town rising high against a blue sky, and the pink petals of the chestnut blossoms falling and drifting on the black waters of the Vltava River. They waited for contacts to be made that would pass them either through Yugoslavia or into Turkey.

That Reinhard Heydrich, Himmler's deputy, should be appointed as Reichsführer over Czechoslovakia at that time was part of the continuing saga of Roger Bushell's ill fortune. Heydrich above all others was the master architect of the Final Solution—the plan to exterminate the Jews of Europe. His task in Czechoslovakia was to induce the puppet Czech government to release the twenty-five Czech divisions for combat duty with the Wehrmacht and the Luftwaffe. He was on the point of achieving this ambition when Czech intelligence, in exile in England, were informed. Somehow this cozy collaboration between Czechoslovakia and Germany must be shattered. Heydrich must be assassinated. Such an unbelievable outrage against the omnipotent powers of the Führer would tear into their swollen nerve system.

Two Czech paratroopers, Jan Kubis and Josef Gabchik, were parachuted in by the RAF. They succeeded, and the fact that Reinhard Heydrich was the only important Nazi leader to be assassinated in the short history of that malignant regime is proof of their determination. As anticipated, the Nazi fury was overwhelming, the sheer barbarity of their reprisals unbelievable.

In the archives of the United Nations lies a heavy volume, one of the record books from Mauthausen concentration camp. Fifteen hundred names are neatly handwritten into its pages, and equally neatly inked through in red lines. They are some of the people who were executed during this frenzied orgy of killing. The two parachutists, along with a handful of others, were eventually betrayed and hunted to their deaths in a church crypt in Resslova Street, Prague. But even before that, the Nazis systematically searched street after street, herding innocent civilians into trucks, then transported them to camps for execution. One did not have to be a suspect; one simply had to be Czech. Those with the merest suspicion attached to them were shot, and all their neighbors were shot. Then came the turn of the relatives of those people, and the milkman, baker, and any others who had the slightest contact with them. But some greater example had to be made, had to be invented, so that all the world would understand that to lift a finger against Hitler and his empire was to strike at a new messiah.

The Germans chose Lidice, a largish village

about twenty miles from Prague. It possessed a nucleus of houses, a fine church, a school, and shops; many farms were nearby. The inhabitants had never heard of Jan Kubis or Josef Gabchik. At dawn the SS troops and bulldozers arrived. They collected the men and boys in a farmyard and machine-gunned them to death. They pushed the women and little girls into trucks and ferried them off to concentration camps. Perhaps five in all survived that ordeal.

Roger Bushell and Jack Zaphok listened to the news flashes over the radio, the shrill invective of the announcer: "This morning of May twenty-seventh at ten-thirty A.M. an attempt on the life of Reichsprotector Heydrich was made in Prague. A reward of ten million crowns is offered for the capture of the culprits. Whoever hides the criminals or gives them any help, or has any knowledge of their identity or description of their appearance and does not inform the authorities, will be shot with his whole family. This is by order of the Oberlandrat in Prague. Other announcements will be made in due course."

Roger's thoughts flew towards the husband, wife, and young son in whose house they were sheltering. They were pleasant, middle-class people, without any deep political motivations, who were helping because they thought it their duty, but now they were caught up in this maelstrom.

Roger said, "Jack, we've got to go. We've got to get out now!"

Jack Zaphok answered quietly. "Too late,

Roger. Every crossroads and street corner are sealed off by police or soldiers. You'd never get a hundred yards."

Roger said in some anguish, "It's too dangerous for our friends."

Jack Zaphok walked across the room and looked down through the curtains. "The Germans don't know we are here. They don't suspect we are here. They can't search every house in Prague."

But they could. And did.

Two days later the door was smashed down and the Gestapo arrested Roger Bushell and Jack Zaphok. Roger never saw Jack again; he later heard he had been tortured and shot. The young couple who had sheltered them were also executed, the son dispatched to a concentration camp.

The Gestapo eyed Roger with malevolence. They did not bother to listen to his story. They did not want to listen to anybody's story; they wanted bloody vengeance. An escaped prisoner of war? He was plainly an Allied agent, one of the conspirators who had planned the atrocity. So Roger Bushell was given the full interrogation treatment in a crowded prison, listening to the screams of the tortured, the dying cries of the innocent, the interrogations in bloodstained rooms. Roger Bushell never broke, and he never forgot. From that moment on he was consumed by a savage anger at the ghastliness of the entire debauched Nazi empire. They shipped him off to Berlin to the Gestapo cells there, and he learned more about their methods of intimidation.

Eventually a hint of caution crept into the interrogations. The knowledge that he was in Gestapo hands would by now have seeped through to the Luftwaffe. Roger, attempting to justify himself as a prisoner of war, had mentioned several well-known Luftwaffe senior officers, among them Kommandant von Lindeiner. These men had powerful friends: the Luftwaffe was still a cosseted service under the second most powerful man in the Reich—Hermann Goering. Was there any point in further exacerbating these relationships by executing this intransigent fellow? He was sent back to Sagan.

And now, defying them once more, he was on a train speeding towards the French border.

Flight Lieutenant Van Wymeersch, the French fighter pilot who had also been one of the first twenty out of Harry, had seen Roger Bushell in the station at Breslau, but had given no signal of recognition.

Traveling alone, Van Wymeersch deliberately took a series of short, circuitous journeys on local trains, deciding that it was a good way of avoiding detection. Then, when the hue and cry died down, he headed straight for Paris, where he would be reasonably safe.

He was arrested at Metz, just across the German border. The Gestapo plainclothes agents were very pleased with themselves; the leader could not keep his mouth shut. "*Ja*, your papers are perfect. Absolutely perfect," he chortled. "We know you terror-fliers are very clever at forging documents. But let me tell you that we are equally efficient in detecting them."

Van Wymeersch immediately realized that this was a nugget of information the forgery department back in Sagan would love to have.

"So," he said pleasantly. "Well, now that you have captured me, tell me how do you do that?"

The Gestapo agent was jubilant. "At this moment a national alert is in operation. You escaped from Sagan probably between midnight and five A.M. on Saturday morning. . . ."

Van Wymeersch nodded.

"By eight A.M. every railway station and every crossing point was alerted."

"But my papers were perfect. You've told me that."

"*Ja*, but our officials are cunning. Now every week, every day sometimes, we add a small and special mark to a document. Yours does not have it. So we are very suspicious and make further investigations."

"Very clever," said Van Wymeersch mildly.

"You are not the first we have caught. Two very clever ones we caught—soon after the escape. Smartly dressed in good suits, briefcases, perfect French and German. Business executives traveling back to Paris? Ha-ha—no special mark—we had them!"

Van Wymeersch felt a sinking feeling in his stomach. That description exactly fit Bushell and

257

Scheidhauer. He tried to keep the conversation flowing.

"Where are they now?"

The Gestapo agent's eyes were suddenly hard and alert. He realized he had said too much. "Where they will never escape again," he answered.

That afternoon Gertrude Schmidt was at her desk in Gestapo headquarters, Saarbrücken, when two tall, good-looking young men were shepherded past her, guarded by two Gestapo agents and the regional Gestapo chief, Obersturmbannführer Dr. Leopold Spann. She was an inexperienced secretary, but she realized that there was something strange about the two men; then she saw that their hands were cuffed in front of them. It frightened her.

Five minutes later Dr. Spann came out of the inner office, approached her desk, and shoved a slip of paper towards her. Two names were written on it. Gertrude was even more frightened. Everyone knew about Dr. Leopold Spann. He had a reputation for not delegating the execution activities of his department to underlings, but of carrying them out—with a certain satisfaction—himself.

He said coldly, "You will type out two death certificates in these names—immediately."

That order was so confusing that without thinking of what she was saying, she stuttered, "B-but, Kommissar—are the two men already dead?"

Dr. Spann's smile was as thin as a razor's edge. "Yes, one of them just died of appendicitis."

With a chill in her heart Gertrude began typing out the death certificates for the two men: Roger Bushell and Bernard Scheidhauer.

That evening driver-mechanic Walter Breithaupt answered the phone to hear the cold, clinical voice of Dr. Leopold Spann: "You will bring the car around to headquarters precisely one hour before dawn. We have recaptured two terror-fliers who escaped from Sagan, Stalag Luft III. We are to convey them to Mannheim and hand them over to the authorities there. Kriminalsekretär Emil Schulz will accompany us. Is that clear?"

"Yes, sir." The phone went dead.

Before dawn, Walter Breithaupt picked up Dr. Spann and Emil Schulz. Both wore their official Gestapo uniform. They drove to the Kripo prison where Roger Bushell and Bernard Scheidhauer had been kept for the night. Their names were high on the list that Dr. Spann had received from Berlin.

Breithaupt drove twenty-five miles along the autobahn in the direction of Mannheim. It was a cold morning and dawn was just breaking when Dr. Spann ordered Breithaupt to stop.

Walter Breithaupt's later testimony related what happened.

"Doctor Spann and Kriminalsekretär Schulz got out and lit cigarettes a few yards away from the car. They talked together for a few minutes.

259

I was left alone in the car with the two prisoners. They sat in the back but were quite powerless because they were handcuffed. Then Doctor Spann came back to the car and asked me to come with him. He said, 'Breithaupt, I have received an urgent teleprint order from Berlin Head Office to shoot both these terror-fliers. You are to say nothing about this incident to anyone, do you understand that? If you do you will be sentenced to death yourself. You don't have to be frightened. Just think of what happens to our wives and children killed during the air raids of these terror-fliers.'

"I went back to the car with Doctor Spann, who told the two prisoners that they could get out of the car to relieve themselves. They got out and went into the bushes to the right and rear of the car. Doctor Spann and Emil Schulz followed, each carrying a pistol, Spann saying as he walked behind them, 'You will be shot if you try to escape.'

"I stood next to the car and I could see everything. Both prisoners were just unbuttoning their trousers, while Spann and Schulz stood a meter behind them with their pistols in their hands. Spann gave a sign, and Spann and Schulz each fired one shot at the same time in the neck of the prisoners. Both prisoners dropped to the earth at the same time."

So died the brave and gallant French pilot Flight Lieutenant Bernard Scheidhauer, and Squadron Leader Roger Bushell, a man of prodigious and uncommon talent, extraordinary leadership capacity, and enduring courage.

And now, beside that deserted road, there was more work to be done: bodies to be disposed of; documents to be forged and falsified; records to be tampered with; ashes to be neatly packed and dispatched. But everywhere the assassins would leave small traces of guilt and witnesses with long memories.

Chapter Sixteen

THAT THE GESTAPO DID not immediately carry out the *Aktion Kugel* directive against Wings Day, Johnny Dodge, Jimmy James, and Sydney Dowse is not all that surprising. As hostages they had a certain value; they might be useful; they could be held for a while—just in case.

More than that, they were now safely incarcerated in Sachsenhausen concentration camp, from which escape was totally impossible, and where in the usual course of events one died quickly from starvation or brutality. Gestapo Chief Anton Kaindl, the present camp commander, had been appointed because his predecessor—a certifiable madman—had seen as his Nazi duty the elimination of every prisoner who entered his gates. This was plainly a waste of useful manpower with nearby factories needing labor. Kaindl improved rations and abolished the evil "Kapo" system, by which the most brutal criminal prisoners were entrusted with keeping "law and order"—thus instituting a reign of terror without any check. Kaindl, being Austrian, and musical, even installed a loudspeaker system throughout the camp so that classical music could be relayed from Radio Berlin, and lift any spirits the prisoners had left.

From Sonderlager A the Sagan four could hear it quite clearly.

In Sachsenhausen and other concentration camps not too far away, the Germans had collected a large group of the most important and famous people in Europe: princes of the blood, statesmen, prime ministers, presidents, dictators, clergymen, field marshals, and generals, including German generals and high-ranking officers who had shown the slightest sign of disagreement with the Führer. They were hostages, at first intended to appear in show trials when the conquest of Europe and the Soviet Union was complete, and thus help illustrate to the world the righteousness of the Nazi cause; but now, as the inevitability of Nazi defeat grew closer, becoming human bargaining chips when the cards were really down.

Compared to the main camp, Sonderlager A was sane and civilized, with decent accommodations for the inmates, reasonable food, privileges of exercise and recreation in the camp grounds, newspapers, books, and the chance to converse quite openly with other inmates. Wings, Johnny Dodge, James, and Dowse knew, however, that whatever sheen the Nazis tried to put upon this place, it was still a prison camp. There were high walls, barbed wire, electrified fences, no vision of the outside world, and inside, armed guards constantly patrolling with their dogs.

They had all heard of concentration camps—after all, camps had existed in Germany from the time the Nazis came to power in 1933. But they had never been inside such a place, had never in any nightmare imagined what went on there. Now they knew. Now, as they were marched into the main camp for their weekly showers, they could see for themselves. In Sagan they had occasionally seen work parties of half-starved Jews, Russians, and Poles, but nothing to compare with this! Hundreds, thousands of men with shaven heads, sunken eyes, and matchstick limbs; living corpses attired in striped pajamas. Posts to hang men by their arms in excruciating pain, whipping posts, gallows, crematoriums. Vicious guards.

Jimmy James and Sydney Dowse shared a room. Their conversation was to the point.

Sydney said, "We're not staying in this bloody place, are we?"

Jimmy James said, "You can say that again. We are not staying here."

"They think they've got us terrorized like those poor buggers locked up in the main camp."

"Which could be an advantage, because they won't think we have the cheek to attempt to escape."

"What do you think—a tunnel?"

"We broke out in the hundredth tunnel out of Sagan. Let's get out on the first one in Sachsenhausen."

Sydney grinned, "Under whose bed?"

"Toss," said Jimmy.

Jimmy lost. They pulled back his bed. Their experienced eyes had already seen that the edges of their hut went down to ground level. If the builders had left a reasonable space between floor-boards and soil, it would be a great place to store excavated earth. But a wire inserted through a crack in the floor disappointed them.

"Damn," said Sydney, "no more than six inches." They tried other soundings around the room: it was the same. Soil dispersal, as at Sagan, was going to be a problem.

"At least it's solid earth," said Jimmy. "It won't need shoring up like Sagan sand." He paused and said, "These SS guards aren't going to care much for our tunnel."

The Gestapo and their elite SS divisions were responsible for all concentration camp security. To impress the inmates of Sonderlager A with the ferocity of their purpose, they had hung a series of metal shields painted with their *Totenkopf* insignia—a grinning skull and crossbones—at intervals along the wire, looking inwards at the prisoners.

"To hell with them," said Sydney. "How far do you think we'll need to tunnel to get under the wall and beyond the guards and dogs?"

"About a hundred feet."

"Jesus, that's almost a third the length of Harry."

Jimmy smiled. "And with only two diggers. When do we tell Wings and the Dodger?"

"Not yet. The fewer who know, the better. Around here gossip is the main occupation."

They were soon to hear two pieces of news that could never be described as gossip. The first was

265

an article in the July 23, 1944, issue of the Nazi newspaper *Völkischer Beobachter,* angrily contesting two speeches that British Foreign Minister Anthony Eden had made in the House of Commons regarding the deaths of fifty officer aircrew. Eden had said:

It is abundantly clear that none of these officers met his death in the course of making his escape from Stalag Luft III or while resisting capture. The Gestapo's contention that the wearing of civilian clothes by an escaping prisoner of war deprives him of the Prisoners of War Convention is entirely without foundation in international law and practice. From the facts there is, in H.M. Government's view, only one possible conclusion. These prisoners of war were murdered at some undefined place or places . . . at some date or dates unknown. H.M. Government must therefore record their solemn protest against these cold-blooded acts of butchery. They will never cease in the efforts to collect the evidence to identify all those responsible. They are firmly resolved that these foul criminals shall be tracked down to the last man, wherever they may take refuge. When the war is over they will be brought to exemplary justice.

The Gestapo reaction had been one of arrogant dismissal. The fifty officers concerned had committed crimes for which they had been executed;

they had been cremated, their urns labeled and dispatched back to the camp from which they had escaped. Their viewpoint was echoed in the *Völkischer Beobachter*, under the headline "ENERGETIC REPUDIATION OF EDEN":

In March this year English POWs broke out in large numbers from different camps in Germany. The measures employed for bringing back the fugitives were completely successful. It became apparent that an action that had been planned partly abroad had been frustrated. In bringing back the prisoners who had fled from one camp (Luft III) the German security forces were repeatedly forced, because of resistance and attempts to re-escape, to make use of firearms. A number of POWs lost their lives.

The Reich government informed the English government of these incidents through Switzerland, which acted as neutral intermediary. In addition it held out the prospects of a final report at the close of the searches. In the meantime the English foreign minister, in a declaration before the House of Commons, did not hesitate to make the monstrous assertion that the British POWs had been murdered in Germany. In a communication made by the Reich government to the English via Switzerland, this unqualified accusation is most sharply repudiated. . . .

Jimmy James and Sydney Dowse could hardly believe it was true. Such an atrocity was inconceivable! Maybe there was some mistake? Yet both remembered those Gestapo thugs arriving at dawn to take away parties of their friends. There was not much conversation between them for the next twenty-four hours.

The second piece of news—good this time—concerned an Allied invasion on the coast of Normandy, in which the heroic panzer divisions were allegedly hurling the American and British troops back into the sea. The reports became completely unbelievable as other names and military alibis cropped up: strategic withdrawals from Caen, heroic escapes through the Falaise Gap, defenders in Cherbourg in complete control of the port.

By this time Jimmy and Sydney had discovered that the space under the floorboards in the corridor outside their room was at least twelve inches deep. They could dig channels under the floorboards of their own room towards it and have plenty of room for soil disposal. They had now told Wings and Johnny Dodge about their enterprise, and both were in full agreement with the plan. They agreed it was better for them to act as watchers rather than diggers.

One morning Sydney decided he would not join the others in their weekly shower trip. They returned in time to hear a shouting match between him and one of the guards. The guard was pointing at the painted shields of the *Totenkopf* guards and shrieking invectives. Sydney had ingeniously extracted them from their positions, and turned them around so that they faced outwards towards the SS guards' quarters, reversing the threat.

Commandant Kaindl summoned Wings Day, as senior officer, to his office. In their first interview, Kaindl had been cold and contemptuous: "You have been sent here because the Luftwaffe cannot stop you escaping. We can. Here there is no escape. Our guards cannot be bribed. Touch the electrified wire and you are dead. Guards patrol night and day and shoot to kill." Now he droned on in a flat voice: "In this matter of a junior officer insulting the *Totenkopf* SS, he could be punished by immediate execution." Wings knew then that Sydney was safe. If execution had been intended Sydney would already have vanished, the sentence having been speedily carried out. No, Kaindl's intentions were to parade his power, to show his ability to control by ruthless terror. Wings Day, through his years of captivity, had met quite a few like Kaindl, and seethed internally at his powerlessness to respond in kind.

But he did know one way of reacting. When he got back to his small group his sole comment was, "Little bastard! Let's speed up the work on the tunnel."

By this time they had received a new and unusual recruit to their endeavors.

It was July 14, 1944: the new arrival walked down from the wicket gate towards their huts. He looked like something out of the cast of a desert adventure movie. He wore a British khaki shirt and shorts. He was of medium height, stocky and powerful, with fair, cropped hair. No one could doubt the determination of the bristly moustache or the bright blue eyes or the lieutenant colonel's insignia on his shoulder tabs. He stuck out a firm, brown hand. "Jack Churchill. Number Two Commando," he snapped. "Didn't know you chaps were here. I've been cooped up round the corner in one of those bloody houses next door to that Austrian chap Schuschnigg—understand he was their prime minister once. Kept throwing them messages but only got a smile back in return."

"Mad Jack" had arrived. His reaction to their plan was, "Escape! Of course we've got to escape. Can't stay in a rathole like this. Now I've been thinking. If we could get to the top of that wall —traverse along the top—drop off—"

"Jack," Wings said pleasantly, "you'd drop off fried. About a million volts goes through that wire along the top."

"Oh, is that so? Got to try something else then. Did I ever tell you the story of how when we went in at Anzio, and we were penned in, I captured that Italian village single-handed?"

Jack was thirty-eight years old. At an early age he had decided that life was for living, not making a living. Sandhurst Royal Military College had turned him into a professional, a commissioned officer, but he found peacetime soldiering boring, resigned his commission, and toured Europe—

France in particular—playing his bagpipes. He liked bagpipes; he was good on them.

When the war came he returned to his regiment. Transferred to commandos, he found himself on a mountainside in Yugoslavia attacking a well-dug-in German parachute brigade. He was cut off, under annihilating machine-gun fire, and decided that the only way he could get back a message to the reinforcements at the bottom—with no wireless transmitter serviceable—was by bagpipes. The astonished Germans a couple of hundred yards higher up heard the sound of bagpipes played by Lieutenant Colonel Jack Churchill, lying on his back in a shell hole. The words to the tune were: "Will ye nae come back again?"

At the bottom of the mountain they did hear the message, but before they could counterattack the war was over for Jack Churchill. He said, "When I saw that stream of scarlet tracer bullets arching over our heads, I knew they'd fastened on our position and were marking us—the target—for mortar fire. Manners, who was commanding, got a bad wound, blood gushing from his femoral artery. Another badly wounded man was screaming his head off fifty yards away. I got to Manners and was trying to stuff a field dressing into his pumping wound. Feathers, another officer, slipped across to help. A bullet killed him immediately and his body slumped across mine. And then another tremendous bang, and that was it!"

As far as anyone knew, Jack Churchill was dead.

A couple of hours later, German boots and hands, prodding to see who was dead or alive on the mountainside, found Jack. He had a bad headache. The shrapnel or bullets that had knocked him unconscious had bent down the rim of his steel helmet like a limp pancake.

"Of course they were jubilant they'd got me," said Jack. "I had a very good but bloody stupid orderly, who was always having trouble collecting my undershorts from the laundry. So, to be certain he always got the right pairs back, he stenciled every pair with black indelible-ink letters about two inches high: 'Major Churchill' [his previous rank]. So the Germans saw that and sent up rockets of joy. They'd heard that Major Randolph Churchill was operating somewhere in Yugoslavia, so obviously they thought they'd captured Winston Churchill's only son. Big story in the German newspapers. They looked after me like a little treasure. Gave me the best bedroom in the house. God knows why they've demoted me to join you lot!"

They all laughed at Jack's story. "We promise not to tell them you're a fraud," said Wings with a grin.

The Dowse-James tunnel moved out towards the wire, and Jack Churchill joined the team.

They had no illusions about what they were doing. If they managed to escape and were then recaptured, it was certain they would not live very long. Gestapo anger would boil over. Their ruthlessness

272

had already been exhibited in the shooting of the fifty officer escapers from Sagan.

Wings had taken each member of his small group individually around the compound after learning of those murders, pointing out the dangers of going out through another tunnel. They would be totally vulnerable. The Sagan fifty were known to the Swiss authorities, and to their own comrades left behind in Stalag Luft III. As far as the outside world knew, the four of them in Sachsenhausen had disappeared; no one knew they were in a concentration camp. All the Gestapo had to do was slip them across into the main camp and like thousands of others they would disappear— "up the chimney."

"No one will think any less of you if you want to pull out," Wings concluded.

No one wanted to pull out. All felt that somehow news of this dreadful place, and this malevolent regime calling itself the Gestapo, should reach the outside world. Why wait here like helpless cattle for the Gestapo to kill them whenever they felt inclined? Let them all get out, and maybe one or two would be left alive to bear witness. Determinedly Sydney and Jimmy went on digging. Johnny Dodge and Wings took turns as lookout; Jack Churchill was earth-disposal officer. His memories of those days are vivid:

"That beautiful September weather drove us all bloody mad. There was the tunnel all ready and waiting, only the last few feet to break through. Jimmy and Sydney had driven under the wall into a new compound they were building next to ours, and we knew we could get over the wall of *that* compound because we could see they'd left a ladder behind.

"But that September weather never stopped. Sunshine. Blue skies. No wind. No rain. And without that we had a problem. Our compound was enclosed by a barbed-wire fence, then a small corridor of grass, then the high wall with the electric wire on top. The guards patrolled that corridor twenty-four hours a day, with nasty big dogs. At intervals they had these air-raid shelters which went about four feet up in the air and four feet down into the ground. In good weather at night the dogs would sit on top of the air-raid shelters, so if and when we came out under the big wall, they were bound to hear us or smell us. But in bad weather, particularly if it rained—they would duck into the shelters with their masters, and go to sleep four feet under the ground. Which would suit us. Beyond that electrified wall was a grassy strip and an asphalt road. We aimed to come up in the grassy strip.

"September twenty-third. Great day. Misty, overcast, cold and raining. Perfect—escape that night. Our two Italian orderlies had even prepared a little celebration supper. They knew all about it; they'd given Wings Day and Sydney Dowse a civilian suit each to escape in.

"We'd made our escape plans weeks before. Johnny Dodge was going by himself and heading west, hoping to hole up somewhere and wait for the Allied troops to arrive. Wings, because he had a bad knee, very swollen, was teaming up with Sydney and they were going by train to Berlin. Jimmy James and I were hard-arsing across country up towards Stettin to try and make a ship to Sweden."

Wings Day had heard about a good contact in Berlin from Andy Walsh, an Irish prisoner whom the Germans had tried unsuccessfully to make an agent of theirs. Andy told Wings Day, "Herr Fullert, sir, he's into the black market in a big way. I was billeted in Berlin while the Germans trained me in sabotage. Fullert owns a fleet of trucks. Loads up with electrical equipment for the Atlantic Wall they're building along the coast of France. Comes back stuffed with contraband: champagne, brandy, wine, cheese, butter. All the palms at every border post have been properly greased, and no one's going to interfere with one of Hitler's pet projects—the Atlantic Wall. 'If you ever want to escape, Andy,' he told me, 'just say the word, and we'll stow you away in one of the trucks and in France, hand you over to the French Resistance.' Fullert lives in a suburb of Berlin—Mahlsdorf. I'll give you his address."

Wings told Sydney Dowse of the conversation. Sydney liked the idea. "With a bit of luck we should be under the wall and running by eleven o'clock at night. That will give us time, won't it?"

Wings knew a lot about Berlin after his long stay there the first time. "Sure. We make for the Oranienburg station near here. Catch a suburban train to Berlin's Friedrichstrasse, and another suburban train back out to Mahlsdorf. Walsh has promised me a sketch map showing how to find Fullert's house."

Jack Churchill continues the story: "At ten o'clock we're all locked up, and off we go. Sydney first, Jimmy next, and me bringing up the rear.

"Sydney had first go at breaking through to the surface. Chopped away at the overhead dirt until he was through about two feet. No sky! Another two feet with the earth and stones falling down over his head. No sky! Maybe he was right and Jimmy had dug us down towards Australia! We were now standing on a pile of rubble to reach the roof and still we couldn't hit the surface. Quiet panic—where the hell were we? Sydney was standing on Jimmy's shoulders jabbing away with our table knife, and then clank—bang! And Sydney said, 'Hell, we've gone too far—we're under that concrete road.'

"That was a bad moment. There in the dark we had a sort of conference, just like a group of submariners stuck in a submarine two hundred feet down.

"Sydney said, 'I think we should go back about five feet and see if we can come up in the grassy strip this time.' Hell, Jimmy and Sydney had been sweating blood carving ten feet of soil from over their heads and now they had to start all over again. Another ten feet and they might find one of those bloody dogs sniffing down the hole!

"Another problem was that we were filling our

tunnel full of debris falling from overhead. I said, 'I'll go back and tell Wings and Johnny Dodge what's going on.' So back I went through the rabbit hole. I began to feel more like a bloody mole than a lieutenant colonel in the commandos, and all the way through I'm bringing earth down onto my head and trying not to think of what it would be like if a hefty fall took place.

"Wings and Johnny D. looked serious but not worried. I said, 'Trouble is, time's passing. It's now three in the morning. We can't break out in *daylight!*'

"Wings said, 'It's now or never. Press ahead. Go for it.'

"I agreed with that, so back went Mole Churchill, and by the grace of God, Sydney had got the table knife through to the surface. We could see the darker gray of the sky and smell the real air. So back I went again to tell the other two, and Jimmy and Sydney followed me to clean up. We cleaned as well as we could because time was now of the essence. We grabbed our escape packs and struggled through. Wings and Johnny D., the last two out, had a damned hard time because the tunnel was now collapsing. When I got out, Sydney already had the ladder against the outer wall of the next compound, so Jimmy and I hauled Wings out first, and hauled him clear. It took all three of us to get the Dodger out; he was really buried in loose earth.

"Then we're all over the second wall and gripping hands in quick goodbyes, and the Dodger is brushing himself off and saying brightly, 'Now, Jack, tell me, in which direction are you proceeding?' I say, 'For God's sake, Dodger, Jimmy and I made our plans weeks ago!'

"There we are with dawn breaking outside one of the most terrible camps in the world, and the Dodger's about to have a polite conversation about points of the compass. I say to Johnny D. very firmly, 'Johnny, see that light in the sky over there? That's the east! The sun's rising. The west is the other way. Keep your back to the east and don't stop walking. Meet you in the Berkeley Grill in a month's time.'

"And, of course, the Dodger did exactly that. Walked away into the dawn, probably whistling his head off, just looking for someone to start a discussion with. The dawn rose and he passed a field where a lot of French POWs were starting work: they were still wearing bits of French blue-gray uniforms. So he walks across to them, smiles, and says, *'Je suis un Anglais,'* and they take him for one of these bloody insane Englishmen, not realizing that actually he's a bloody insane American. And the French prisoners are naturally horrified that he's making these remarks in a loud voice, because they have a nasty German NCO in charge of them—fortunately at that moment he's being nasty in the next field. But the Dodger goes on in his best French, 'I understand you have a very good French Resistance system.' And they say, *M'sieu,* we have a very good French Resistance movement in *France*. This is *Germany!* Now if you will step this way. . . .'

"They took him over to a mound of turnips they were building up, and hid him inside, buried him in turnips so to speak, probably popping one in his mouth to prevent him singing 'The Star-Spangled Banner.' They promised him they'd come back and rescue him that night. Johnny D. goes straight to sleep because he's been awake all night!"

Jack Churchill's summing-up of Johnny Dodge's escape is romantic, but not accurate. Certainly he met up with the French, who hid him in barns and pigsties, cow sheds and cottages, protecting and feeding him at the risk of their own lives, until eventually someone spotted him, betrayed him, and the German police arrived.

Meanwhile, Wings Day and Sydney Dowse had caught the 6:00 A.M. train to Berlin. There were no checks at the ticket barrier for the local trains, which was lucky, for by this time the *Totenkopf* SS would be aware that four individuals had escaped from Sachsenhausen—the terrible camp from which there was no escape. Wings wondered if the icy look always apparent behind Kommandant Kaindl's glasses had changed to a glare of anger yet.

The Mahlsdorf train left promptly at 8:15. By nine they had reached the drab, sprawling suburb. The house they were looking for sat on a long straight road that reached towards the countryside. Andy Walsh need not have bothered to draw them such an accurate map: there was simply a long corridor of gutted houses. Not a roof remained, not a single person stirred. It was a derelict area. They identified the house and eyed its decay; it had plainly not been habitable for at least a year. They looked at each other and said nothing. The house next door looked as if it contained a dry cellar. Wings's swollen knee was giving him hell again. "Let's go in, have a bite, and rest for a bit, eh?" he said.

"Okay," said Sydney. All their bright plans were shattered. Now they had to think again. But there was to be no time for second thoughts.

An old lady living in one of the cellars in that gloomy road had seen them pass, and enter the cellar. These days there were villains and murderers everywhere. As soon as Wings Day and Sydney Dowse had settled down inside, she hopped out and scurried along to the warden at the nearest air-raid shelter. He telephoned the police. Twenty minutes later Wings and Sydney were looking down the barrels of the policemen's revolvers.

They were taken to the local police station and interrogated. Both claimed they were escaped air force officers from Sagan, Stalag Luft III. Yes, they had been imprisoned in Sachsenhausen, but they were RAF from Sagan. The civilian police heard this with some interest. They were under the impression that all escapers in that mass escape had been dealt with by the Gestapo. Sydney

Dowse also gave them something else to think about by announcing loudly that not only were they from Sagan, and prisoners of war, but that he had written and mailed letters to the Swiss Red Cross in Geneva, and to the Luftwaffe commandant in Sagan, Stalag Luft III, and to other addresses that he was not prepared to divulge.

The Kripo had already heard the radio announcements about the escape of dangerous prisoners from a German prison. That afternoon they were taken under escort to Berlin and the next day picked up by four Gestapo thugs. They were separated, and Wings wondered if he was going to make it back even to Sachsenhausen this time. Finally he recognized the wall and the main gate. But he did not recognize the low brick building or the dimly lit corridor lined with cells. His cell was stinking and dreadful: a pile of dirty blankets on the floor, a lavatory bucket in one corner, a short, heavy-link chain, cemented to the middle of the floor. When he was handcuffed and linked by one ankle to the chain, the door was slammed behind him. The place was called Zellenbau—the death block. The Gestapo had decided that those with but a short time to live did not deserve or need comfort.

Jimmy James and Jack Churchill shot off in a northwesterly direction, passing quickly through a built-up suburban area, skirting houses, sliding over fences, crawling across lawns. They reached their objective, the railway station at Oranienburg, used by Sachsenhausen personnel in their travels to and from Berlin. But unlike Wings and Sydney, they were not traveling by train.

Earlier Jack had proudly shown Jimmy his map. "Swiped it out of Major General Bessanov's atlas. [General Bessanov was one of the prized Russian prisoners.] Our needs are greater than his. Look: here's Oranienburg; up there, on the sea, is Rostock, about a hundred and fifty miles as the train flies. First boat home, just in time to meet the Dodger at the Berkeley Grill."

"First-class?" said Jimmy with a grin.

"First-class."

Overhead they could hear the distant drone of aircraft.

"A lot of people still at war," said Jimmy.

They followed the railway tracks for about twelve miles before the increasing daylight made them seek shelter in a small coppice. There they slept and waited for night. And so it went. When they heard a train approaching they dived for cover down the embankment or under a hedge. On the fourth night they arrived at a small station with shunting sidings. They found a "sleeping nest" in the undergrowth nearby, and Jack went off to do a reconnaissance. He returned with rutabagas, carrots, turnips, and potatoes. He found a rusty can that held water, and produced a vegetable stew. He had also collected elderberries, which he designated as "the fruit course."

"There were small disagreements," said Jack. "I was ten years older and a bit more up on living outdoors than Jimmy. Jimmy would say, 'It's too dangerous to have a fire.' And I would say, 'Of course we can have a fire. We're in woodland and no one can see the bloody smoke.' And after the third day Jimmy decided that smoke was okay. So we always had vegetable soup, because if you're hard-arsing you need a little hot nourishment. It was September—harvesttime—and there was a lot of sense in our following the railway lines, because railway workers all over the world love to cultivate the spare pieces of land which you find around railway stations and along their lines."

They made good progress to Waren, a largish town on their route, and decided to take a chance by walking straight through. They looked like tramps. So did a lot of other people. No one stopped them, and they rejoined the railway track outside the town. In the darkness they reached a small station perched on a high embankment. It looked empty and they decided they would refill their oil bottle from a signal lamp there. They had just started when they saw an old man watching them. As he seemed to be alone, Jimmy gave him a cheerful *"Guten Abend"* and he went away. Jimmy had a sense of unease, but Jack was determined to fill the bottle. It was a mistake. Out of the darkness rushed two large men armed with heavy staves. Jimmy reacted, grabbing his pack and taking a run and a jump down the embankment. Churchill, still fiddling with his oil bottle, was clutched by one of the men while the other beat him with his stave.

Jimmy dashed back up the embankment to the rescue. One of the heavies was holding Jack while the other got in several punishing blows. But Jack, twisting and turning, now managed to twist his captor into a position to take three or four powerful blows from the stave himself. Then Jimmy, who had played good football back at Sagan, went in hard at the man with the stave, at the same time grabbing one of the handles of Jack's bag, which the man had been clutching. Now Jimmy was receiving the blows that were intended for the colonel. Jimmy fought furiously, dragging his assailant back towards the edge of the platform and the embankment. With a last major wrench, Jimmy tumbled backwards and rolled head over heels down the embankment, taking the bag with him. The diversion enabled Jack to pull himself free from the other man, and with a leap and a roll he was sprinting away with Jimmy into the darkness. They were not pursued.

They stumbled into a thick wood, then found a grassy glade by the side of a small lake hemmed in by autumn-colored trees. Dawn was breaking, and the morning sun was warm. They examined their injuries. Jack had a colossal black eye, scalp wounds, and a lot of big bruises, but he brushed off such things as mere inconveniences. They bathed and shaved in the lake, then slept in the sun.

The next night they tried a new routine and decided to walk across country; they found themselves marooned in acres of freshly ploughed land that clung to their shoes. Returning to the railway tracks, they moved onwards at their normal speed, and suddenly the air was salty on their lips. They were getting close; they could smell the sea. But a little breeze moved in the mist, and they lost their bearings. They returned to the fields again and found themselves moving through a ghostly column of figures: a straggling line of Polish women, slave laborers moving off to work. Before they knew what was happening, the German overseer was at their side. Who were they? What were they doing? He did not believe they were French workers going to a local farm. But he wasn't very bright. He told a fourteen-year-old boy to escort them back to his headquarters for examination. The column disappeared into the mist; they followed the boy. The fog thickened. Jack stared down the uncertain youth, saying, "Thanks for showing us the way, young man," and both Jimmy and he took off at top speed. They thought the youth was quite pleased to have lost them.

When they seemed to have put a safe distance between themselves and the German overseer, they slowed to a walk. As the fog was clearing and the sky brightening, they found shelter. They did not know that the German radio was constantly broadcasting descriptions of the two English desperadoes who were still on the loose.

The overseer later realized their importance and contacted the police. A search was mounted. Jimmy and Jack were awakened that afternoon by voices and saw the barrels of three rifles pointing down at them. They belonged to members of the Volksturm, the local Home Guard. The guards were quite agreeable, pleased that they had captured two British officers rather than notoriously savage Russian runaways. They took them to an inn and bought them mugs of excellent beer. But conviviality vanished when six armed Gestapo thugs arrived in a large Mercedes.

The Gestapo left them for the night in the Güstrow jail. Jack, after fourteen days in the rain and cold, considered the night in the Güstrow jail the best sleep he had ever had in his life. Jimmy James always slept like the proverbial baby.

Like Wings and Sydney, they were placed in death cells. Johnny Dodge was out for a month —the longest of all. He joined them on death row two weeks later.

Chapter Seventeen

WINGS DAY LOOKED AROUND his cell in the death block—four by eight feet, the only light from a small barred grille high up near the ceiling. It looked and felt like a place where—knowing his time was up—a man would wait to hear the hangman's footsteps.

Wings's main fear, and it was very real, was how he would behave when he reached this point. They had taken a considered risk; they had figuratively kicked the *Totenkopf* in the groin, and it was plain they would be shown no mercy.

In Berlin, at the central office of the Kripo, Inspector Peter Mohr could now concur with that opinion. He had just been handed a secret telex message. It came from Heinrich Himmler, head of the Gestapo, and informed Mohr of the escape of five officers from what was supposed to be the absolutely secure camp of Sachsenhausen. The order stated that upon capture the five officers were to be subjected to interrogation under torture, and then executed. The commandant of Sachsenhausen, his second-in-command, the duty officer on the night of the escape, and the architect who designed Sonderlager A were also to be executed.

Wings saw two guards enter the cell. That there

were two was unusual. He was led down the dark corridor and brought to a halt at a door on the left. A pulse beat in his head. The door was pushed open. Wings half expected to see a guillotine or a hangman's noose. His previous months in the Sonderlager had made him aware of such eventualities. Instead, with an overwhelming sense of relief, he saw a man sitting behind a table. He was obviously an interrogator, and Wings Day had met many of those. The man indicated a chair, and Wings sat down facing him.

Wings realized then how precious life had become. Any misery was better than the final curtain of execution. Interrogation after his recent thoughts was like a reprieve.

He hoped his face showed none of his emotions. The man opposite him was about forty years old, and—surprisingly—not in Gestapo uniform. Nevertheless the face was harsh, emotionless. It was also scarred with saber cuts. Only later did Wings realize they must have been inflicted in duels staged at Heidelberg University, where the Nazis had resurrected these grotesque charades of macho courage. A Heidelberg scar was worn just as proudly by a German male as any degree conferred by that old and beautiful university.

Wings observed his interrogator closely. After all, in a minor capacity as an RAF officer, he had attended many selection boards and committees of inquiry, and knew some of the tricks. One of the oldest was silence. This interrogator knew that: he looked at Wings and said nothing. Wings noted the short-cropped hair, the artistic and well-kept hands, the large signet ring.

"You are the senior officer of this party, are you not, Wing Commander Day?"

Wings took his time replying to that. He, Sydney Dowse, Jimmy James, and the Dodger had discussed the problem of interrogation a hundred times; they had even indoctrinated Jack Churchill. The ground rules were simple. You told the truth when the story could be checked; you invented a feasible story when it could not.

But Sydney Dowse and he had been at liberty for not quite twelve hours. Had the others been recaptured yet? He sensed danger in the question.

"Not necessarily."

"But you will admit that you were in command of your party?"

"Totally untrue. We escaped as individuals and split up. Two of the officers who escaped with me from Sachsenhausen were of equivalent rank. They were not even from the same service. Army men."

The interrogator was writing all this down, and at least he was being reasonably polite. He addressed Wings as "Herr Oberst," thus acknowledging his proper rank. But Wings was not reassured. He knew he had to exist from minute to minute and hour to hour. His sole comfort was that being alive to answer questions was far preferable to facing a noose.

Wings also thought that, these days, the war was frequently a confrontation between two men, often with one handicapped by lower rank or captivity. He was in that latter situation now. He lacked sleep, the pain in his swollen knee was constant, and deep down was the certainty of execution. Why should he offer any resistance, or even bother to answer any questions, if the outcome was to be the same? Why should he have to concentrate with such fierce intensity? But he knew the answer to that. There was always a tiny seed of hope and optimism. Thousands—even millions—of men and women had had no alternative but to face death. Their only choice was the way they went to their death: screaming, protesting, or with dignity. Wings drew in a long, deep breath. When he got down to it, *that* was his primary anxiety. Whether anyone knew about his death was not the point at issue. Could *he* face it with courage and dignity?

The interrogator put down his pen, and his dark eyes flicked up, "You escaped from Sachsenhausen on the night of September twenty-third together with Flight Lieutenant Dowse?"

"Yes."

"You caught a train to the Friedrichstrasse station in Berlin?"

"Yes."

"You had contacts in Berlin?"

"No."

"Then why did you choose to catch a train to Berlin?"

"It was the first train to arrive at six o'clock in

the morning. We wanted to get as far away from Sachsenhausen as possible."

"What did you do then?"

"We caught another train in a different direction. As I say, anywhere to put distance between ourselves and this camp."

"But you got off at Mahlsdorf. Why did you get off at Mahlsdorf?"

"Simply to confuse the enemy. To go in a different direction."

Wings knew he had to skate very carefully now. He had to protect Andy Walsh and the Fullert connection.

"But you only stayed on that train for forty-five minutes. You were not very far from Berlin. You had a contact there?"

"No."

"Herr Oberst. You go to Berlin and then make a side journey to Mahlsdorf. Doesn't that strike you as very odd?"

"Not really. We had escaped from a narrow dark hole. We were exhausted, hungry, and cold. We had no sense of direction. A small bombed-out town like Mahlsdorf would be a good place to hide."

"Or a good place to meet your contact."

"There was no contact."

"Perhaps your contact had once lived in that bombed-out town?"

Wings knew this was getting too close for comfort.

"I have been a prisoner of war since 1939. My

291

only contacts have been with POWs in camps. How could I possibly have contacts—as you call them? You are trying to make your evidence fit your facts—not the truth of events. I would suggest that two escapers who only manage to spend eleven hours of freedom are totally lacking in contacts of any sort."

"Herr Oberst. The dossier detailing your first escape from Sagan Luft III informs me that you spent quite a long period of time in Berlin. You are asking me to accept the idea that you existed without money, papers, or identity in the capital city of Germany for that period?"

"We moved around from place to place," said Wings wearily. "We stayed up nights. We were on the run. Who is likely to give a British prisoner of war a night's rest in the capital city of Germany?"

This time the pen remained poised, the eyes steady.

"British intelligence, perhaps? A saboteurs' organization? A group of partisans?"

"No," said Wings. Now he knew where the interrogation was leading. One slipup here and he was done for.

The questioning went on hour after hour until the first light of the September dawn eased through the barred window. The interrogator carefully screwed the cap back on his pen and shuffled his notes into a pile. Wings realized the other man was just as tired as he was. The guards took him back to his cell and manacled him again.

The door closed. Wings knew he had made it at least for a few more hours. Rationally he knew that their taunting humiliation of the SS by daring to escape had closed their last avenue of survival. This interrogation was probably one last hypocritical subterfuge in legal justification. He was aware that his life hung by a spidery thread. It was fortunate he did not know just how tenuous that thread was—that upon the result of this interrogation certainly hung his own life, and probably the lives of all of them.

Wings Day later wrote:

"As they pushed me back into the cell, and fastened my right ankle to that obscene post embedded in the floor, the sun was glowing through the window. I fell asleep. A peace destroyed in what seemed to be only seconds, the door reopening and a sudden return of fear . . . a fear which slowly subsided as I realized it was only 5:00 A .M reveille; time to take your night bucket down to ablutions and wash. A return then to sweep out your cell; your privileges as a POW all gone; now you are a common criminal. Food: thin soup, a bit of bread, smelly cheese, or sausage; that to last you twenty-four hours.

"Through the cell window I saw a circle of shaven-headed prisoners circling the small square. I waved my handcuffed hands at them—anything to make human contact. Nobody waved back; only the guards threatened and shook their fists at me. Later I learnt that they were all SS awaiting trial, awaiting execution, undergoing sentences for serious offences. The SS had to remain irreproach-able, the elite; a serious crime and you were ex-ecuted." This reinforced Wings's awareness that to mock the shock troops of the Führer's glorious empire was a crime of similar seriousness. The Nazis executed more than 30,000 of their own troops for desertion or other offenses during the war.

"Midnight again . . . the cell door opens with such a quiet swiftness that it is a terrible shock to your system. The swiftness with which the ankle manacle is unfastened, the way you are yanked to your feet, thrust through the door . . .

"And the dreadful silence of that corridor. Dark, tiny lights, a sense of blackness. That si-lence was always my most terrible impression of Zellenbau. It must have been specially sound-proofed; the floor was black rubber; the trolleys had rubber wheels; there was never any shouting or raised voices; conversation was forbidden; the guards never spoke; they were like dumb mutes. You were manhandled but quietly. It was like being dead! Now I was being hurried along, but not towards the interrogation room. Outside, the route to the main gate and the main entrance to Sachsenhausen where all the black and obscene things took place. This, I knew, must be it! My time was up."

Then, to Wings's surprise, he was hustled not through the main gate but into the main Kom-mandantur building, and into a big room with a long table, a single chair facing it. The guards hurried him across, unfastened his handcuffs, and he looked up at the five men facing him across the table. The stony-faced man in the center wore a black gown; the two on either side of him were in dark uniforms. In the mock naval jacket he'd worn since his escape from Sagan, Wings did not feel happy. He thought, "This looks like a court-martial. But why in the dead of night?" He also saw that an interpreter and a stenographer were present.

The judge in the black gown did most of the talking. The interpreter wasn't much good, and Wings was able to give himself a certain amount of time by arguing with him about his skill. They went over and over the same ground covered by his first interrogator, the inference always that Wings had "outside contacts," and was somehow engaged in spying, sabotage, and subverting their guards.

"The questions went round and round in circles. I suppose they were trying to trip me up. My knee was giving me hell and I had a good row over the inhumanity of not giving me medical aid. They seized on that at once. 'You were given the best medical attention possible, and once your condition was alleviated you seized the opportunity to escape. You are plainly a spy in direct communication with British intelligence. You were plainly under strong pressure from England to put into action the plans they had made for you—no matter if it cost you your life.'"

Daylight was again flooding the dreary outlines

of the concentration camp as Wings was led back to the black hole of Zellenbau. He had two more midnight sessions with the interrogator, another midnight session with the tribunal, and each time the shock was the same: the feeling that this exit might be his last. From a whispered conversation with an orderly in the ablutions he knew that normally one left his cell only for the three s's—shave, shit, or shower. There was a fourth s—it stood for "shot."

But at least his solitary confinement gave him time to think. Wings knew that something was going on that he did not understand. Some trap was being laid for him. But why? He had busted out of Sachsenhausen, and the SS did not put up with that sort of thing. The smoking chimneys of the camp crematorium were eloquent proof of that. So what was the purpose of all this careful chronicling of his activities? Why get a special interrogator, and a whole tribunal of black-uniformed Gestapo, up all night asking the same questions? Plainly their methods were intended to break him.

Wings had a feeling that his interrogator was a trained policeman. He acted like a policeman; he took careful notes like a policeman. Did the Gestapo merely want a legal reason to execute him?

Wings wrote: "These two points made me think. As interrogation followed interrogation—always during the early morning hours—my thoughts crystallized. Whatever happens to me—my fate—will seal the fate of the other four. Break me, pin anything on me, spying, sabotage, links with British intelligence, and we are all for the high jump."

But how to convince them that his only loyalty was to his fellow officers and his country? The next midnight tribunal went on hammering at these well-established points, but with one new addition: Was it not true, they suggested, that part of his mission was to spy on the nearby airport? Wings replied he had not even seen an airfield, let alone spied on one. He did not admit that during his stay in Sonderlager A he had seen some odd goings-on in the air about three thousand feet above the camp: what looked like rocket planes towed by other aircraft to that height, and then somehow ignited, trailing a brilliant flame behind them before they ran out of fuel and came in at a shallow angle to land. Plainly they had landed at the airfield in question. Later, Wings realized he was watching the trials of the robot bombs that were to create much damage in London.

Wings refuted their accusation. He had been at liberty for less than twelve hours. Most of that time he had spent on trains or hiding in a cellar. How could he have *reached* the perimeter of any airfield, let alone spied on it?

The tribunal were unimpressed. Ah, yes, and that brought them back to the point of what he was doing in Mahlsdorf in the first place.

The judge was plugging away relentlessly, repeating the familiar accusations. Wings knew that he was sweating. His hands were clenched together, but he could still feel the pain of the handcuffs. This was too much. He knew he had reached the bursting point. Why in the name of God were they doing all this to him? Why not just execute him?

He was hardly aware that he was standing up, then hobbling up the line of the long table and back again, protesting angrily and bitterly. For Christ's sake, didn't they understand the truth when they heard it?

"I am a professional soldier—do you understand that?—a professional soldier. My father and grandfathers were professional soldiers before me. My father's brothers, my uncles, were professional soldiers. In the Crimean War one of them won one of the first Victoria Crosses ever awarded. Do you understand what that is, or don't you? It's equivalent to your '*Pour Le Mérite*,' which your soldiers receive for great gallantry."

He stopped for a second to catch his breath.

"I have served as a soldier in two world wars, and during peacetime all over the British Empire. When the war broke out I deliberately got myself transferred from a cushy desk job to a fighting command. Commanding a flying squadron in battle."

He shook his fists at them. "And what happens! What happens! I stupidly get myself shot down on my very first operation. Can you imagine that? All those years and I'm shot down the first time I'm over enemy territory. For five years I've been a prisoner of war. Do you understand what that

298

means? The lowest sort of life. A vegetable. No chance of serving my country in a profession which has occupied my entire life. My contemporaries—and I was at school with some of them—have risen to high office and high rank. And where am I—do you understand that?"

He made another hobbling journey up and down the table.

"I've got to get back. Don't you understand that? Do you really think I'm going to contaminate myself trying to contact partisans, becoming a spy, a saboteur, a secret agent? That's not my style or trade. I'm an RAF serving officer and that's where my personal honor and pride will always remain.

"Doesn't the German Army have pride and tradition and brave soldiers? Doesn't it follow an equally praiseworthy code? What I have said goes for myself and my four companions; they are British officers doing their duty. And if you want to know why we escape: we prefer death to the dishonor of sitting around passively as prisoners. Do you understand that?"

He found he was back at his chair. He collapsed into it, overwhelmed by the force of his own rhetoric and vehemence. He did not know where it had all come from. From his deep subconscious or his own heart. It didn't matter. He had said his piece, and he didn't bother to search their faces for any result.

Then he heard the judge's three quiet words. "We do understand," he said.

Wings wrote: "The court adjourned, and I was

led back to my cell. It was broad daylight as I crossed the parade ground. This was my last session with them, although I did not know it. About a week later I was moved to a new cell, better furnished, an iron bed with a straw palliasse. A small table and chair. Usual eating things. The handcuffs were removed, the leg irons left off."

From his "new abode," as he termed it, he was taken as usual to the ablutions, and there, at last, he was allowed to meet—his face white with a prison pallor—Sydney Dowse. They were not allowed to speak. Only their eyes could communicate. And Wings Day was indescribably moved!

Wings did not know until long afterwards that he was not, as he thought, being tried by a Gestapo tribunal. The Geheime Staatspolizei did not bother with such superfluities as trials; one simply disappeared. He was being cross-examined—with all the seriousness and concern for the law of the German legal system—by the Kriminalpolizei.

The revelations to the Kripo police in Mahlsdorf of both Sydney Dowse and Wings Day that they were escaped POW RAF officers from Sagan, Stalag Luft III, had been dutifully logged and passed on to Kripo headquarters in Berlin. The Kripo by this time were not only incensed by the sheer brutality of the killing of fifty Sagan officers, they could perceive quite clearly that the Gestapo were unloading guilt on their shoulders—the first indication being the fact that Kaltenbrunner had ordered his subordinate, General Nebe, head of the Kripo, to select the officers for execution.

This conflict was increasing.

As Obersturmbannführer Max Wielen, head of the Kripo in Breslau, made clear in his testimony at the Nuremberg Trials, the Kripo were well aware of what was happening: "The urns containing the ashes of the officers who had been shot were transmitted by the Gestapo to the Kripo. By this means the fact that the Gestapo were connected with the matter was to be camouflaged."

The Kripo were certainly not going to pass five more officers over to the Gestapo without making their own investigation of guilt, and recording their report. They found Wings Day to be what he said he was: an RAF officer doing his duty. The Kripo could not cast a protective blanket over him or his comrades; on the other hand, many of the Gestapo, seeing that the war was lost, were already planning their routes of escape, and their methods of avoiding responsibility.

There was a new wind blowing through Germany. The voice of the Führer was no longer a clarion call. There was now a confusion of voices—military and civilian—trying to find a way out.

In January 1945, Wings Day, Jimmy James, Sydney Dowse, and Jack Churchill were returned to Sonderlager A. There they were greeted with some emotion and firm handshakes by the other imprisoned soldiers who understood the chances they'd taken and the courage involved. But what had happened to Johnny Dodge?

In the dawn hours of a cold January morning, the door of his cell in the Sachsenhausen death block was thrust open. At that moment he was handcuffed, filthy, unshaven, and fastened by leg manacles to a steel post embedded in the concrete floor. He knew that his time had now come. Stolidly the warders began to unlock him. They knew as well as he that the end of a stay in that evil place was death. Taken by each arm, he was hurried along the quiet corridor and through into the open air. They tugged him towards the outer gate, and so, Johnny Dodge surmised, towards the main camp, where executions were assembly-line productions. Thrust through, he blinked in utter surprise. A smiling, smartly dressed young German officer stood next to a huge shiny Mercedes. He hurried forward to grasp Johnny's hand, saying, "Welcome, Major Dodge. We are going to Berlin."

Three hours later, sitting in a smart, undamaged Berlin apartment, bathed, shaved, and wearing new civilian clothes, Johnny sipped a large Scotch and soda and listened to a very attentive high German official. "Major Dodge," he said warmly, "we have decided to send you back to England."

Johnny Dodge replied, "Oh, good. Why?"

The official explained that they knew he was a *close* relative of British Prime Minister Winston Churchill. Therefore he would quickly be able to arrange a meeting with Mr. Churchill, and pass him a message of the highest importance. Germany was now holding out the hand of friendship towards the Allies. It must be obvious to the Americans and the British that unless they joined the German armies there was no way of stopping this tidal wave of Soviets washing across Europe. The Reich was prepared to come to a quick agreement on this. Naturally there would be small problems to overcome: the Allied demand for "unconditional surrender" would have to be rephrased, as would the alteration and adjustment of European borders. But that could all be solved. Would Major Dodge return to England and deliver that message?

"Certainly," said Johnny Dodge. He had met Winston Churchill a few times and could well imagine the gust of laughter which would greet this suggestion. "How do you intend to get me back?"

That would take a little time, travel towards the Swiss border being a little perilous these days, but it would be managed.

It was. Johnny Dodge was put over the border into Switzerland and made his way back to London several weeks later. In London, Major Dodge got in touch with U.S. Ambassador Winant, who arranged a dinner party with Churchill. It was a great success. The prime minister congratulated Johnny Dodge on getting home in time for the victory celebrations. In forty-eight hours the Allies would be accepting the unconditional surrender of the German armed forces.

In those final months of the war there were

many German leaders trying to find a way of contacting the Allied High Command and arranging an armistice. Several POWs were approached in this way, the plan being that they should be released into Switzerland, contact General Dwight Eisenhower, and arrange radio communications with the SS so that a deal could be worked out. Like Johnny Dodge they were too late and nobody wanted to listen.

In South Compound, Bub Clark remembers, the order to evacuate reached them at around 11:00 P.M. on January 26, 1945. "We knew when the Russian offensive crossed the Vistula they might be at our front door at any moment, and we guessed the Germans would have to evacuate. We gave orders that everyone should be prepared to march at a moment's notice. So everyone built packs, and made hoods; packed whatever clothing was available and what food they could carry. But the whole compound went crazy."

Davie Jones had real trouble on his hands: "My job at the time was to collect and hold all the money that shot-down aircrews brought into the camp. I had thousands of U.S. dollars, thousands of British pounds, thousands of French francs—a holy fortune. Rojo Goodrich, who led the South Compound evacuation, comes in and says, 'Got to be out of here by midnight, Davie.'

"I say, 'But I've got all this money . . .'

" 'Where is it?'

" 'I've buried it in certain locations all over the

compound. Couldn't leave it under my bunk. This place doesn't have any safe-deposit boxes.'

" 'Well, get it.' And Rojo's gone.

"I had a map of the places I'd buried the damn stuff. But everybody's going mad. It's pitch-dark. There's a foot of snow on the ground, and the ground's frozen solid. I'm going around like a hooded zombie with kettles of boiling water, pouring it into the hidey-holes, and trying to collect that loot. I got it all out. Nobody bothered to wonder whether I'd gone mad. They were all too busy. On the march I managed to pass back the dollars and pounds to their rightful owners, but no one claimed the francs. I guess I had twenty thousand dollars' worth. When we got back to France after the march, I managed to get a week in Paris. I still had all these francs; I kept them in a shoebox. Not my money. Didn't spend a sou of it. So I fly back to the States still carrying my shoebox. I'm ordered to report to the building which is now the Pentagon. I'm being debriefed by this second-rate captain. I hand him the shoebox and explain how I came by it. What does he do? Opens the lid, peers inside as if it contains horse manure, says, 'Oh! Foreign money,' and empties it all into his wastepaper basket. I sit there thinking of those days in Paris, and what we could have done with that dough."

Jones's memories of the journey itself are no less vivid. After the German command had given the order to evacuate and each general had gotten his men together, "We started marching along that damn road away from the camp. There was a foot of snow at first and then as the days went by it turned to slush. Every mile along the road things were thrown away—musical instruments, books, food. I always admired Bub Clark's determination: he was pulling a sledge assisted by two or three like-minded 'librarians,' loaded with camp records. He got them back to the States; they now reside in the Air Force Academy in Colorado Springs. Guys were dying by the roadside, every hour and every day. Some wandered off. We ran into lines of other refugees—they came from every part of Europe, as far as I could ascertain—all sorts staggering along in this endless gray world of fog and ice and snow.

"They put us in barns, in cement works, in factories. That night in the factory I'll never forget. We were all as far down as we could get. I was ground down—worried about me—no one else. Now with us we had this Colonel C. V. Jones. He was a very late arrival in Sagan and did nothing else but talk about how he and General Cannon had won the goddam war. He was from Jackson, Mississippi, and we thought old C. V. was nothing more than a bag of Southern wind.

"Well, we started on that march. And the longer we went on, and the more tired we got, the more old C. V. talked. And by the time we got into the factory that night, I guess old C. V. had saved at least twenty lives; he just talked them up off the ground and onto their feet again. 'Come on, kid, if I can do it, you can. I'll carry this bit for you

306

Sure, lean on me for a few steps and you'll feel better.' Where he got the strength from I'll never know. And it didn't finish there. On one occasion this big tough colonel was giving a young kid hell. And C. V. turned on him and said, 'Leave the kid alone, you son of a bitch!' Which was fighting talk even between colonels. And this big bastard turned on C. V. and started to increase the problem, and suddenly there was a knife in C. V.'s hand as he said, 'Lay a finger on me, man, and I'll cut your guts out!' Funny how adversity turns pompous bores into goddam heroes. I can tell you, by the time we ended that journey Colonel C. V. Jones was one of our genuine leaders.

"That's when we reached a railhead and they stuffed us into boxcars. There isn't enough room for most of us to sit down. Pitch-dark. Who's here? Sound off. Name and rank? Then I find I'm the senior officer. Great command, a pitch-black boxcar full of about a hundred starving, freezing airmen. 'Let's number off. Now, even numbers sit down, odd numbers stand up. Alternate in shifts.' Then someone finds a blanket, and we manage to rig it as a hammock so that the sick guys can get a bit of a rest. We were in that boxcar for four or five days. No food or water to speak of. They opened the doors very occasionally, and ten thousand guys jumped out and dropped their trousers. I don't think Hollywood would want to film those scenes."

Wally Floody, George Harsh, Bob Tuck, and Peter Fanshawe, all members of the Escape Committee, all seething at the thought of missing the mass escape, and then realizing with very mixed feelings that their lives had been saved by this odd quirk of fate, left Belaria Compound along with 150 other POWs. Wally and George decided to travel as partners, and included one other good friend, Kingsley Ewart Brown. Their clothes were mainly rags, and the soles of their boots began to flap after the first thirty miles or so. All the time they were wet and cold and hungry. The German officer in charge did not seem to know where they were going, and with every day's march, and every night spent in a drafty barn, discipline evaporated. Soon their column had dwindled to a hundred men; fifty had decided to strike out on their own. At one point Kingsley Brown left the column and they thought he'd gone too, but he reappeared after a few hours, holding something beneath the blanket he used for a shawl. He opened it a fraction to allow Wally and George to glimpse his treasure. Three loaves of rock-hard, German black bread.

"My God," said Wally, "where did you get that?"

"Bunch of Frenchmen back there. Slave laborers but know their way about. Got a whole cart full of bread. I traded my watch for these three loaves. They're crazy for watches."

"Right," said Wally, peeling his off. "Here's mine."

George said protestingly, "Wally, that's a real Rolex!"

"Goddam it, George, you think you can eat a bloody Rolex?" Wally roared. "Give Kingsley your watch."

Floody, Harsh, and the others ended up at a small town a few miles south of Potsdam.

"There was George and me, Hornblower, everybody else from Belaria," said Wally. "About twelve hundred RAF types, plus American fliers, about forty-five hundred U.S. troops, and about five hundred Danes. The only thing you learn from a situation like that is that a human being is a very adaptable creature. We were always hungry, and you had to learn to live with that; you were frozen in wintertime and you had to learn to live with that; and when the Russians arrived and overran us, we had to learn to live with them. They came in thousands in or on every sort of conveyance—jeeps, armored cars, weapons carriers, trucks, horses, bicycles, and on these enormous Stalin tanks which seemed mainly to be crewed by Mongolian troops, squat little guys who knew what they were after. Every tank had a mattress on it because every German broad they found they heaved on and everyone took their turn, and maybe they kept her until next day or maybe they tossed her off . . . because they were raping the countryside.

"They were fine with us, because we were on the same side. They didn't bother about feeding us; we had to feed ourselves. Ten of us formed a small group and our job was to feed the Allies and ourselves. The Russians gave me three trucks and three drivers and a Russian captain to go along with us, and my job was to get six tons of potatoes every day—from somewhere. Some other group's job was maybe to get ten head of cattle, another's to get flour—and so on. We scrounged around the countryside to get food.

"Things changed entirely when the Soviet commissars arrived about two weeks later. At a knife stroke everything was cut off—communications, friendships, everything. General Patton sent a bunch of trucks through to pick us up. No way —the Russians lined the road with machine guns and said, 'Turn round and go back . . . or else.'

"We were just the bargaining counters. The Russian thinking was that the Allies had thousands of Russian prisoners in their hands; they were prepared to do an exchange deal—one Allied body for one Russian. As far as the Russians were concerned, that was logical. By now we'd thrown the camp open and refugees from everywhere just poured in. And there were some pretty unusual liaisons. There was this Belgian girl with a year-old baby; she came trundling along the road and took refuge with us. She'd been the mistress of a Luftwaffe captain, and he'd been killed, and within a week she met this New Zealand POW and they were married! Married! I'll never forget it because she couldn't speak one word of English and he couldn't speak one word of French.

"Eventually we were all driven to the Elbe in a convoy of Russian trucks. An American pontoon bridge had been thrown over the river and the prisoner exchange was on. Three Russian prisoners one way, three Allied the other. George Harsh, Kingsley Brown, and I crossed together. We had a hard job believing it was all over. George was having a sharp word with an American officer who thought we were all blue-blood Brits and imitating the accent. Brownie looked at me and said, 'Well, what d'you know?' And I said, 'By God . . . we made it!' "

The Sachsenhausen Group, the last remaining kriegies of the Sagan escape—Wings Day, Jimmy James, Sydney Dowse, plus commando Jack Churchill—faced the most dangerous journey.

At dawn on April 3, 1945, they were bundled into buses along with other prisoners they had never seen before and driven down to the Oranienburg railway station. They were guarded by soldiers; in overall charge was Kripo inspector Peter Mohr, who had been a member of Wings Day's examining tribunal. At Oranienburg, shepherded into Pullman coaches with corridors, lavatories, and soft upholstery, they reflected that at least being among the Important People hostages gave them privileges.

The train took them through Berlin, where the sight of the devastation was awe-inspiring. Farther south, Leipzig was no better: the town a shambles, the station deluged by refugees seeking to get aboard the train, people even clambering onto the roofs of the carriages. They spent the night on a siding, and next morning rattled southwards again through beautiful mountain country. At some point they changed trains—this one running on a narrow-gauge track, with smaller compartments and wooden seats. Someone said that they were hard against the Czechoslovakian border—in Bohemia, in fact.

Faces brightened. Everybody had heard of Bohemia: singing students and surging violins. They all clung to omens and gossip and hope. What else was there to cling to?

One of the Russian hostages, General Bessanov, was not so optimistic. The Gestapo were holding the Russians as bargaining chips to wring a few concessions out of the approaching Allied armies. But the Allies would not play that game. The Nazi guards would certainly be under orders to liquidate all the Important People hostages if the Allies closed in. That was now highly likely. Why bolster themselves up with false hopes? That point of view was confirmed when they arrived at Flossenbürg concentration camp, where the commandant informed Peter Mohr that the camp was overcrowded and he had orders from the highest authority in Berlin to exterminate all new arrivals as swiftly as possible. He intended to do that with this party.

Peter Mohr produced documents that countermanded those instructions, and suggested the commandant ring Berlin if he doubted them. By the narrowest of margins they survived.

They spent several days at Flossenbürg, knowing that the extermination of hundreds of prisoners was continuing at all possible speed, before the rest were moved on by bus to another concentration camp, Dachau. And now the number of hostages grew in number as they were rounded up from other camps, many women and children among them. Their guards were increased by the addition of a special group of SS troops under a sadistic commander, Obersturmbannführer Bader. It did not take Wings and his group long to discover that this was an elite execution squad. The only point at issue now was when, and how, they proposed to slaughter all the prisoners, for with the new additions the Important People group had now risen to more than a hundred and fifty.

In a column of buses they left Dachau and crossed into the Austrian Tyrol. They journeyed on through the mountains and finally ran out of fuel near the pretty mountain village of Niederndorf. For them, the last act of the war was to be played here.

By this time, Jack Churchill was fed up. He was a soldier. There was still a war on. He could not continue to be bused through the countryside with all these women and children like a goddam tourist. He was going to make a break for it and see if he could bring help. Did Wings agree? He did. But the Sagan three decided to stay with their group, because now they were close to Italian partisan country, and it appeared that the partisans were able and willing to engage the German guards and free the hostages. The women and children

313

might need protection. Besides, no one would notice Jack Churchill's absence; they could cover for him, whereas four missing might invite Bader's retaliation.

Jack slipped away through the trees and traversed the steep slopes of the mountainsides, living roughly, hungrily, and happily for almost a week. On the seventh day he saw a convoy of trucks passing along the narrow white road that bisected the valley. The Yanks had arrived.

Jack scrambled down to intercept them, waving madly at the leading truck. A fresh-faced young U.S. lieutenant stared down at him. Jack raised his voice above the growl of the engine: "I'm a British officer—escaped from a prison column. Can I come aboard?"

The young lieutenant grinned and said, "Sure. Come on up. I guess you're hungry?"

"Starving," said Jack.

The young lieutenant reached behind him and began producing rations. "What do you want: cheese, ham, bologna, sardines, salmon . . .?"

"Thanks, one will do," said Jack.

The column restarted, and Jack sat back reflecting ruefully upon the fact that the territory it had taken him a week to cover was now being devoured in a couple of hours. His reverie was disturbed when he saw they were approaching a German roadblock and a large .88-millimeter anti-aircraft gun pointed directly at them. If it opened fire on this unprotected column of trucks, they would be blown to kingdom come. He began to speak, but the young lieutenant was already ambling forward to parley with the enemy. Jack sat tightly on both hands, fingers firmly crossed. Damn it, this was no way to end a war.

The lieutenant returned, smiling. They had reached agreement. The Germans had not seen an American column of trucks, and the Americans had not spotted a roadblock. Both sides would retreat a couple of miles to the rear, face and honor saved, have supper, and take their time consulting with higher-ups about what action should be taken. If they played their cards right, the war might be over by then.

For the first time in about two months Jack found his face splitting in a broad smile. "Now, damn it all—that is a good way to end a war!"

Oddly enough, it was the German generals who came to the rescue. The night of Jack's escape Bader moved the SS truck containing his weaponry into the center of Niederndorf, and his drunken SS troops began to make threats that the prisoners would all be shot within a few hours. In Neiderndorf the Wehrmacht still operated the telephone exchange, and one of the Important People captives, an assertive German officer named Colonel von Bonin, got a message through to a German Army group still fighting a rearguard action in the mountains. The commanding officer promised that a unit of Wehrmacht troops would arrive before dawn. What did arrive was only a small detachment armed with machine guns, but plainly it felt no affection for the Gestapo, and Bader and his group, faced by grim-faced young men and an equally grim-faced Colonel von Bonin brandishing a revolver, dropped their weapons. Disarmed, they were allowed to drive on from Niedernforf into Italian partisan territory. They did not last very long.

It was a young Austrian, Tony Duccia, a leader of the local Austrian partisans, who approached Wings Day with his scheme. This mountainous territory had for centuries been fought over, divided, and redivided by feuding bands of Austrians and Italians. This animosity was certain to surface again and in that situation none of them was safe. He had an old car. He believed he could get Wings and himself through territory held by the Austrian partisans and, with his documents, through the retreating German troops. Duccia's problem, however, was that when they got to Italy and, hopefully, the advancing American troops he, Duccia, would be treated as an enemy. Could Wings take over then, and get the Americans to send a special rescue mission to keep the hostages safe? Wings Day was completely in favor of making his ninth escape attempt, not through one of those filthy dark tunnels, but through the sunlight in a battered old Volkswagen.

As they drove south through Bolzano they glimpsed the headline in the local newspaper: "HITLER DEAD!" To Wings it gave no feeling of either relief or exhilaration. This world tragedy had surpassed analysis and emotion. The desperation and the deaths, and the condition of friend and enemy alike, defied human reason. Only a sense of numbness remained.

It was a feeling reflected in the scenes they had witnessed earlier on the narrow road south of the town of Bressanone: lines of horse-drawn carts, worn-out German transport, sometimes one truck towing two or three others, weary soldiers trudging back towards the Brenner Pass, streams of Italian workers from Austria and Germany walking home in the opposite direction.

At one crossroads an SS Unteroffizier commanding a platoon of troops waved them to a halt, and shoved his head through the window. "I am commandeering this vehicle," he announced truculently.

"No, you're not," retorted Tony Duccia, brandishing a sheaf of papers in his face. "These papers give us the right to proceed to Trento on an important mission."

With that he was in gear and roaring away. Wings Day crouched lower in his seat, his borrowed overcoat concealing the fact that he wore what was left of his RAF uniform with flying brevet and medals, hunching his shoulders against the expected fusillade of bullets. None came. But five miles short of Trento the engine began to make grating noises and stopped. They had run out of oil.

They walked into Trento where, to Wings's immense relief, he realized that Tony spoke perfect Italian and quickly got them escorted to guerrilla

317

headquarters. There Tony made the announcement that they had matters of immense importance to communicate to the advancing American forces, and here was a real live RAF high-ranking officer to prove it. The partisans were very impressed. Certainly they would provide a car to carry them onwards. The Americans were still some fifty miles to the south, and getting through the Germans, still fighting fiercely in retreat, was dangerous.

The car took an hour to appear. It was small and plainly had been hiding in someone's garage for the past few years. It spluttered into action and proceeded for at least two hundred yards before coming to an eternal halt. Another long wait, and another car appeared. This one lasted as far as the first steep hill, where the rear axle broke. Tony and Wings walked back to town, and after a lengthy wait a third car was produced. This time they refused the guerrilla heroes who wished to stand on the running board or sit on the roof, and took only the driver and a local guide. They needed the guide, for after an hour and a half driving along the mountainous road, the clutch of the third car burned out and there was no alternative but to walk. Fortunately the guide knew the mountain trails very well. They spent that night in a mountain hotel—the first guests in two or three years.

Next morning, leaving at dawn, they found they had been provided a bodyguard. He was carrying a captured German rifle and wearing a German parachutist's smock. The bullet hole in the back explained how he had acquired the outfit. Wings began to pray they did not fall into the hands of a German patrol.

Now whenever they stopped at a farm for refreshments they were accosted by belligerent guerrilla bands claiming authority over the territory. They managed to convince the guerrillas that their journey would not breach that authority, and asked one band if there was any way of getting through the German lines.

Yes, they could cross the valley behind the Germans, climb up into the mountains, and traverse for a few miles along the other side. Then it would be a simple matter to descend and make contact with the Americans. As long as the Americans didn't mistake them for enemies, it would be all right.

The Americans did not mistake them for enemies. From their high traverse along the slope of the mountains they could see the German and American positions quite clearly. They descended cautiously, and Wings decided that they must have been seen through American binoculars. He hoped the Americans recognized an RAF uniform, and when they reached the scrub cover in the valley, he strode firmly ahead. Eventually he spied a soldier behind a bush some fifty yards away. The soldier called without much enthusiasm, "Who goes there?" And Wings shouted, "A British officer and party. Can we come over?" "Oh, sure," replied the American voice. "All come over."

The young commanding officer got in touch with his headquarters. A small, fast jeep convoy guided by Italian partisans made sure they got through to Niederndorf without hostilities. Jimmy James and Sydney Dowse were among those who welcomed them.

For the thousands of Sagan, Stalag Luft III, survivors, the war was at last over. As they were collected at various bases preparatory to being shipped or flown home, it took some time to sink in. It took even more time before they could start to think about peace.

For others, left behind in Germany or newly arriving, different conflicts were just beginning.

Part Four

A Question
of
Justice

Chapter Eighteen

WING COMMANDER WILFRED "FREDDIE" Bowes
of the RAF's Special Investigation Branch was
forty-two years old, a cheerful, powerful character
with a hard face and deep-set blue eyes that could
be as intimidating as the twin barrels of a loaded
shotgun. A Yorkshireman still trailing vowels of
that gritty accent, it had taken him twenty years,
starting as an ordinary aircraftsman, to reach his
present rank. Most of his important decisions were
empirical and intuitive; more often than not
they were right. His language was inevitably
blunt, corrosive sometimes to both superiors and
subordinates—occasionally primordially obscene.

Flight Lieutenant Francis McKenna, Bowes's
chief assistant and soon to be squadron leader,
was thirty-eight years old. Born in the adjoining
northern county of Lancashire, he was a quieter
and more contemplative man than Bowes, a Catholic with conceptions of law, justice, and com-
passion that often disturbed his own conscience
more than anybody else's. He had been a senior
police officer in Blackpool, but felt he should be
doing more, and towards the end of the war managed to transfer to flying duties with the RAF. He
flew his tour of thirty missions across the lethal

night skies of the Reich, and at the end of it was posted to the RAF's Special Investigation Branch in London under Wing Commander Bowes. Their overall commander was Group Captain W. V. Nicholas—"Nicky" to Bowes. McKenna always remembered that first conversation. Nicky looked up from his chair.

"Get through the files, Lieutenant?"

"Yes, sir."

"What do you think?"

"No hope, sir."

Nicky allowed his eyebrows to lift slightly. "You know Germany?"

"Only from thirty thousand feet, sir."

"Speak the language?"

"Only three words, sir: *ein Bier, bitte.*"

"Great," said the group captain. "You'll never go thirsty. Besides we shall supply you with a first-rate interpreter."

"With respect, sir," said McKenna, slowly, "I don't think it will work. The Gestapo have had years to cover their tracks; they're experts in providing new identities, false papers, aliases. I've gone through that great pile of papers you gave me, sir, with a fine-tooth comb. . . ."

Group Captain Nicholas knew that Flight Lieutenant McKenna was a first-rate cop, quiet, patient, thorough. Interrupting, he said, "Tell you what, McKenna: go across to Germany for a couple of weeks. Take Flight Sergeant Williams with you as assistant. He's ex-Portsmouth police, you'll like him. Nose around, the two of you. Then after two weeks report back and we'll think about it. How's that?"

"Yes, sir," said McKenna, saluting his CO and turning to leave. In the outer office Wing Commander Bowes was grinning broadly. "Now, Sherlock, you've got a great chance to examine all the clues, the fingerprints, the bloodstains, the forensic evidence, just like they do in the movies."

"Yes, sir," said McKenna, trying to keep a shade of asperity out of his voice. "I'll do my best."

McKenna knew what the jurists would say: No chance of catching the Gestapo criminals responsible for murdering the fifty RAF officers. Didn't the Special Investigation Branch understand that Germany was awash with millions of displaced persons, plus millions of Germans fleeing from the east, where the Russians were in control? Did they really imagine the Russians would allow them to investigate *anything* in their territory? To make matters worse, Sagan itself—renamed Zagań —was now part of Poland, also under Russian control. Besides, who the hell cared about an investigation into the deaths of fifty officers? They were dead, weren't they? Nothing could bring them back. What were the lives of fifty Allied airmen compared with the millions of civilians who had been slaughtered? Didn't they know that the Russians had executed fifteen thousand Polish officers and buried their bodies at a place called Katyn? Didn't they know that when the D day invasion took place, Hitler had signed a manifesto sentencing more than two hundred thousand French Resistance workers to death?

Technically, the United Nations War Crimes Commission, set up in October 1943, were responsible for bringing to justice the men guilty of the murder of the Sagan officers. In reality, they did not have the staff, the experience, or the facilities to handle the huge task confronting them. In addition, the Soviet Union had refused to join in such investigations, preferring to set up their own war crimes tribunal—thus ensuring disorganization and confusion from the very start.

The RAF did not deliberately decide to go it alone. They had no choice. They found themselves in a situation where, if they did not act, it was unlikely anyone else would. But they also felt a deep and personal sense of responsibility for their dead comrades, plus an intense determination that the murderers should be caught. So in the final outcome, it was the RAF's Special Investigation Branch (S.I.B.) working in conjunction with the Judge Advocate General's office, and with considerable help from the United States Counter Intelligence Corps and U.S. War Crimes Liaison, that were responsible for the entire investigation.

McKenna arrived in the British zone of Germany after a bumpy flight in a drafty Dakota on September 5, 1945, almost six years to the day after the outbreak of war. On the drive to Rinteln, where the S.I.B. had their headquarters, he discussed the task at hand with Flight Sergeant H. J. Williams, who had also been assigned to S.I.B.

"Let's review what and who we've got on our side," McKenna began. "We've got Wingco Bowes back in London coordinating information from a variety of sources, and he should be out here pretty soon. We've got War Crimes Commission units; we've got investigators from the S.O.E. [Special Operations Executive, a secret intelligence organization] and material coming in from M19 [an organization attached to S.O.E.]; and the Judge Advocate's office. We've got Lieutenant Colonel Scotland's special setup. . . ."

"The London Cage?" asked Williams.

"Precisely. Set up as a holding prison for Nazi war criminals, with our requirements high on their priorities list. They've got special interrogators there, fluent linguists. When we've got a recalcitrant suspect we need not waste days trying to sweat it out of him; we fly him back to London for the experts."

"But first we've got to catch a suspect."

"Dead right. So now we do tours of the zone, making friends and influencing people. And going through everyone's files: War Crimes Commission, International Red Cross, displaced persons, mayors. . . . We'll make friends with the Yanks, and we might even try the existing German civil police."

McKenna knew where to start. In the office allocated to them at headquarters he spread out a map.

"This is the area we've got to look at very carefully. Here's Berlin. About a hundred and eighty miles to the southeast of it is Breslau, which is eighty miles from Sagan. Twenty-nine of the fifty Sagan officers murdered were probably murdered in that area. Breslau, headquarters of that region, was the main base for the Gestapo and the Kripo and they control all those suboffices, Görlitz and Liegnitz and Hirschberg, from whose crematoriums the urns containing the ashes were sent. All the escapees from Sagan scattered into that triangle . . . only a few made a quick getaway by train. Those urns are a giveaway to where the officers were murdered. The urns of Bushell and Scheidhauer were sent from Saarbrücken, for example."

Williams asked quietly, "You've got the names of some of these Gestapo thugs?"

McKenna fished in his inside breast pocket and produced a notebook and papers. "A list of more than a hundred wanted men, extracted from the documents amassed by the Judge Advocate's office. We start with the Breslau connection. The first alarm concerning the breakout was flashed from there by the local criminal police chief, Obersturmbannführer Max Wielen. He was the man who decided that this was a mass escape and called this a national emergency, all forces alerted . . ."

"You think Wielen's got something to do with the murders?"

"I know it." Williams's brow furrowed as McKenna told him the story. After the British forces had crossed the Rhine they had picked him up near Cologne, and he was now in jail in the British zone. He was sixty years old, a professional police officer in the Kripo. His great rival was local Gestapo chief Dr. Wilhelm Scharpwinkel. The Gestapo and the Kripo hated each other, but were sometimes forced to work together in an organization they called Sipo. In Breslau, Wielen alleges, he was trapped into collaboration by the Gestapo. His statement details how he was ordered to Berlin to meet General Nebe, the Kripo chief. McKenna consulted his papers again. "This is what he says. 'General Nebe gave me a teleprint signed by Kaltenbrunner which read: "On the personal command of the Führer, reference the Sagan escape affair, more than half the recaptured English officers will be shot. The Gestapo will receive the appropriate orders from Gruppenführer Müller. Everything is to be avoided which might bring to light the action of the Gestapo.'"

McKenna went on. "Wielen makes the usual claims: that this was contrary to the Geneva convention; he would not do such a thing, and declined to accept responsibility for any part of it."

"So?" asked Williams.

"General Nebe gave him the usual dirty look, and told him it was a direct 'Führer order' and could not be disobeyed. If he as a Kripo officer raised difficulties he could expect the usual treatment: court-martial and a firing squad. So Wielen went back to Breslau, and there Scharpwinkel, much to Wielen's relief, had taken over. Even-

329

tually Scharpwinkel outranked Wielen, and Wielen was posted to Cologne."

"And Scharpwinkel?"

McKenna's voice was level and emotionless: "No evidence for the court yet, but there seems to be a big possibility that Scharpwinkel enjoyed his power, and that he gunned down at least half a dozen of our officers *himself.*"

"Has it occurred to you, sir," said Flight Sergeant Williams, "that there are a lot of angry and embittered Germans still lurking in the undergrowth?"

"Oh, sure," said McKenna.

A week or so later, driving home, he turned off a side road and saw what Williams had meant. He braked to a halt and walked to the front of his car, where his headlights had caught a glittering line of light across the road. It was a thin steel cable stretched across between the trees. It would have smashed the flimsy windshield of his aged car and taken his head off. All five officers who formed the core of the investigation team— Bowes, McKenna, Arthur R. "Dickie" Lyon, Stephen Courtney, and Harold Harrison—were aware of the danger.

One of McKenna's first acts was to spread the word that the S.I.B. were on the job and looking for Nazi villains. Seeking help to catch them, he circulated the names, ranks, and particulars of every wanted man to the relevant offices in the American, British, and French zones (it was pointless sending anything to the Russians). His own attention was focused on the third level of Gestapo command, the regional offices and the men in charge, especially Venediger in Danzig; Gmeiner in Karlsruhe; Smidt in Kiel; Schafter in Munich; Spann in Saarbrücken; and Ziegler in Czechoslovakia.

They could be hiding anywhere. There were thousands of prisoners of war and German internees in POW and concentration camps—now used for a far different purpose—throughout the Reich. None of the four powers that had divided Germany into zones wanted to be responsible for holding, housing, feeding, and clothing these men through a long, cold winter. Less than half had been identified, but the relevant authorities were screening and releasing them with a minimum of formality, their philosophy being: get them off our hands, back home, back to work, so that German society—released at last from the Nazi terror—can establish a measure of normality.

McKenna knew this and knew he had to hurry. First he had to make personal visits to these camps. Interrogators were still turning up evidence that could prove vital in McKenna's search. Cold winter or not, he had to get on with it.

He sent his first report back to Group Captain Nicholas ten days after his arrival in Germany. He asked to stay. There would be months of work (he did not dream it would go into years), but the job could be done. He would report again as soon as they had their first break. That was what he needed above all—one small break.

"Pack your bags," said McKenna to Williams and Wilhelm Smit, ten days after they arrived. "We are driving to Düsseldorf."

Wilhelm Smit had been loaned to them from a liaison corps of the Netherlands air force as an interpreter. His German was perfect, his English excellent; one of his jobs was to teach McKenna German.

As McKenna drove the jeep, he outlined his objective. "As we know, Breslau was the coordinating center for our part of this investigation. Breslau Gestapo were also in direct command of other smaller centers, such as the nearby town of Görlitz. From the testimony of other Sagan escapers who were imprisoned there, we know that thirty-five airmen reached its jail. Twelve were returned to Stalag Luft Three. Twenty-three were murdered. At Breslau, working with that bastard Scharpwinkel, was Ernst Schmauser and his deputy, a Colonel Seetzen. Plus one other important figure, a Doctor Günther Absalon, who arrived in Stalag Luft III after the escape and poked around for a couple of weeks. He was certainly present at several of the executions, and probably took part in some."

"He might be in Düsseldorf?" asked Flight Sergeant Williams.

"His parents live there," said McKenna. "I have their address."

Herr and Frau Absalon were elderly, and worried, and scared. No, they had not heard from their son for almost a year. He had been fighting in Breslau during that last battle—they feared he might have been killed.

McKenna passed the next question to Smit.

"Ask them, would they mind if we searched the house?"

Wilhelm Smit's eyebrows flicked up at that. How would they reconcile that with the opening politeness?

"Has to be done," said McKenna severely.

The search revealed nothing of interest. Outside McKenna said, "We have another address nearby. Doctor Absalon had a wife."

The younger Frau Absalon was a good-looking woman in her early thirties. She also wanted to contact her husband—mainly to divorce him. He was a Nazi through and through, and she hated both Dr. Absalon and the Nazis. If they ever discovered him, she would be glad if they would let her know.

They returned to Rinteln through a succession of bombed cities. For the next few days they made other visits. Working on the theory that Belsen concentration camp, which now held a collection of Gestapo prisoners, might turn up a suspect, they paid it a visit. For sanitary reasons much of it had been burnt down, but it still retained a residue of hell—piles of human ash and human bones, and the inescapable odor of human smells. McKenna never forgot the recollection of a colleague who had been there in the first week: naked corpses stacked neatly like rows of cordwood;

333

scores of live children already recuperating on Red Cross feeding. They played hide-and-seek and tag among the corridors of the dead. What else was normal?

Up to his neck in files, reports and index cards, McKenna had a thought: a good policeman started his investigations at the beginning—at the source. The source in this case was Breslau. But that lay in Soviet-held territory, and the clash between Soviet invaders and Nazi defenders had been apocalyptic, the city smashed, raped, burnt, destroyed. A bastion of defense lying on the route to Berlin, it had been defended desperately. But knowing this, the Germans would have stripped the city of all but its military capability. Women and children, the old, sick, and wounded, would have been evacuated. To *where?*

McKenna's eyes widened in disbelief when he heard the Bürgermeister's cheerful answer. "Why, here to Rinteln, Herr Major. The evacuees wished to be as far away from the Russian advance as they could, and we were almost as far as they could get considering that the British and Americans were advancing from the West. An overspill in Minden, but mainly the people from Breslau were evacuated to Rinteln."

"They're still here?"

"Of course. Who wishes to go back to East Germany, Poland, and the Russians?"

"You have their addresses?"

"Of course. My efficient staff will be pleased to provide you with all that information." The

334

records and addresses of the Breslau evacuees were available from the Bürgermeister's staff within hours. McKenna consulted Wilhelm Smit.

"It's a house-to-house, door-knocking chore," said McKenna. "You take one street. I'll take another. Just check my German on, 'Do you have anybody evacuated from Breslau here?' If I can't cope I'll come screaming for you."

The first day was rainy, cold, and miserable. Lots of inquiries, no results. The second day was rainy, cold, and miserable, and McKenna was re-checking doors on which he had knocked and received no answer. But then, footsteps in one of the doorways. A timid middle-aged woman answered. Between McKenna's fractured German and her schoolgirl English, he managed to work out that, yes, she did have an evacuee from Breslau, but he was not home, and might not be back for another hour or so. His name was Klaus Lonsky. McKenna asked if she would mind if he came into the house and waited for Klaus. She smiled. Of course he could do that.

She led him to a small front room and left him alone. McKenna sat on a hard seat. He thought longingly of the centrally heated RAF mess not all that far away; the chatter of the pretty Waafs who always seemed to drift in; the six brands of Scotch gleaming behind the bar—with a name like McKenna, that amber liquid was part of his inheritance. At last the door opened. Klaus Lonsky came in. He was a tall, good-looking young man in his mid-twenties. He looked at McKenna with interest, not fear. He shook hands and smiled. McKenna decided he might just as well start with the sixty-four-dollar question.

"Do you know a man named Scharpwinkel?"

"Yes."

McKenna decided that God was smiling on him at last. And another thing. He'd answered in English. Klaus Lonsky spoke good English. How did he know Scharpwinkel?

"By sight only. But I've seen him often. He was head of the Gestapo. In 1943 I was in the Wehrmacht, and posted as a lieutenant to the military police in Breslau. There was a great deal of fighting. I never spoke to Scharpwinkel, but I knew him well, and many others in the Gestapo there."

McKenna could not believe his good luck. McKenna pulled out his bunch of photographs from his inside pocket, and handed one to Klaus. "Can you tell me who that is?"

"Doctor Absalon." Luck was getting better. McKenna went on asking questions: Where was Scharpwinkel now?

"Dead."

"Why do you say that?"

"Breslau towards the end was declared a fortress. All military forces were banded together to man the front lines. First, trenches were dug in the suburbs, then as the Soviets drove us back, there was house-to-house fighting through the streets. Scharpwinkel formed his own company of Gestapo officers and Kripo police to fight to the last. They were practically all killed. He must have been among them."

"But you never saw his body."

"No. But eventually the city surrendered, and we fled."

"What other important Gestapo or Kripo leaders did you see or know in Breslau?"

"Well, there was Doctor Kah, Obersturmbannführer Ernst Kah, head of the SD—the Sicherheitsdienst, the SS intelligence service. Then there were Wielen and Seetzen."

"So Absalon, Scharpwinkel, Kah, Seetzen. You believe they are all dead."

"They are all either dead or captured by the Russians, which amounts to the same thing."

McKenna had one more question. "Do you know anyone else around here who served in Breslau?"

Klaus thought about that. "Yes, I have a friend, another infantry lieutenant like myself. His name is Hubertus Zembrodt, but I do not know his address or where he is. These are troubled times, Herr Major."

"They certainly are," agreed McKenna. "Confusing, too." After his interview with Lonsky, McKenna felt he had at least made a few human contacts. Cross-filing and cross-checking indicated that there was a possibility that either Kah or Seetzen might be hiding in the Hamburg area. After all, with the Russians pushing through past Berlin, that was the only area left to them, and it was plain they all preferred to be captured by the Americans or the British.

He circulated all available names, photographs, and descriptions to the RAF special police units and Special Investigation Branch. And although the Judge Advocate's office in London was very wary about his intentions in approaching the recent enemy, he began to make contacts with the German civil police, who were still under the direct control of the Allied military government. Many of them, now cleared of any sinister Nazi motivation, seemed to McKenna to belong to the "decent-cop" type, and were genuinely, perhaps penitently, anxious to assist.

The name Zembrodt had not been turned up in his filing and cross-checking, but that was not unusual: Zembrodt was not a wanted man, but an ordinary army lieutenant doing his duty. Like Klaus Lonsky, he must have been evacuated from Breslau, and be now residing somewhere in the district. McKenna scrutinized his maps. As far as he could see, the only small town he had missed was a tiny place some eighteen miles from Rinteln called Barntrup.

In the office he said to Wilhelm, "May as well make the trip. Make a change from losing our eyesight going through files." They arrived at the Bürgermeister's office. He had a pretty secretary who took quite a fancy to Wilhelm, one that was reciprocated. Delighted to oblige two army-of-occupation officers, she fished out the file on former members of the armed forces living in the district.

"Zembrodt? Certainly." She flicked over the pages. "Here he is. Hubertus Zembrodt. Wehrmacht. Alverdiessennerstrasse 20. Our local police will be happy to show you the way."

Hubertus Zembrodt lived in a small cottage. About thirty years old, the young army lieutenant was very helpful. He remembered Klaus Lonsky very well. And the man named Scharpwinkel?

"He's dead. Killed by the Russians."

"You're certain of that?" asked McKenna.

The young man shrugged his shoulders. "I'm not. But my wife is. She will tell you."

Frau Gerda Zembrodt was eighteen and attractive. And she had a talent for drama. She had met and married her soldier husband during the bloody battle for Breslau. He had been wounded twice, the second time seriously, and as she had nursing experience she got a job in the hospital to be near him. On the day after Breslau surrendered, the tenth or eleventh of May—she couldn't quite recall—two Russian officers came into the wards with Dr. Mehling, who was in charge of the hospital. With them was a Russian woman in civilian clothing, memorable because she carried a large revolver in her hand. The doctor led them into a ward and the woman screamed, "Which one is Lieutenant Hagamann? Speak up!" There was little hope of his disguising his identity, and a man in a corner bed raised his hand. "I am."

The Russian woman rushed furiously towards him, threatening him with the pistol, and tore back his covers.

"You are a liar! A liar! You are Scharpwinkel, the Breslau chief of Gestapo. Get out of that bed! Out!"

"But I am wounded. My leg is wounded."

The pistol was shoved into his ear. "If you don't get out now, you will be dead!"

Shouting back at the top of his voice, he stumbled to the center of the ward. He appealed to Dr. Mehling. That was no use. The doctor too was under arrest for sheltering him. As they were being pushed out of the ward, a nurse put an army greatcoat over Scharpwinkel's nightclothes.

A minute or two later they heard a burst of machine-gun fire. "Scharpwinkel was dead," said Gerda.

McKenna scratched his ear. "You saw him being shot?"

"No, we were all too frightened to even look out of the window. But everyone knew he was killed."

"You saw bloodstains afterwards, the body?"

"No, they took it away in a car."

McKenna nodded, and after a few more questions thanked the Zembrodts for being so helpful, and asked them if they would mind signing a formal statement about this evidence. They had no objection. Wilhelm wrote it all down, and they both signed.

On the train going back to Rinteln, Wilhelm sensed McKenna's mood. "You don't think Scharpwinkel is dead?"

"No. No sign of Scharpwinkel or Doctor Mehling. No bodies; no bloodstains, witnesses, or corroborative evidence. The Russians want him as much as we do. He's got to answer a lot of questions. We'll have to get our top brass in Berlin to make a request."

The phone rang in the Royal Air Force S.I.B. office in Hamburg; Sergeant Taylor picked it up. The voice was hoarse and muffled, and spoke with a guarded German accent. "I have something of interest to report to you. An SS Obersturmbannführer named Ernest Mercier is hiding in the Swedish Mission Hostel in Hamburg." The phone clicked dead. Taylor was not surprised. Citizens had not lost their Nazi-indoctrinated duty of betraying each other. The only thing different on this occasion was that Taylor had just read McKenna's circular giving new details of Nazis on the wanted list. Taylor made inquiries. The desk clerk at the Swedish Mission Hostel verified that Herr Mercier had indeed stayed there but had gone. However, he had left a forwarding address. Taylor was at the front door of a boardinghouse, Number 23 Gurlittstrasse, within the hour. Mercier's landlady expected him back that evening and, anxious to assist British authorities, promised to telephone them when he returned. The telephone rang at 7:00 P.M. Half an hour later, Taylor put the man under arrest.

Ernest Mercier was furious.

"Here are my identity papers. As you can see, I am a displaced person of French nationality.

341

Here is my supplementary ration card stamped by your military government. And here is my permit signed by your military superiors authorizing me to travel through Germany on behalf of the British Army to buy wine for the officers' messes." He gave Sergeant Taylor one of the cold-eyed stares typical of the German officer class, and Sergeant Taylor began to ask questions. Herr Mercier did not intend to answer questions. Taylor decided Mercier should spend the night in the local civil jail, while he made more inquiries. An hour after Taylor got back to his unit, the phone rang. It was the German civil police. Mercier had made a determined effort to escape. He had not succeeded. Sergeant Taylor sent back his two NCOs to make sure he did not try a second escape. Next morning Sergeant Taylor began his interrogation. He was an ex-policeman, thorough and patient. Ernest Mercier admitted he was Dr. Ernst Kah, formerly of the Sicherheitsdienst.

After further interrogation, Kah, now almost anxious to implicate anybody who could help his case, admitted he knew the whereabouts of one other SS officer hiding in Hamburg.

"His name?" asked Taylor.

"Standartenführer Seetzen, a Gestapo security police colonel." One of McKenna's most wanted men! Sergeant Taylor managed to keep his face very still and very cold.

"You know his address?"

"Yes, but he must not know that I've—I've—"

"If you follow our instructions he will never

know that you informed against him," said Sergeant Taylor. "Now this is what you will do. . . ."

Midnight. A narrow half-gutted street of tall, high-gabled houses in a seamy area. The lights of the two black Capitan police cars dimmed as they moved into position. Dr. Ernst Kah with his police escort sat in the second car. The first drew up at a doorway. Taylor and his police posse moved swiftly up the stone steps, picked the lock, and were through in seconds. Seetzen was asleep. He woke to find a revolver at his head. He was allowed to dress, was handcuffed and then bundled down the steps. Outside the headlights of the second car suddenly held them in its blaze. Kah stared through the windshield and nodded his head. An RAF special policeman got out and gave Taylor a thumbs-up.

Still handcuffed, Seetzen was placed in the back seat of the first car, an escort beside him. Taylor sat in front next to the driver. They headed towards the headquarters of the police unit. Halfway there Taylor heard a crunch, and felt the impact against the back of his seat as Seetzen's body arched forward and his feet hit the upholstery. Immediately he knew what had happened, and cursed himself for his carelessness. But who could have known this one was important enough and evil enough to need to bite into the cyanide capsule concealed in his teeth? Taylor shouted, "Hospital, quick!" But even as the car changed direction and increased speed, Taylor knew it would be too late.

One of his mates had been there when Himmler bit into his capsule at Second Army headquarters, Lüneburg, and took very few minutes to die.

Sergeant Taylor telephoned McKenna in Hanover to give him the news. McKenna said, "Well done, laddie. Two in one go. Kah was Number Twelve on my list, Seetzen Number Seven. I suppose Kah never mentioned Scharpwinkel."

"Not in any of my interrogations, sir."

"Obersturmbannführer Kah had got himself covered with a pretty good alias, don't you think? Buying wine for British Army clubs . . ."

"A very good one, sir."

Kah had not only gotten himself a good alias, he could prove his complete back of knowledge or cooperation in the Sagan murders. Ferried back to England to the London Cage, and interrogated by the best experts in the business, he was found to be in the clear.

Chapter Nineteen

IN THE MIDDLE OF December, some three and a half months after McKenna had started his investigation, Wing Commander Bowes arrived at Rinteln, full of zeal. He had now been promoted to chief of the Special Investigation Branch, British Forces, occupied Germany. McKenna, meanwhile, found himself promoted to squadron leader, which meant he could function more efficiently: station commanders and officials did not like being cross-questioned by officers of comparatively junior rank.

They also received a new recruit.

Flight Lieutenant Dickie Lyon was twenty-eight years old, tall, thin, intelligent, and thoughtful. He smoked a pipe. He had graduated at the top of his class at the officer-oriented Hendon Police Staff College, and had served as detective-inspector in various stations of London's Metropolitan Police. He had volunteered for the RAF, and at the end of the war was working for the Air Directorate of Intelligence, interrogating scientists in the Luftwaffe and the aeronautical industry about the technological advances they had made. On one trip his plane was weather-bound at Brussels and he spent the night at a hotel. There he bumped into a Major Pancheff, who was second-in-command to Lieutenant Colonel Scotland, the formidable head of the London District Cage of the War Crimes Investigation Unit. They talked for a long time. As Lyon was fluent in German, Pancheff suggested he transfer to Bowes's outfit.

Bowes's first destination was Czechoslovakia, to which country he intended to take Lyon to break him in. The journey made a lot of sense: seven of the Sagan officers had been murdered there, and the Czech government had promised cooperation. Officials in the Czech government had strong feelings about two of those murdered Sagan officers: Flight Lieutenant Ernst Valenta, one of the Escape Committee's most brilliant officers, was a Czech fighter pilot flying with the RAF and had been a member of their intelligence operation; and Tom Kirby-Green, a regular RAF officer, had been squadron commander of the Czech training units in Britain. The Czechs had uncovered links to both those murders. One had come up, strangely enough, through a letter from a Dr. van der Bijl, who had written to the British ambassador in Prague. During Tom Kirby-Green's months with the Czech air force Dr. van der Bijl and Tom had become great friends. The news of his death, and that of Canadian pilot Flying Officer Gordon Kidder, his escape partner, had sickened him, and when he had returned to Czechoslovakia he had determined to seek out the guilty men.

"Quite extraordinary," said Captain Vaca of the

346

Czech army and intelligence branch, who had been assigned to Bowes and Lyon for their investigation. "We knew of course, that Kriminalrat Hans Ziegler was chief of the Gestapo in Moravia, where both Squadron Leader Kirby-Green and Flying Officer Kidder were killed, but we hadn't really had time to go into the details."

"They made a pretty good escape break, didn't they?" asked Lyon thoughtfully. "Moravia, Brno—Vienna less than a hundred miles to the south."

Captain Vaca nodded. "They certainly did," he agreed. "Doctor van der Bijl discovered that it was Ziegler who received the Berlin teleprint from RSHA; he arranged the executions, and took great precautions to cover up the crime. He ordered four Gestapo agents to carry out the killings. Two cars, two drivers: Kiowsky and Schwartzer. Two executioners: Erich Zacharias and Adolf Knippelberg."

"No arrests?" asked Bowes.

"We have Friedrich Kiowsky in custody."

That evening over dinner, Captain Vaca gave Bowes and Lyon the relevant details.

"Eat well," he said, raising his glass of red wine. "Tomorrow I take your appetite away."

"Great," said Bowes. "What are you doing, showing us the torture chambers?"

"More or less," said Captain Vaca. "The Gestapo occupation gave the Czechoslovakian people a very bad time. We are driving to Zlín, where we hold Kiowsky, and before that to Brno, where we hold two hundred Gestapo prisoners, the interrogation of some of which may be of interest to you. And I will show you some of the sights which the Czech people are trying to forget."

At a place called Pangratz, Captain Vaca showed them a section of the prison that the Gestapo thought was totally efficient. A long corridor was lined with thirty small cells. At the end was a "courtroom." At the back of the courtroom, behind the judge's dais, a long black curtain stretched completely across the room. Verdicts of guilt took only a few seconds to pronounce. Prisoners were then thrust through the curtain into the death chamber. There, a long rail was attached to a series of nooses that glided along it. Bodies could then be slid away like the carcasses of animals into another curtained-off room. There was also a guillotine, and cells five feet long and two feet wide, into which three or four men could be stuffed.

Bowes closed his eyes. By this time Lyon's pipe had gone out and he did not relight it. These had been men—real human beings, innocent, with wives and children, with distant hopes unrealized . . . cattle hung on wires. Bowes took a deep breath; Lyon put his pipe in his pocket.

They had yet to meet Kiowsky, who was being held in another prison. First there were the interrogations of the Gestapo officials in Brno. Most of the men they interviewed were small fry, hopeless, diminished human beings who had been caught up in the swirl of Gestapo activity.

Only one was of any interest—Franz Schauschutz, a thirty-three-year-old SS Hauptsturmführer attached, with the equivalent rank of detective-inspector, to the Gestapo. Captain Vaca had saved him until last. Schauschutz talked forever. Bowes and Lyon both knew that he was held on various serious charges by the Czechs; they also knew that he thought his only hope of survival was to impress Bowes with his revelations, and hope to be transferred as a material witness to the British zone, where he might receive a more lenient sentence. He maintained he had taken no part in the murders of Kirby-Green or Kidder. His sole responsibility was to act as Zlín Gestapo chief while Hans Ziegler went on leave. He did admit he had worked on the teleprint that had to be sent to Berlin, but he swore he was absolutely innocent of any part of the conspiracy.

That evening Captain Vaca gathered a few of his army friends together and took Bowes and Lyon out to dinner. They ate well and drank well, and for the first time in what seemed to be a lifetime both Bowes and Lyon managed to laugh. "Now," said Captain Vaca, "let's go for a last drink at one of Brno's famous bars. The Gestapo adored it. You'll enjoy it too."

It was a cellar bar, its arched walls covered with murals. One was a Rubenesque panorama of full-breasted naked women. "The faces belong to some of the secretaries the Gestapo brought here," explained Vaca. "They are the nymphs being chased by the Gestapo satyrs. Obviously their duties were amatory as well as clerical. And plainly the artist must have been Gestapo, to be allowed to depict his senior officers in such wanton caperings. You will notice the faces adorning the satyr bodies . . ."

"Jesus Christ!" said Bowes, staring. "I know him! I know that face. That's the man we've been interrogating all afternoon!"

"Schauschutz," confirmed Vaca. "Another gentleman in the scene is your missing link, the second murderer, Erich Zacharias. And here's the driver, Kiowsky. And Knippelberg. They had no fears. They knew their Führer's Reich was going to last a thousand years—believed they would be remembered that long."

"They will be," said Lyon, "but for different reasons." He paused and looked at Vaca. "Zacharias and Knippelberg? The question is, where do we find them?"

Captain Vaca said, "Perhaps Kiowsky might be able to tell us." He went on: "You will also meet the local judge—Judge Molowsky. You will like him. He cannot wait to observe two British policemen—he hopes from Scotland Yard—interrogating a suspect. I hope you don't disappoint him."

Dickie Lyon grinned. "I shall restrain the formidable Inspector Bowes of Scotland Yard from tearing Kiowsky limb from limb."

Friedrich Kiowsky was scared. They brought him into Judge Molowsky's office and he stood at attention, tall, white-faced, dark-eyed. He had watched Gestapo interrogations many times, and if these officers in blue uniforms were anything like that then he was in for a very bad time indeed.

Captain Vaca had provided Bowes with many pictures. The first one Bowes pushed into Kiowsky's hand was that of the mural. Lyon did the translation.

"You know that man," said Bowes pugnaciously, pointing his finger. His voice did not sound friendly.

"Yes, Herr Major," Kiowsky confirmed. "That is Kriminalsekretär Adolf Knippelberg."

"And this man?" Again the stubby pointing forefinger.

Kiowsky's voice wavered. "That is Hauptsturmführer Schauschutz."

"You were present when the two RAF officers were shot?"

"Yes."

"Then start your story at the beginning and tell us exactly what happened." Kiowsky was anxious to help.

His Gestapo boss, Herr Ziegler, had told him to prepare the car for a drive to Breslau, nonstop, to convey two English terror-fliers to prison there. They would take one prisoner in their car; the other would be taken in a second car coming from Brno. The second driver would be a man named Schwartzer, accompanying Gestapo Kriminalsekretär Knippelberg. They set off at midnight. At about twelve miles short of Moravská Ostrava,

351

they stopped. The officers' handcuffs were removed and they were told they could relieve themselves. As they stood by the ditch, first one then the other made a dash for freedom. Zacharias and Knippelberg fired at them as they ran away and they were killed.

He stopped. There was a long silence.

Bowes said, "This bugger's trying to sell us the official version straight from Gestapo files."

Judge Molowsky, who was a rather plump, round-faced, cheerful individual, had, before the interrogation began, ordered several flagons of beer and a giant bottle of slivovitz to be placed on his sideboard. Lyon could not follow this legal ploy, especially as Judge Molowsky's only comment had been, "It will help our concentration."

"Let's do it all over again," said Bowes. "This time in greater detail."

Kiowsky looked nervous as Lyon translated. This business of questions and answers, the whole thing being typed out by a secretary, plainly puzzled him. Two men, both sitting astride reversed chairs, arms across the backs . . . no rubber truncheons, nooses, threats of torture. But now the questions were quicker, harsher, Lyon sometimes shooting in a question of his own, sometimes translating Bowes's quick interjection: How fast did they run? What did they look like as they ran? Were their arms pumping up and down like sprinters'? Bowes imitated the action.

"Yes, yes. Of course they were."

"What about the handcuffs?"

Kiowsky was puzzled. "I told you we took them off."

"Were they handcuffed in front or behind?"

"In front."

"Then why remove them? You don't have to do that just to have a pee."

Kiowsky was still considering that point when Bowes asked quickly, "How much petrol had he got in the tank?"

"A full tank," Kiowsky answered.

"How far would that get him? How many miles could he get on a full tank?"

"Two hundred miles."

"In that rough country? Steep hills? Ice and snow? What time were the officers shot?"

"Four A.M."

As the torrent of questions continued, Kiowsky began to get very uneasy. He could not fathom in which direction the questions were leading.

"You had been driving for four hours! You hadn't even reached Moravská Ostrava! You weren't even a quarter of the way to Breslau! Where were you going to refuel?"

Bowes thrust his face close to Kiowsky's and yelled, "Where were you going to refuel?"

Kiowsky's face was gray and sweaty. He swallowed convulsively several times.

Bowes thrust home his point, his voice violent.

"You said you were going to drive nonstop to Breslau. You had no chance of reaching Breslau on a single tank of fuel. Because you were not going to Breslau, were you? You knew those of-

353

ficers were going to be shot long before you reached Breslau. You were driving them to be murdered and you are as guilty of those murders as either Zacharias or Knippelberg."

Kiowsky slumped in his chair, browbeaten and defeated. Lyon glanced at Judge Molowsky, indicating the drinks. Molowsky nodded; Lyon poured out a full tumbler of slivovitz and handed it to Kiowsky, who drank it greedily. He still did not understand what was going on. The Gestapo did not hand you a glass of slivovitz; they kicked your teeth in. Both Bowes and Lyon understood that he was only a small cog in the huge Gestapo machine, a machine that was beyond his comprehension. He drank his slivovitz slowly and they gave him time. And Kiowsky decided that a free confession was easier than trying to maintain a cardboard deck of lies.

"I admit they were still handcuffed. They did not try to escape. But I was still in the car when they were shot. I had nothing to do with their murders."

"Right," said Bowes affably. "We'll go over it once more, and now we want the truth. I expect you'll wish to alter the deposition which the secretary is typing?"

Yes, he wished to do that. He had asked Ziegler what he should do about petrol, as one tankful would certainly not take them as far as Breslau. Ziegler had said that they did not have to reach Breslau, and he was not to ask questions but just do what he was told.

354

On the journey he drove and Zacharias sat in the front seat with him. He asked Zacharias what was going to happen to the two officers, forgetting that one of them could speak German. Zacharias had not forgotten, and simply turned his thumb down. Then Kiowsky knew that the two officers were going to be shot.

Bowes and Lyon, helped by Judge Molowsky and Captain Vaca, collected more evidence. They took Kiowsky out to where the shootings had taken place. They took statements from the crematorium attendant, who said he had no way of identifying the bodies except by his notes and making sketches of their wounds. He added, "At the end of the war I reported what I had done to our authorities, as I was sure, someday, there would be inquiries." But both Bowes and Lyon knew they were no closer to catching the murderers. There were plenty of rumors. One was that Ziegler had committed suicide at the end of the war; another was that he'd been killed in the bombing raids. Much more likely was the report that said he had been seen in the Zell-am-See area, in Austria, a place he had been particularly fond of in wartime. As for Knippelberg, records showed that he had been held by the Americans before they moved out of Czechoslovakia. But the most important clue concerned Zacharias, and was offered by Judge Molowsky. He had the address of Zacharias's wife in Zlín.

Bowes dispatched Lyon immediately. Zacharias's wife was a pretty Czech woman of twenty-five, and she hadn't a good word to say about her husband. He was a swine, a deceiver, a liar, a cheat, and a murderer; life had been pure hell living with the man; the sooner they caught him the better, but all she knew of his whereabouts was that he was living somewhere in northwestern Germany.

Bowes and Lyon then took the train to Prague. They would ask McKenna to meet them in Wiesbaden; McKenna could take over the hunt for Zacharias in the north, while they headed south to Austria and Zell-am-See.

When they arrived at Wiesbaden, McKenna was in the bar sipping Krug champagne, which cost five marks, the equivalent price of one cigarette on the black market. Bowes briefed McKenna with photographs and papers relating to Zacharias. He had also received information that suggested Zacharias might be working in Bremen, which was used by the Americans as their port of entry, and therefore identified as an American enclave in the British zone. McKenna was delighted. He got on well with the Yanks, and found them extremely helpful.

Captain Leather, a tall, lean Texan, was civil administrative officer for the port of Bremen. McKenna met him in his office just before closing time. Leather listened politely, hung his hat over the office clock, and said, "If there's anyone here by the name of Zacharias, we'll find him."

They went through the files. It was long past

midnight when Leather's finger lighted upon an entry. "Does this sound like him? Erich Hermann Zacharias. Arrived here September 1945. Now working as a clerk in Refrigeration Plant Two-eighty-three in the docks. Got his home address too. Shall we pick him up now?"

"No," said McKenna. "Might be an old address, and if anyone sees us snooping round they might give him a tip-off. Let's get him while he's at work."

The next morning McKenna had to admit the Americans were thorough: they had armed guards at every entrance and exit to the refrigeration building. Inside the clerk's room was a long row of desks topped by green lights. From Bowes's photographs McKenna recognized Zacharias immediately. He walked up behind him and tapped him on the shoulder. "Are you Erich Zacharias?"

"Yes."

McKenna said, "I am a British officer in the Royal Air Force investigating the Sagan, Stalag Luft III murders. I have reason to believe that you were involved in the murders of Squadron Leader Kirby-Green and Flying Officer Kidder, and I am taking you into custody."

Zacharias did not try to resist arrest—the sight of the armed U.S. patrol prevented that possibility. He was taken to the local civilian prison for holding purposes.

The next morning a disgruntled Captain Leather was on the phone. Zacharias had escaped. There may have been collusion with the civilian police, but there wasn't much point in going into it—the fact was, Zacharias was gone. The U.S. military police were doing their damndest to track him down. McKenna blew out his breath in exasperation, and did not think they had much chance.

He was wrong. Captain Leather's boys knew what they were doing and retained an adequate network of informers. And ex-Gestapo were not popular. Three weeks later they intercepted a letter addressed to a friend of Zacharias who had worked in the same refrigeration plant. The letter had a return address, a house in Fallersleben, a small town close to the Russian zone. The letter said only, "Erich has been ill but is improving and will soon be on his way."

They raided the house at Fallersleben and found Zacharias dressed and about to disappear into the Russian zone. They had captured him with only minutes to spare. This time McKenna escorted him back into the British zone. He was taking no more chances with the man who had helped to murder Tom Kirby-Green and Gordon Kidder. He sat with him on the noisy Dakota bumping its way back to England and, still handcuffed wrist to wrist with his prisoner, handed him over at the London Cage.

He explained Zacharias's propensity for escaping to Colonel Scotland, and suggested they look after him carefully. Rather loftily, the colonel pointed out that the London Cage was guarded by the Scots Guards and that escape was very unlikely. McKenna said he was happy to know that.

His plane had scarcely landed back in Germany when he received a signal from Colonel Scotland asking for all available photographs of Zacharias to be flown to London immediately. Zacharias had escaped.

Fortunately, Zacharias had jumped from a window, hurt his foot, and lost a shoe; he was easily recaptured. It also turned out that, tired of trying to escape, tired of trying to duck the charges, he was prepared to admit he killed one of the officers—but, he said, only because of Ziegler's explicit orders.

Then Dickie Lyon brought important news. "Natzweiler," he said.

The name of Natzweiler concentration camp was burnt into McKenna's brain. High in the Vosges mountains, Natzweiler was the only death camp the Nazis had built on French soil. It was the site of vile experiments; prisoners died there by the thousands of exhaustion, starvation, and execution. It was also the only concentration camp in the Nazi empire where they left the gas chambers intact, the guards having fled before the Allied advance. They had sent Flying Officer Dennis Cochran's ashes back to Sagan from there. Tall, quiet, sensitive, easygoing, and intelligent, Cochran had changed the color of his uniform to that used by the displaced persons' labor corps. Van Wymeersch, who eventually got back to England, noted seeing him coolly sweeping a street in

Frankfurt. He had made it to the very edge of the Swiss frontier before recapture. He had been twenty-four years old.

"Major Barkworth," said Lyon, "our friend in the War Crimes Investigation Unit, reports that in connection with his own inquiries he picked up two suspects and lodged them in the civil jail at Wuppertal. One of them was Ganninger—"

McKenna sat up. "Adjutant at Natzweiler?"

"Correct. Who after his first interrogation was returned to his cell, where he cut his throat with a razor blade he'd sewn into his jacket. The other, Herberg, let slip not only that he had been a member of the Karlsruhe Gestapo, but had known about the cremation of a British officer in Natzweiler in 1944. Nothing to do with him, naturally."

"When are you leaving?" said McKenna.

"Now! To the U.S. zone it's three hundred miles round-trip."

"Let's get moving," said McKenna. "We can't trust the civil police to hold a man of that importance."

McKenna's interrogation tactics were very simple. He interviewed Kriminalkommissar Walter Herberg in his cell in Wuppertal jail.

"You were," said McKenna quietly, "on the staff of Oberregierungsrat Josef Gmeiner, chief of the Gestapo at Karlsruhe?"

The corners of Herberg's mouth drooped. At last it had all caught up with him.

"Yes," he said.

"Were you there in March and April 1944?"

"Yes."

McKenna's voice was still quiet, and Lyon could make out its soft Lancashire burr. "Have you anything on your conscience from that time?"

No bullying. No threatening. McKenna had looked at the man and sensed his inner despair. Herberg's eyes had met McKenna's and retreated. He began to speak, stumbled over the first words, put his hands over his face, and wept. McKenna gave him a long time to recover. Then he told his story.

Herberg ended: "I hope I have remembered every detail."

As far as McKenna was concerned, he had. He had given him names: Karlsruhe Gestapo head Josef Gmeiner; Heinrich Boschert, the driver; Kriminalsekretär Otto Preiss, who fired the gun. He believed Preiss to be in the U.S. zone, Boschert in the French zone.

"The matter has been dreadful to me," Herberg continued. "I have tried to block it out of my mind. It is horrible how a man can be thrown into agony by orders that destroy his peace of mind and leave his conscience tortured. It was impossible for me to let the officer escape, because I could not give orders to that effect to my subordinates. If I had let him escape the concentration camp would have been waiting for us, and I could not be expected to let myself down in front of my subordinates."

McKenna then went into the American sector,

where help was immediate. Preiss was a common name but he took one camp at a time: Dachau, Ludwigsburg, Mannheimm, and Darmstadt. There were half a dozen Preisses in those camps, and McKenna swiftly dismissed five of them.

The sixth he looked at with special interest. He was big, blond, truculent, about forty years of age.

"You are Otto Preiss, former Kriminalsekretär, Gestapo, Karlsruhe?" said McKenna.

"No, Herr Major," said Preiss.

"Oh! Where do you come from, then?"

"Heidelberg. I served in Heidelberg, Herr Major."

"In what department of the Gestapo?"

"Department 4(1)C, Herr Major. Foreign labor and economic sabotage."

"Who was the head of Department 4(1)C?" Otto Preiss hesitated, and McKenna prompted him, "You weren't going to say Kriminalkommissar Reise?"

"No," said Preiss, plainly concerned.

"Or Kriminaldirektor Faber, boss of Department Four?"

"No, Herr Major." Preiss was very worried.

McKenna's voice expressed concern. "It's this awful camp," he said. "I think it's affecting your memory. Now I have a piece of paper here, and it has a very good description of you. It says that you were *born* in Heidelberg, not that you served in it. It says that you were a Kriminalsekretär under Reise and Faber. Now the reason I am interested in you is that I am an officer of the Special

Investigation Branch of the Royal Air Force and I am making inquiries into the murder of Flying Officer Cochran of the Royal Air Force who was shot in the neighborhood of Natzweiler concentration camp at about eleven o'clock in the morning of April first, 1944. Now I know you know something about it, but I want to tell you something of what *I* know. I know that you and Herberg and Boschert were in it together, and I know who did the shooting. I know it was not your idea. I know that Gmeiner ordered the shooting because Himmler ordered him, and Hitler ordered Himmler. Now you tell me what *you* know about it."

Preiss made his confession. There were significant differences between his and Herberg's story. Cochran had been led along the path by all three of his escorts: Preiss on the right, Herberg on the left, and Boschert in the rear. Herberg had told Cochran to turn right and face the woods, then nodded to Preiss. Preiss had shot him twice. Death had been instantaneous.

Preiss boasted about other executions he had carried out. Naturally he was only obeying the orders of his superiors.

McKenna took Preiss to join Herberg at Minden's secure prison. Herberg had already told him that he thought the French had taken Boschert prisoner. McKenna contacted them. Yes, they had held him, but he had been cleared by them and passed along to the Americans, who also wanted him for interrogation. The Americans swiftly replied to McKenna's inquiry. Boschert was in Number 2 Internee Hospital in Karlsruhe.

McKenna found him there, suffering from a broken back. While in the French prison he had fallen down a flight of stairs and broken his spine. "Fallen or been pushed?" McKenna inquired. Boschert said nothing. The French tended to remember the two hundred thousand of their compatriots, men and women, executed in concentration camps and prisons when the Allies invaded. They also remembered how in Fresnes prison in Paris, a favorite sport of Gestapo interrogators was to handcuff a prisoner with his hands behind his back, take him to the top of a flight of stone steps, and push him down. Boschert was ready to talk. The only significant alteration to the story was that he had stayed in the car while Herberg and Preiss got out to do the shooting.

Finally, Gmeiner himself was handed over by the French on the understanding that if the charges did not stick, he would be returned to them. The charges did stick. Gmeiner's defense, like all the others, was that he was simply carrying out orders.

At his trial, Boschert admitted that both he and Josef Gmeiner had been instrumental in sending six English agents, all women, to a death camp. The British prosecuting counsel said, "I presume you were given that duty because as Gmeiner's adjutant you were his biggest and best thug?"

As Boschert was considering that statement, the

prosecutor continued: "You agree that the Gestapo were a lot of thugs, do you not?"

"I never regarded myself as one of them," Boschert replied.

"How long do you have to be in the Gestapo before you become one of them? You were there from 1938."

"I was a member of the Gestapo from the first day I joined it."

"And you considered yourself a member of the Gestapo, and you strutted around Karlsruhe in the Gestapo uniform, and you were proud of your uniform at that time, were you not?"

"Yes."

"It is only when you lose the war that you become a timid little mouse, or when you allegedly hide in the car waiting to hear the shot which killed Flying Officer Cochran?"

Boschert was found guilty, as was Oberregierungsrat Josef Gmeiner, who maintained his legalistic stance to the end: "To refuse to obey an order and to inform Berlin that the unit was not prepared to carry out the order would have had the result of immediate arrest and a subsequent condemnation by an SS and police court."

It was the defense of every Gestapo official. Orders were orders. If you disobeyed them, you were executed.

Chapter Twenty

FLIGHT LIEUTENANT HAROLD HARRISON, young and enthusiastic, was the last to join Wing Commander Bowes's investigating team. Summoned to Bowes's office, he saluted, announced his name, and stood at attention until Bowes waved a hand at him, saying, "For God's sake, sit down. I'll be with you in a second."

Wing Commander Bowes, like all good policemen, was methodical. He kept records. And one record he kept very carefully indeed.

It had been discovered in a Gestapo records office in Munich after the U.S. forces overran the city. It was headed simply, "Decrease of Prisoners of War in Sagan, Stalag Luft III"—"decrease" being the euphemism used for the murder of fifty officers. It contained a long typed list of names, many of them misspelled, in the left-hand margin, and other columns beside it. What enraged Bowes most was that all the columns were empty except for the two little black marks signifying "ditto." Opposite the first name was "Cause of Death," and beneath it, "Shot While Trying to Escape"!

Bowes added other columns, carefully writing in the name, date of arrest, and sentence after trial of every Gestapo official implicated in each murder. That, he decided, kept the record completely straight.

Bowes turned his attention back to Harrison.

"Glad to have you with us, Lieutenant." He picked up Harrison's papers. "I see you did a tour in Bomber Command?"

"Yes, sir."

"Any experience with police work?"

"No, sir. I was working in a solicitor's office before I was called up. I suppose that gave Air Ministry the clue when bomber pilots became redundant, and they had to find something for us to do while we served out our time."

"Dead right, and we've got plenty for you to do. I'm sending you to join Dickie Lyon—he'll show you the ropes. He's interrogating Gestapo suspects at a camp at Esterwegen, near the Dutch border."

In Esterwegen Dickie Lyon looked at Harrison with appraising eyes. Harry Harrison had yet to find out how depressing these first postwar winters in Germany really were. The weather was awful. The misery of literally hundreds of thousands of people was not only a day-to-day reality, it was atmospheric, like a fog that choked you. And no matter how hard you worked, or how much you tried to rationalize, the terrible problems of millions of displaced people and a whole nation in ruins could not be avoided. Lyon knew that one of the ways of keeping sane was to adopt a tunnel-vision viewpoint, to concentrate on just one thing—your job. Young Harrison would have to find that out.

Over a drink, Harrison said hesitantly, "I've never been trained as a police officer; in fact, I'm not sure I've got that sort of inquiring, disbelieving mind."

Lyon chuckled. "The basic art of interrogation is to understand what is required and why it's required. The man who's being interrogated is usually holding something back. These Gestapo are still full of arrogance. They're cowed but they're often fighting for their lives; and with their police background—because that's what the Gestapo were supposed to be, the secret state police—they are very accomplished liars. Interesting, though . . . this morning we're going to talk to one who heard that I was here. A man called Achterberg. He approached Camp Registry, saying he might have information for me."

"Is that strange?"

"Very strange. Usually they're hiding in the woodwork."

Ex-Sturmbannführer Kurt Achterberg, as Lyon had suggested, had little left of his arrogance. He was tall, thin, sharp-featured, with eyes that flitted in all directions. He announced that he had worked at the headquarters of the Danzig Gestapo—he had done nothing wrong, of course—but he had some information that might be useful. Did the major know that the head of the Danzig Gestapo had been Dr. Venediger?

Yes, Lyon did know that.

And his mind was alert. The whole team knew that four Sagan officers—Henri Picard, Gilbert Walenn, Edward Brettell, and Romas Marcinkus—had been murdered in Danzig. The whole team were furious that the Polish and Russian authorities had refused admittance to that area.

Did the major know the name Hauptmann Bruchardt?

No, the major didn't.

He must beware, then, when and if they caught up with him. Bruchardt was a terror. He had shot men dead in his own office and in the street. He'd had a rawhide whip in a pail of water beside his desk, and used it often. "He is a dangerous man, Herr Hauptmann, and is always armed. I advise you to shoot him dead as soon as you meet him."

Lyon's face did not alter. Why draw such a colorful picture of someone who must have been a Gestapo colleague? Lyon wondered why he should be the recipient of this valuable information. Plainly there was a grudge buried somewhere. "You have Bruchardt's address?"

"It's here, I have written it down. He lives in Hamburg."

Flight Lieutenant Lyon immediately dispatched an armed unit to pick up the brutal Bruchardt. He was not there. But they found—as usual—an angry and vindictive wife. The brute had deserted her, run away with his mistress, and she knew the name of the town where he was working, doubtless under another name. It was deep in southern Germany, a town called Kempten.

By coincidence, McKenna had also decided to try hard to dig out a few details on the Danzig Gestapo. He was interrogating prisoners with Danzig connections at a camp called Neuengamme, some distance from Esterwegen. Having no luck, he telephoned the documentation clerk to tell him he was leaving. The clerk said, "Oh, there's one more who's not on your list. He's only been here a couple of days. You want to see him?"

"Might as well. What's his name?"

"Achterberg—he's Danzig Gestapo."

Achterberg was quite put out. "But I've been answering questions about this matter all over Germany."

McKenna read him a list of names. He knew none of them. McKenna came to Bruchardt. "Bruchardt?"

McKenna knew from the look that flashed across Achterberg's face that there was something here to be investigated. He also knew Achterberg was keeping something back. After a long pause Achterberg said, "Yes, I know Bruchardt."

"You don't like him?"

"No."

"Why not?"

"He's having an affair with my wife."

"Can you help us trace him?"

Achterberg thought for a while, then said, "I can give you a lady's address in a place called Kempten."

370

McKenna returned to Rinteln and bumped into Lyon. "Hi, Dickie, I've got a lead on a man called Bruchardt in a town—"

"—called Kempten," interrupted Lyon. They both went in to see Wingco Bowes.

"American zone," Bowes instructed them. "Two good Yanks there in the field office of the U.S. Counter Intelligence Corps: John Kiselyk and Roger Cope. Both of you go; Bruchardt sounds like a toughie."

The woman in Kempten turned out to be a Frau Blum. Roger Cope found her without difficulty. She claimed not to know anyone called Bruchardt.

McKenna was a little peevish. He had worked close to fifteen hours a day for four days on this project, and he was very tired. "Oh yes, you do," he told her. "You also know a woman called Frau Achterberg who is his mistress. Now, why don't you be sensible and give us his address, if he's not living here? Then we can all go home and get some sleep. Otherwise *you're* going to be up all night, and *we're* going to be up all night. And we'll catch him eventually, and you may not be left out of that scene. It may get you into serious trouble."

Frau Blum looked at the flinty faces of the four investigators and decided that Herr Bruchardt was not really worth this obstinacy. He had changed his name to Brandt, and was living at 22 Rathausstrasse.

They approached Number 22 cautiously. Lyon had apprised them of Achterberg's warnings.

"Goddamit!" said McKenna. "She's taken us for a ride!" Number 22 was a police station.

"Hold it," said Roger Cope. "There are apartments above it."

With caution they awoke the caretaker to question him. He was less amused than Frau Blum. Of course there was a man named Brandt living in a flat there—what did that have to do with him? Then he noticed that both Cope and Kiselyk were carrying submachine guns, and Lyon an automatic revolver. McKenna didn't like guns; he never carried one.

A submachine gun nuzzled the caretaker in the ribs; he said he would gladly lead them to Herr Brandt's room and unlock the door very quietly.

It was dark inside the room. A little light filtered in from the corridor. There was heavy breathing from inside that suddenly became suspended. McKenna peered in. A figure was sitting up in bed. "Now!" McKenna yelled, and the combined weight of American and British jurisdiction hurled themselves at the huge man who had leapt like an animal towards a corner cupboard. He was enormous. Only a submachine gun jammed into his stomach, and Lyon's revolver at his temple, slowed him down. McKenna opened the cupboard and removed the heavy-caliber revolver lying there. Bruchardt's wrists were far too large for their handcuffs, but their weapons kept him covered. In the local jail McKenna related the story of the escape of Zacharias from a similar jail, and Roger Cope smiled grimly. "We have other ways," he said, installing two enormous armed American guards in Bruchardt's cell with him. "If he wants to tangle with these guys, it will probably save the hangman a job."

Wing Commander Bowes was very pleased with the performance of his two civvy cops and their friends in the U.S. Counter Intelligence Corps. Clearly, however, he was even more elated about something else.

"The Russians have got Scharpwinkel. They won't bring him to us. But we can go to Moscow and interrogate him there."

"Who's going?" asked McKenna.

"I am—with the great German-speaker, Dickie Lyon." McKenna nodded. Bowes's grin evaporated. "You're not jealous?"

It was McKenna's turn to smile. "I'll lay bets you never get near him. The Soviets haven't done a damn thing to assist in our investigation since we started. They've got Scharpwinkel, and they intend to use him for their own ends. Probably make him head of intelligence in East Germany."

McKenna was pretty well right in his assumptions. Neither Bowes nor Lyon were allowed access. Neither was Captain Maurice Cornish, a member of Colonel Scotland's staff at the London Cage and a dedicated member of the investigation. He was in Moscow for three months, and in that time was allowed to get only two formal statements from Scharpwinkel, and then only when German-speaking and English-speaking Russians were present. They prevented Captain Cornish from exerting the slightest interrogational pressure on Scharpwinkel. "You must not use that tone of voice," he was told.

To Bowes and McKenna's surprise, however, the Russians said they would exchange Scharpwinkel for a certain baron who was now running a small industrial firm near Cologne. The Foreign Office repeatedly asked the Russians for details of what war crimes the baron had committed. The Russians refused any information. The case was dropped.

Later, McKenna heard that the Russians were applying for the extradition of Anton Kaindl, commandant of Sachsenhausen concentration camp, a man well known to Wings Day, Jimmy James, Sydney Dowse, and others in that group. The British were prepared to hand him over. "Why not ask for Scharpwinkel in return?" suggested McKenna to the Foreign Office.

"We do not barter in human flesh" was the Foreign Office's lofty reply.

Despite the fact that Captain Cornish's three months seemed almost wasted, Bowes and McKenna scrutinized the two statements Scharpwinkel had made very carefully.

"At least Scharpwinkel gives us the names of the various towns where the Sagan officers were held captive and interrogated by the Gestapo," Bowes said thoughtfully.

"And one we did not know about," added McKenna.

"Exactly! Kiel!"

"I know they're still holding a group of Danzig Gestapo in the jail there."

"Get Dickie Lyon and young Harrison on it at once," said Bowes. He stared across at McKenna. "You've got other things to do, I understand."

"Saarbrücken, sir," said McKenna. "The urns of Squadron Leader Bushell and the Frenchman Bernard Scheidhauer were sent from there. Our S.I.B. man in Frankfurt has picked up a lead through the Americans. He's arrested a driver named Breithaupt—a driver who might have driven Bushell and Scheidhauer to their executions."

Bowes tapped his desktop with an urgent pencil. "Get onto it, Mac—now!"

In Kiel, Dickie Lyon knew exactly where to start. He drove Flight Lieutenant Harrison straight there. "Oh, God," said Harrison. "Not another crematorium!"

"Sorry," answered Lyon, "but one thing I admire about the Germans—they kept such marvelous records. Even when you're dead, they've got you checked in, identified, and located. Don't bugger around with a morgue attendant or a crematorium official—he's got you identified."

If one could use such a term in a place as somber as a crematorium, one could almost say they were made welcome.

"What date? Around March twenty-fourth? Sir, we have exactly what you want. Now you have solved the mystery! Come!" The crematorium manager was overjoyed.

The huge ledger was produced, the thick vellum pages turned. A finger pointed triumphantly. "Four bodies for cremation. Roman numerals— one, two, three, four!"

"Roman numerals?" said Lyon. "No names?"

The manager explained. At 1830 hours on March 29, 1944, four officials from the local Gestapo headquarters had arrived with four bodies for cremation. Their leader was an Obersturmbannführer, a big violent man—no, none gave their names. "We asked for their authority for the cremation. They had none. We asked for the names of the men to be cremated. They refused to give them. We said we could not cremate the bodies without proper authority and authorization. They went away in a rage. The next morning the crematorium rang the civilian police, the Kripo, and asked them how we should behave. The Kripo said they did not issue permits for the Gestapo, and they wanted nothing to do with the matter. The Gestapo then contacted us and told us the bodies could be cremated under the insignia I have now shown you."

"So you never knew their identities," said Lyon in a disappointed voice.

"We could always find that out if necessary," said the manager. "We were told that they were French—secret agents."

"How could you find out their identities?"

The manager's eyebrows rose. Didn't Lyon

know the answer to a simple question like that? They were captured at Flensburg, right on the Danish border. The local police would have all the details.

Lyon and Harrison got back into the car. At Flensburg the police were quite happy to open their records. Yes, the four men were escaped aircrew officers from Sagan, Stalag Luft III—here were details and photographs. They'd had no alternative but to hand them over to the Gestapo.

"Let's talk to the Kiel Gestapo they're still holding in the Neuengamme camp," said Lyon grimly. It was not hard to find the four men who had brought the bodies to the crematorium. They were simply told to deliver them. They also came up with the names of the two local men who had driven the cars: Struve and Denkmann. But the really guilty men, the ones who had arranged everything, were Kiel Gestapo chief Friedrich Schmidt and his deputy, SS Sturmbannführer Johannes Post.

Struve and Denkmann were arrested without trouble. Denkmann was ill and Lyon placed him in hospital under guard. Struve made his guilt quite clear. When arrested, without being charged or knowing what crime he was supposed to have committed, he kept protesting that he had not shot the Royal Air Force officers.

Schmidt and Post had disappeared without a trace. Lyon and Harrison combed camps and towns without results. Lyon made several visits to Copenhagen when he heard that they might have taken refuge there. Nothing. They had learned that Post had kept a pretty blond mistress named Marianne Heidt, but she too had vanished. She did have parents in Kiel, however. Lyon led the raid on the house. As was so often the case, they were ordinary middle-class people without any idea where their daughter might be. Only one clue emerged from the house search: a small photo of the loving couple in ski clothes at a German ski lodge.

In May 1947, Dickie Lyon's demobilization papers came through, and although he spent his last few weeks in a frenzy of tireless searching for Schmidt and Post, he discovered nothing. He handed the case over to McKenna, gave him the snapshot, and returned to London to resume his duties with the Metropolitan Police.

A month later McKenna was visiting Minden, the holding camp for Nazi war criminals, on official business.

"Any new arrivals?" he asked.

"Only one," the duty officer said. "He's not even been charged yet. Don't think he's got anything to do with your investigation."

"Name?" asked McKenna.

"Johannes Pohlman, a haulage contractor from Celle."

"I'll just take a quick peep through the spyhole," said McKenna.

The man was big and broad, with a florid face and an angry expression. McKenna knew he had never seen him before, but there was something there he could not quite place. He went for a stroll and then it struck him. He fished in his wallet. He pulled out the picture of the ski slope, and people turned to stare as he ejaculated, "My God!"

Back in Johannes Pohlman's cell, McKenna asked a series of minor questions, which the man answered arrogantly.

McKenna then countered sharply. "I think you are a liar! I think you are SS Sturmbannführer Johannes Post."

"I most certainly am not."

"I have a photograph of you here with your girlfriend, Marianne Heidt. Do you deny that's you?"

Post looked and grinned. "Yes, that's me." His bitter arrogance grew with interrogation. He had no regrets about arranging the shootings of those four terror-fliers.

Later during his interrogations by McKenna, Post made his brutal cynicism quite clear. When McKenna demanded to know how he could be so inhuman, he replied, "Inhuman! I was dealing with subhumans. Yet I always gave them a full night's warning before I shot them, so that they could prepare to meet their fate. For the glory of the Führer I have killed any number of subhumans. I have liquidated non-Aryans, Gypsies, vagrants, Jews, and political unreliables. The Führer has shown his appreciation by personally awarding me the highest political decoration in the realm. For the glory of the Führer I only regret that I have not killed more. I wish I had the chance to wipe out more people like you, who have left cities in ruins and killed our women and children. These terror-fliers I disposed of were of no more good to the Reich than all the other subhumans whom I sent on their journey to heaven."

Post was without scruples, without mercy, with only the tunnel vision of his personal goal: the destruction of other human beings, for his beloved Führer. He was tried, found guilty, and hanged.

In 1945, when McKenna first arrived in Germany, he had made friends with Lieutenant Ernest Neidorf, a U.S. Army war crimes investigator, with whom he exchanged information. McKenna told him that both Roger Bushell and Bernard Scheidhauer had been shot in the vicinity of Saarbrücken, and since that was in a part of the French zone very near the American zone, he would be grateful if the lieutenant could learn something about those killings. Neidorf worked hard on the case. He discovered that Obersturmbannführer Dr. Leopold Spann had been Gestapo chief of Saarbrücken at the time. He had arrived in a truck with the bodies of two RAF officers at Neue Bremm concentration camp near Saarbrücken one morning, demanding that they both be cremated. With him was another Gestapo official, Kriminalsekretär Emil Schulz, and the driver was Walter Breithaupt. This all came out when the French arrested a German police officer named Fritz Schmoll, who had been in charge of execution and cremation records at Neue Bremm. Schmoll remembered the case well: bringing in the bodies of RAF officers for cremation was an unusual occurrence. All three men had disappeared. The trail had gone cold. Lieutenant Neidorf had returned to America, but the U.S. War Crimes Investigation Branch still kept in touch, and one morning RAF S.I.B. Sergeant Stuart Greet got a call from them. They had the address of a Walter Breithaupt in Frankfurt. Might he be their man?

When McKenna arrived, Greet had already made the arrest. McKenna patted him on the back and said, "Well done, Sergeant. Did he give you any trouble?"

"None at all. I took another sergeant with me and stationed him around back, and then went and knocked on the front door. The parents didn't seem too worried by my arrival. They simply said, 'Oh, he's upstairs in bed.' No trouble. I just walked up the stairs, and he got up, dressed, kissed his mother on the cheek, and came like a lamb."

"He's made a statement since then?" asked McKenna.

"A very thorough statement. The usual routine, though. A drive into the countryside, a stop so the two officers could relieve themselves. Spann and Schulz follow them and shoot them in the back."

McKenna nodded with sad resignation. "No wonder the Gestapo leaders got infuriated. How could every regional Gestapo office be so bloody stupid? Every single one used the same excuse. Handcuffed officers allowed out of the car to relieve themselves, then shot 'trying to escape.'"

"Now we've got to track down Spann and Schulz, sir."

"We're getting luckier lately," said McKenna. "They're starting to betray each other. The blood-brother oath of the valiant Gestapo seems to be dripping away."

All three investigative arms of the U.S., France, and Britain had put out feelers for Dr. Spann. All three produced the same result: Dr. Spann had been killed during an air raid, at Gestapo headquarters in Linz, Austria. Fifty other Gestapo were killed in what was one of the last raids of the war. The deaths were registered. Eventually McKenna investigated for himself, and found the evidence irrefutable.

Evidence now suggested that Emil Schulz must be in the French zone, which made things a bit sticky, because the French did not care much for handing over prisoners; they had more grievances to settle than either the Americans or the British. Nevertheless, in Saarbrücken, where McKenna met up with his old friend Flight Sergeant Williams—now a warrant officer—they were cordial. They helped to trace an Emil Schulz to a drab apartment building where he had been living with his wife and two daughters. He was not there. His wife and daughters were rumored to be living in a small village near Saarbrücken called Frankenholz.

With Williams, and Sergeant Jean van Giessen as interpreter, they drove the seven miles to the village. The door was answered by a young woman whose dress and face were white. Two small girls clung to her apron. All appeared terrified. Neither McKenna nor Warrant Officer Williams liked this very much. Mrs. Schulz admitted her husband had been in the Gestapo during the war. Where was he now? She didn't know. Maybe he was dead. Apologetically McKenna said they would have to search the house. They began with clothing. No man's clothing that had been recently worn was found. Then they turned to drawers. In the bottom of one they found a single sheet of ruled paper with a serial number at the bottom. The faces of both the small girls and their mother were tragic. An illegible signature. McKenna said quietly to van Giessen, "Ask them to leave the room for a minute." The mother and daughters went out. It was a letter written by a man to a wife and children he loved. A letter of yearning and despair. "Tell her to come back," said McKenna.

"This is from your husband, isn't it?" he asked the woman. Frau Schulz was holding back her tears. No, it was from a friend. No, she didn't know where Emil was. She didn't know anything. "I am afraid we shall have to take this with us," said McKenna quietly. As they closed the door they could hear the little girls crying.

There was no jubilation as they drove the car back to the French security office. The French officer was polite and helpful. McKenna handed over the letter. "It's some special sort of paper, isn't it?"

The French officer took one glance. "Prison paper," he answered.

There were several prisons around Saar-brücken; they went to the closest one first. McKenna asked to see the prison commandant. He was tall and swarthy. He looked at McKenna's brevet and the squadron-leader rings around his cuffs.

"What rank is that?" he asked.

"The same rank as yours," McKenna answered. The commandant nodded. McKenna thought, Funny how officers seem happier communicating with men of the same rank. He went on to tell the commandant about his quest. He did not mention Bernard Scheidhauer—that was a French matter, and the commandant might well close the subject altogether. "We want this man Schulz for the murder of an English officer, Squadron Leader Roger Bushell." McKenna hoped the commandant would note the equivalent rank.

"His nationality was English?"

"Born in South Africa, but of British nationality, serving gallantly in the British RAF."

"It's murder?" ·

"He was shot by this man Schulz."

"How can I help?"

"I have a letter here, unsigned, which may have come from your prison. There is some sort of signature—but it is certainly not 'Emil Schulz.' "

"A prisoner has to put his name somewhere on

the letter," said the commandant. "Let me see. Yes, the paper could be from here. The signature could be—Ernst Schmidt." His eyebrows raised. "A common enough name, don't you think?" He consulted a register. "Yes, we have an Ernst Schmidt here."

"Can I interrogate him here—in front of you?"

"Certainly."

Ernst Schmidt was brought in. He was probably close to forty, of medium height, medium looks, medium size, medium everything. He did not look like a bestial killer.

No, he was not masquerading as Ernst Schmidt; his name was not Emil Schulz; he had never known anyone called Dr. Spann or Walter Breithaupt. . . .

McKenna held out the letter. "This was written by you to your wife, Frau Angela Schulz, was it not?"

Emil Schulz glanced hopelessly from the commandant to McKenna, and his resistance crumbled. He should have been a store clerk, a shoe salesman, a decent man bringing his wages home to Angela every week. Instead, the lure of the smart uniform with the scarlet swastika, the power, the great leader whose flame drew him like a moth to disaster.

McKenna said, "We know the man really responsible for this crime was Doctor Spann, but he is dead. Did Spann order you to commit this crime?"

Schulz admitted everything. But McKenna

needed more than that. He needed to remove Emil Schulz from the prison. And that might take months.

Van Giessen had not yet translated Schulz's admission that he had shot Squadron Leader Bushell himself, while Dr. Spann had shot Bernard Scheidhauer. Van Giessen caught and understood McKenna's glance as McKenna said loudly, "I am going to repeat his admission once more, so you can translate clearly into French." He looked hard at Emil Schulz, saying, "Tell us about Squadron Leader Bushell. I should like the commandant to hear what you say. *You shot Squadron Leader Bushell?*"

Van Giessen translated. The commandant listened and nodded, as Schulz repeated his admission.

McKenna had seen the pack of Gauloises cigarettes on the table. "Ah," he said, "I smoke those occasionally. A bit strong for me, though."

The commandant smiled for the first time, showing tobacco-stained teeth. He offered McKenna the pack. McKenna took one, put it between his lips, then fumbled in his pockets. "Perhaps you'd like to try our English cigarettes, Commandant. And thank you very much for your assistance." He placed two packets of Players on the desk. The commandant nodded and murmured his thanks. McKenna struck while relations were cordial. "As you hear, Commandant, this is a clear case of murder of a British officer.

I would like to get this man back to my base camp as quickly as possible."

"If you sign the necessary documents for his custody, I will hand him into your care, Squadron Leader."

McKenna had never filled in documents more quickly in his life.

In August of that year McKenna escorted Emil Schulz to England. The train to London was crowded with holidaymakers; there was only standing room in the corridors. Everybody was far too sunburned and happy to notice that the tall RAF man and his companion were linked by handcuffs. Emil Schulz was a quiet and resigned prisoner. Eventually he said shyly, "Could I write a letter to my wife?"

McKenna said abruptly, "That's entirely against regulations."

Schulz nodded. "I thought that perhaps—you might do me a great favor and deliver the letter yourself. I know that this is the end of the road. I shall have to pay with my own life for what I have done. My wife will never see me again, and I should like to write her a letter."

McKenna said, "It would have to be translated before I could possibly do such a thing."

"I would be very grateful," said Schulz.

McKenna remembered the long sessions of interrogation that had occurred between him and Emil Schulz when he was taking his statement.

"How could you do it?" he had asked. "There was Roger Bushell, shot in the back, fallen to the ground, rocking in agony, his knees drawn up, rocking back and forth in absolute agony. And you get down on the ground, steady your pistol in the crook of your elbow, wait till his temple comes round against it, and then you pull the trigger. You say it was a coup de grace. I call it willful murder. How could you do it?''

Emil Schulz had revealed he was not a very good policeman; he'd managed to climb only three lower ranks in the Gestapo. "I never fought at the front," he answered. "I had never killed a man before, and haven't killed anyone since. I tried to get out of this killing. I told Doctor Spann that what he was asking me to do was wrong, but all he said was, 'Just do as I tell you.' He said, 'Remember, this man was a terror-flier. Think of what our wives and children had to suffer in the German cities.' What else could I do? If I'd not done it, someone else would have done it. If we had all refused, we could have been shot." He ended sadly, "But I have always expected to answer for this . . . this deed I never wished to do. And now it is the end of the road."

McKenna unlocked Emil Schulz's handcuffs and scrabbled around to give him room to sit on the floor of the corridor beside him. He tore a sheet out of one of his notebooks and gave him a pencil. Children, mothers, fathers, stepped around and over them as they went to the lavatories.

Emil Schulz wrote: "Dear Angela, dear Ingeborg, dear Helga, you dears of mine. I am already

388

in England now, and alas, could not say goodbye to you. I am here as a prisoner because I carried out an official order in the spring of 1944. I never on my own initiative acted against the laws of humanity. Had I not taken part then I should have gone down at that time. I was on guard duty with Ludwig Weiss. Ask him.

"I am waiting for justice. I only ask to be treated as I deserve and judged according to my position. In that case I'll be all right. Do what you can for me. You, dear Angela, have courage and live only for the children. . . . How much easier it would be to suffer death three times in order to prevent all this happening to you and especially to the children. Maybe it will be all right, because I was not, and am not, a criminal. Be brave with the children. . . . Ever your faithful husband, your Daddy and your Emil."

McKenna went back to Frankenholz and knocked on Frau Angela Schulz's door. He said, "I cannot leave this letter which your husband has written you, because it is against the regulations under which I serve. But I will wait while you read it as many times as you wish to."

McKenna sat down in a chair and waited. Angela Schulz read the letter carefully, a dozen times, a score of times, committing it, as McKenna knew, to some secret compartment of her heart, so that one day she could tell her daughters that . . . that. . . ?

Then she stood up and handed the letter back to McKenna, saying softly, "Thank you."

McKenna did not know what to say, but he had to say something, so he told her, "I wish you well." Then he put the letter back in his pocket and went back out to his car. The sun was shining as he drove away, and his face was grim. He said aloud, "Sometimes I hate this job. I really hate this bloody job."

He knew they would hang Emil Schulz.

McKenna knew a precept was at stake; "exemplary justice," to quote Anthony Eden's pledge, had been achieved. Not by lynchings and summary executions, but by the slow and relentless process of the law. Twenty-one Gestapo were executed, eleven committed suicide, six were killed by air raids in the last days of the war; seventeen received long sentences of imprisonment, a handful were acquitted; Scharpwinkel remained in Soviet hands and is alleged to have died in 1947. Friedrich Schmidt, the Kiel Gestapo chief, escaped prosecution until 1968, when he was arraigned before a German court and sentenced to two years' imprisonment. His plea: he was only obeying orders.

Epilogue

THE YEARS HAVE PASSED, the passions diminished, the old heroes are still around, remembering the old days, enjoying their reunions.

Certainly that modest hero Johnny Dodge did not deserve to drop dead running for a bus that was a bit too quick for him. Wings Day, irrepressible to the end, retired from the RAF with the rank of group captain, and spent a lot of that retirement traveling around Canada and the United States, making his merry presence known to many of his old friends. George Harsh, security officer of empirical wisdom and good nature, died in his seventies.

Bub Clark and David Jones reached high rank in the U.S. Air Force and, now retired, live in Colorado and Florida, respectively. Jimmy James, Jack Churchill and Sydney Dowse keep themselves busy in England and Europe. Wally Floody lived in Toronto, Canada, until his passing last September.

Of the three escapers who made the "home run" immediately after the Sagan breakout, Peter Bergsland and Jens Müller still live in Norway, and Bram van der Stok became a doctor and now lives in retirement in Hawaii.

And all over the Commonwealth, and indeed the world, they look back—the old heroes—remembering when their eyes were shining and their limbs were young, and there was a big important war to be won. Remembering, too, their comrades, the heroes who did not make it.

The Fifty

FLYING OFFICER HENRY J. BIRKLAND, Royal Canadian Air Force, b. 8/16/17. Recaptured near Sagan, transferred to Görlitz; last seen alive 3/31/44.

FLIGHT LIEUTENANT E. GORDON BRETTELL, RAF, b. 3/19/15. Recaptured at Schneidemühl, killed by Gestapo 3/29/44.

FLIGHT LIEUTENANT LESTER J. BULL, RAF, b. 11/7/16. Recaptured near Reichenberg, d. 3/29/44.

SQUADRON LEADER ROGER J. BUSHELL, RAF, b. 11/30/10. Recaptured at Saarbrücken, d. 3/29/44.

FLIGHT LIEUTENANT MICHAEL J. CASEY, RAF, b. 2/19/18. Recaptured near Görlitz, d. 3/31/44.

SQUADRON LEADER JAMES CATANACH, DFC, Royal Australian Air Force, b. 11/28/21. Recaptured at Flensburg, d. 3/29/44.

FLYING OFFICER ARNOLD G. CHRISTENSEN, Royal New Zealand Air Force, b. 4/8/22. Recaptured at Flensburg, d. 3/29/44.

FLYING OFFICER DENNIS H. COCHRAN, RAF, b. 8/13/21. Recaptured at Lörrach, d. 3/31/44.

SQUADRON LEADER IAN E. K. P. CROSS, RAF, b. 4/4/18. Recaptured near Görlitz, d. 3/31/44.

LIEUTENANT HALLADA ESPELID, Royal Norwegian Air Force, b. 10/6/20. Recaptured at Flensburg, d. 3/29/44.

FLIGHT LIEUTENANT BRIAN H. EVANS, RAF, b. 2/14/20. Recaptured at Halbau; last seen alive 3/31/44.

LIEUTENANT NILS FUGLESANG, Royal Norwegian Air Force. Recaptured at Flensburg, d. 3/29/44.

LIEUTENANT JOHANNES S. GOUWS, South African Air Force, b. 8/13/19. Recaptured at Lindau, d. 3/29/44.

FLIGHT LIEUTENANT WILLIAM J. GRISMAN, RAF, b. 8/30/14. Recaptured near Görlitz; last seen alive 4/6/44.

FLIGHT LIEUTENANT ALASTAIR D. M. GUNN, RAF, b. 9/27/19. Recaptured near Görlitz; last seen alive 4/6/44.

Flight Lieutenant Albert H. Hake, Royal Australian Air Force, b. 6/30/16. Recaptured near Görlitz, d. 3/31/44.

Flight Lieutenant Charles P. Hall, RAF, b. 7/25/18. Recaptured near Sagan, d. 3/30/44.

Flight Lieutenant Anthony R. H. Hayter, RAF, b. 5/20/20. Recaptured near Mulhouse, d. 4/6/44.

Flight Lieutenant Edgar S. Humphreys, RAF, b. 12/5/14. Recapture near Sagan; last seen alive 3/31/44.

Flying Officer Gordon A. Kidder, Royal Canadian Air Force, b. 12/9/14. Recaptured near Zlfn, d. 3/29/44.

Flight Lieutenant Reginald V. Kierath, Royal Australian Air Force, b. 2/20/15. Recaptured near Reichenberg, d. 3/29/44.

Flight Lieutenant Antoni Kiewnarski, RAF, b. 1/26/1899. Recaptured at Hirschberg, d. 3/31/44.

Squadron Leader Thomas G. Kirby-Green, RAF, b. 2/28/18. Recaptured near Zlfn, d. 3/29/44.

Flying Officer A. Wlodzimierz Kolanowski,

RAF, b. 8/11/13. Recaptured near Sagan; last seen alive 3/31/44.

FLYING OFFICER STANISLAW Z. KROL, RAF, b. 3/22/16. Recaptured at Oels; last seen alive 4/12/44.

FLIGHT LIEUTENANT PATRICK W. LANGFORD, Royal Canadian Air Force, b. 11/4/19. Recaptured near Görlitz; last seen alive 3/31/44.

FLIGHT LIEUTENANT THOMAS B. LEIGH, RAF, b. 2/21/15. Recaptured in Sagan area; last seen alive 4/12/44.

FLIGHT LIEUTENANT JAMES L. R. LONG, RAF, b. 2/21/15. Recaptured near Sagan; last seen alive 4/12/44.

FLIGHT LIEUTENANT ROMAS MARCINKUS, RAF, b. 7/22/10. Recaptured at Schneidemühl, d. 3/29/44.

LIEUTENANT CLEMENT A. N. MC GARR, South African Air Force, b. 11/24/17. Recaptured near Sagan; last seen alive 4/6/44.

FLIGHT LIEUTENANT GEORGE E. MC GILL, Royal Canadian Air Force, b. 4/14/18. Recaptured in Sagan area; last seen alive 3/31/44.

FLIGHT LIEUTENANT HAROLD J. MILFORD, RAF,

b. 8/16/14. Recaptured near Sagan; last seen alive 4/6/44.

FLYING OFFICER JERZY T. MONDSCHEIN, RAF, b. 3/18/09. Recaptured in Reichenberg area, d. 3/29/44.

FLYING OFFICER KAZIMIERZ PAWLUK, RAF, b. 8/1/06. Recaptured at Hirschberg; last seen alive 3/31/44.

FLIGHT LIEUTENANT HENRI A. PICARD, RAF, b. 4/17/16. Recaptured at Schneidemühl, d. 3/29/44.

FLYING OFFICER JOHN (POROKORU PATAPU) POHE, Royal New Zealand Air Force, b. 12/10/14. Recaptured near Görlitz, d. 3/31/44.

LIEUTENANT BERNARD W. M. SCHEIDHAUER, Free French Air Force, b. 8/28/21. Recaptured at Saarbrücken, d. 3/29/44.

PILOT OFFICER SOTIRIS SKANZIKAS, Royal Hellenic Air Force, b. 8/6/21. Recaptured at Hirschberg, d. 3/30/44.

LIEUTENANT RUPERT J. STEVENS, South African Air Force, b. 2/21/19. Recaptured at Rosenheim, d. 3/29/44.

FLYING OFFICER ROBERT C. STEWART, RAF, b.

7/7/11. Recaptured near Sagan; last seen alive 3/31/44.

FLYING OFFICER JOHN G. STOWER, RAF, b. 9/15/16. Recaptured near Reichenberg, d. 3/31/44.

FLYING OFFICER DENYS O. STREET, RAF, b. 4/1/22. Recaptured near Sagan; last seen alive 4/6/44.

FLIGHT LIEUTENANT CYRIL D. SWAIN, RAF, b. 12/15/11. Recaptured near Görlitz; last seen alive 3/31/44.

FLYING OFFICER PAWEL TOBOLSKI, RAF, b. 3/21/06. Recaptured at Stettin; last seen alive 4/2/44.

FLIGHT LIEUTENANT ERNST VALENTA, RAF, b. 10/25/12. Recaptured near Görlitz; last seen alive 3/31/44.

FLIGHT LIEUTENANT GILBERT W. WALENN, RAF, b. 2/24/16. Recaptured at Schneidemühl, d. 3/29/44.

FLIGHT LIEUTENANT JAMES C. WERNHAM, Royal Canadian Air Force, b. 1/15/17. Recaptured at Hirschberg, d. 3/30/44.

FLIGHT LIEUTENANT GEORGE W. WILEY, Royal Canadian Air Force, b. 1/24/22. Recaptured near Görlitz, d. 3/31/44.

SQUADRON LEADER JOHN E. A. WILLIAMS, Royal Australian Air Force, b. 5/6/19. Recaptured near Reichenberg, d. 3/29/44.

FLIGHT LIEUTENANT JOHN F. WILLIAMS, RAF, b. 7/7/17. Recaptured near Sagan; last seen alive 4/6/44.

Sources and Acknowledgments

MY SINCERE THANKS ARE due to a great number of Sagan, Stalag Luft III, survivors from many countries, and specifically to Wally Floody in Canada; Major General "Bub" Clark and Colonel John Bennett at the Air Force Academy in Colorado Springs; Major General David Jones, Joe Consolmagno, and Maurice Rosener in Florida; Bill Nance in Texas; and Peter Fanshawe, Jimmy James, Sydney Dowse, and Colonel Jack Churchill in Britain, all of whom gave generously of their time in long recording sessions. I am also grateful to the scores of other Stalag Luft III ex-kriegies who took the time to write to me about their personal experiences.

Many others provided invaluable assistance, including Peter Murton, Keeper of Aviation Records at the RAF Museum, Hendon; Duane Reed, Head of the Collections Unit at the Air Force Academy; the Ministry of Defence Air Historical Branch, Lacon House, London, and the Provost Branch of the RAF, the Imperial War Museum, and the Public Record Office. Also, Miss Elizabeth Harrison of the RAF Escaping Club; Mrs. Virginia Spivey; and Mrs. June Bowerman, Wings Day's daughter, who gave me permission to browse through Wings Day's manuscript and notes in the twenty-nine boxes kept at the RAF Museum.

Finally, a number of books furnished important anecdotes and background information: Jimmy James's *Moonless Night,* Colonel Jerry Sage's *Sage,* Sydney Smith's *Wings Day,* Aidan Crawley's *Escape From Germany,* Larry Forrester's *Fly for Your Life,* and Allen Andrews's *Exemplary Justice;* Kommandant von Lindeiner's unpublished memoirs, and the invaluable *Camp History of Stalag Luft III (Sagan) Air Force Personnel, April 1942-1945.*

I would also like to thank Mark Polizzotti for the superb job he did in editing the manuscript.